UNIX®

Primer Plus
Third Edition

Stephen Prata, and Donald Martin
Revised by Mike Wessler and Dan Wilson

Waite Group Press
A Division of Macmillan USA, Inc.
201 West 103rd St., Indianapolis, Indiana, 46290 USA

UNIX® Primer Plus, Third Edition

International Standard Book Number: 1-57169-165-0

Library of Congress Catalog Card Number: 99-65431

Printed in the United States of America

First Printing: December 1999

02 01 00   4 3 2 1

Trademarks

All terms mentioned in this book that are known to be trademarks or service marks have been appropriately capitalized. The Waite Group Press cannot attest to the accuracy of this information. Use of a term in this book should not be regarded as affecting the validity of any trademark or service mark.

UNIX is a registered trademark of AT&T Corporation.

Warning and Disclaimer

Every effort has been made to make this book as complete and as accurate as possible, but no warranty or fitness is implied. The information provided is on an "as is" basis. The authors and the publisher shall have neither liability or responsibility to any person or entity with respect to any loss or damages arising from the information contained in this book.

EXECUTIVE EDITOR
Don Roche

DEVELOPMENT EDITOR
Susan Shaw Dunn

MANAGING EDITOR
Charlotte Clapp

PROJECT EDITOR
Andrew Beaster

COPY EDITORS
Pat Kinyon
Linda Morris

INDEXER
Craig Small

PROOFREADERS
Beth Rago
Linda Morris

TECHNICAL EDITOR
Paul Love

INTERIOR DESIGN
Gary Adair

COVER DESIGN
Alan Clements

COPY WRITER
Eric Borgert

PRODUCTION
D & G Limited, LLC

CONTENTS AT A GLANCE

TABLE OF CONTENTS

PREFACE

The world of computers has changed radically in the last 10 years. It has seen perhaps the most rapid and widespread developments in information technology. Several paradigm shifts have occurred to place computers in virtually every aspect of industrialized civilization. What seemed technically impossible a decade ago is now commonplace. The understanding and appreciation of computers is no longer just for "nerds" or "geeks"—it's a nearly required skill for everyday life. Business, entertainment, education, and the social interaction of almost everyone has been affected. Indeed, computers are reshaping the way we live.

When the last edition of this text was published, the terms *Internet* and *Web page* would have drawn puzzled looks from the average person. Today, of course, you are seemingly in the minority if you don't surf the Web or, even worse, don't have an email account. Although statistically this isn't true, the Internet is certainly on the minds of most businesses, students, and ordinary people. These groups may not fully understand the Internet or the implications of its use, but they certainly are not afraid to merge into the information superhighway.

Hand and hand with the growth of the Internet is the proliferation of inexpensive PCs and GUIs. It would be impossible to ignore the impact these easy-to-use systems have made on the general public. These systems have often been the first contact people have with computers, whether it's in the office, school, or home. For less than $1,000, anyone can have direct access to the Information Age. The result is that people of all ages are jumping on the computer bandwagon. This involves everyone from great-grandmothers learning Java (yes, this is true!) to little kids surfing the Web for the first time. And this trend is growing.

Where does leave UNIX? Stronger than ever. UNIX is growing to support the Information Age in every facet. Here are a few examples:

- Many, if not most, Web servers are powered by UNIX. TCP/IP—*the* communications protocol of the Internet—owes its birth and childhood to UNIX. Not only is UNIX largely responsible for the birth and the recent growth of the Internet, but it will likely be responsible for the Internet's continued growth.

- Although many people have purchased PCs with the traditional preinstalled GUIs, a growing number of people are buying PCs specifically to use with Linux. Created by Linus Torvalds in the early 1990s, this UNIX lookalike for PCs is catching on quickly with more experienced computer users. It provides many of the features of UNIX for those who can't afford a server costing several thousand dollars.

- UNIX finds itself in a good position in terms of its size and scalability. The decline of mainframes means UNIX has room to grow to accommodate more users. Individual servers with multiple processors or clusters of these servers working together can facilitate this. On the other hand, UNIX can be put in powerful workstations to support just a few users or resource-intensive applications.

We could go on about other environmental factors that are friendly to UNIX, but that would do injustice to the merits of this fine operating system. Although many trends have helped create a hospitable environment for UNIX, this system can stand on its own.

UNIX is an elegant and powerful computer operating system developed at AT&T's Bell Labs. It is one of the world's most successful operating systems. An *operating system* is the software that breathes life into a computer. It gives the computer a personality, manages the system's resources, runs programs, and handles the interaction between you and the computer. Compared with other operating systems, UNIX offers much greater freedom of action and much more comprehensive services. UNIX's sophisticated modular structure lets you expand its abilities even further. UNIX's features spoil its users and make them reluctant to use other systems.

What are these powerful, alluring features? First, UNIX is a *multiuser* OS (operating system), meaning it allows many users to share the resources of one powerful computer system. Second, UNIX is *multitasking*, meaning it allows users to perform several processes simultaneously. Thus, you can edit a file, print another file, and check the spelling of a third file, all at the same time. But what's most important is that UNIX is comprehensive. UNIX also is an open system. You can customize it to meet your needs—you aren't locked into an inflexible system.

With the fading away of BSD UNIX in favor of AT&T's implementation, the surviving vendors have battled to create several interesting UNIX flavors. Whether it is Sun's Solaris, IBM's AIX, or HP's flavor of UNIX, you will often find one of these implementations where it matters in mission-critical systems. When business and profits are on the line, many experienced companies rely on UNIX.

Given all that we've just said, is it any wonder that UNIX is so big? Or why it is such a good idea to learn it? Clearly, it would be in most people's best interest to at least understand the role of UNIX, if not actually learn how to learn it. We've tried our best to give you a good guide to this exciting operating system. We've attempted to keep this text at the level of a UNIX beginner but have assumed familiarity with computers in general. Some older topics have been removed and newer ideas and topics have been added. Overall, we have tried to create an easy-to-read guide that anyone who is somewhat familiar with computers can use to learn UNIX. We certainly hope our efforts have paid off and that we've given you, the UNIX apprentice, a valuable guide into the UNIX Information Age.

UNIX continues to thrive, which means there's a need for good introductory texts. We've tried to meet that need with this book. Our primary aim is to present the basic features of this fascinating operating system and yet not overwhelm you with *all* the ramifications. (That's why we call the book a *primer*.) But we also introduce you to some of UNIX's most interesting advanced features. (That's where the *plus* in the title comes in.) Throughout, we've used plain language, examples, and figures freely to make the important points clear. We began learning UNIX through a trial-and-error approach that brought us a lot of surprises, some of them pleasant. Then we tried to pass on the benefit of our labors by teaching others to use the system. These experiences have helped us identify with the problems of a new user. We think that we can steer you around the pitfalls that await an unwary beginner. We find using UNIX a joy and we have tried to infuse our writing with that pleasure.

We hope this book helps you fully appreciate and enjoy the powers of the wonderful UNIX operating system.

ABOUT THE AUTHORS

Stephen Prata is a professor at the College of Marin in Kentfield, California, where he teaches physics, astronomy, and the C++ programming language. He received his B.S. from the California Institute of Technology and his Ph.D. from the University of California, Berkeley. His association with computers began with the modeling of star clusters. Dr. Prata is author of *C Primer Plus, Third Edition*, and *C++ Primer Plus, Third Edition*.

Donald Martin is a retired professor of physics and computer science at the College of Marin in Kentfield, California, where he served as director of the Computer Science Center for several years. He received his A.B. from the University of California, Berkeley, and his M.A. from San Jose State University. Mr. Martin is coauthor of *UNIX System V Primer*, *UNIX System V Bible*, and three hiking books.

Mitchell Waite is president of The Waite Group, a developer of computer books. He is an experienced programmer, fluent in a variety of computer languages, including C, Pascal, BASIC, Assembly, and HyperTalk. He wrote his first computer book in 1976 and is the coauthor of *New C Primer Plus*, *C: Step by Step*, *Microsoft Quick Programming*, *UNIX System V Primer*, and many other titles.

Revision Authors

Michael Wessler received his B.S. in Computer Technology from Purdue University in West Lafayette, Indiana. He is now the senior Oracle database administrator working on clustered Sun Solaris UNIX computers running Oracle Parallel Server (OPS) at a satellite programming provider. Michael has programmed professionally in COBOL, SQL, and some PL/SQL. Michael is coauthor of *Oracle Unleashed, Second Edition*, and *COBOL Unleashed*. He can be contacted at mwessler@yahoo.com.

Daniel Wilson is a technical manager with Oracle Corporation with the Indianapolis practice. His background includes UNIX Systems Administration and Oracle Database Administration in SMP, UNIX Cluster, and three-tier Internet environments. Dan is now working as Oracle's technical architect on Encyclopaedia Britannica's Internet project. He has programmed in C, C++, COBOL, and SQL. A graduate of Ball State University in Muncie, Indiana, Dan is a coauthor of *UNIX Unleashed, Systems Administrators Edition*; *Oracle Unleashed, Second Edition*; *UNIX Unleashed, Third Edition*; and *COBOL Unleashed*.

Contributing Author

William Pierce received his B.S. from Ball State University in Muncie, Indiana. A system programmer with 21 years of experience, he has been involved in the design, development, programming, and implementation of numerous hardware systems and software applications. His programming experiences have involved numerous languages with **awk** and MASM—the assembly language of Unisys mainframes is his favorite. He currently works as an independent contractor with Alternative Resources Corporation based in Cincinnati, Ohio. He enjoys system administration work on Hewlett-Packard and Sun UNIX computers. William is a coauthor of *UNIX Unleashed, Third Edition; UNIX Unleashed, Systems Administrators Edition;* and *COBOL Unleashed.*

DEDICATION

To my family and friends for the endless support they provided while I was working on this book during a difficult time. Their efforts and the advice given will not be forgotten.

—Mike Wessler

To my wife, Angela, who has always supported my efforts, both good and bad. Her intelligence exceeds my own and for this I am fortunate as I have always counted on her advice. Also, her strength and dedication to our family has made it possible for me to work in a very demanding and rewarding field. For this I can't thank her enough—although I'm sure I'll soon find a way.

—Dan Wilson

ACKNOWLEDGMENTS

Any book attempting to teach the use of a computer operating system to beginners would surely be useless without extensive technical editing of the manuscript. This is especially true for the UNIX system because of its large number of built-in facilities and commands. Further, because UNIX is becoming so popular (even as a 16/32-bit operating system for micros), it is critical that the teaching of its operation be carefully explained and completely tested. We have been fortunate to have several people contribute to the testing and critiquing of our original manuscript and we would like to pay tribute to them here.

First, we would like to thank Jon Foreman, Dan Putterman, and Michael Lindbeck at the College of Marin for their participation in the many technical discussions we held regarding UNIX. We are particularly indebted to Brian Harvey, who made numerous technical contributions to our first edition. Thanks also to Michael Forte for his technical assistance with the `emacs` chapter.

The people at Sams gave us the strong support necessary to make this book a reality, and we would like to give them our sincere regards. We also wish to thank our colleagues at the College of Marin for their help and support: Bob Petersen, Dick Rodgers, Bernd Enders, Fred Schmitt, and Nancy Zimfirescu. And, of course, our sincere appreciation to the numerous students who struggled through our earliest efforts at creating a user-friendly introduction to UNIX. Finally, thanks to Bob Johnson for his fantastic cartoons.

Even with this wonderful support, we may have allowed an error or two to creep into this book. For them, we are responsible.

From Mike Wessler: I want to thank Matt Coffey for his contributions on this project. I also want to thank the people at Sams for their support.

From Dan Wilson: I want to acknowledge the great team at Sams for excellent work on this book: Don Roche, Susan Dunn, Andy Beaster, and Pat Kinyon. Thanks to my grandmother Alma Johnson who has always been the true writer in my family. I also want to thank Matt Coffey for bringing this opportunity to my attention. Thanks to Jim Beatie and Doug Shuck of Encyclopaedia Britannica for allowing me to have a part in building the coolest Web site around. And finally, thanks to the Oracle team: Chris Sarjent, Paul Singleton, Len Kucharski, Udhay Parerikkal, Lisa Hong, Jorge Garcia, and Yonghe Xue.

TELL US WHAT YOU THINK!

As the reader of this book, *you* are our most important critic and commentator. We value your opinion and want to know what we're doing right, what we could do better, what areas you'd like to see us publish in, and any other words of wisdom you're willing to pass our way.

As an associate publisher for Sams, I welcome your comments. You can fax, email, or write me directly to let me know what you did or didn't like about this book—as well as what we can do to make our books stronger.

Please note that I cannot help you with technical problems related to the topic of this book, and that due to the high volume of mail I receive, I might not be able to reply to every message.

When you write, please be sure to include this book's title and author as well as your name and phone or fax number. I will carefully review your comments and share them with the author and editors who worked on the book.

Fax: 317-581-4770

Email: `office_sams@mcp.com`

Mail: Michael Stephens, Associate Publisher
          Sams Publishing
          201 West 103rd Street
          Indianapolis, IN 46290 USA

INTRODUCTION

UNIX Primer Plus, Third Edition will help shape computer novices into proficient UNIX (and Linux) end users. All the basic skills are covered, plus some advanced features for the more daring. The technical information is supplemented with the authors' personal experience and advice. This text provides an excellent starting point for anyone starting a UNIX/computer science class or a new job that requires UNIX. You will have the benefit of many years of experience so you can avoid the more common errors.

In this book, you'll learn basic and intermediate UNIX commands and functions. (Most of this information is transferable to Linux.) After reading this book, you will be able to operate in a normal UNIX environment as an educated end user. This book will give you a good introduction to the UNIX operating system and to many of its important application programs whether you are new to computers or an experienced programmer. The best way to learn UNIX is to use it. When you start reading the book in earnest, sit down at a terminal and duplicate our examples and improvise your own examples. You may be surprised occasionally, but you won't hurt the system.

Use this book as a reference book. Command summaries (in shaded boxes for easy look-up) document a large number of UNIX commands. Or, you also can use this book as a lead-in to the official UNIX manual. The manual is rather terse and is written for knowledgeable users; the summaries and examples that we provide can help clarify and expand on the manual. Use the tear-out reference cards for a concise summary of the most important UNIX commands.

However you use this book, we hope that you will enjoy it as much as we have enjoyed writing it.

Who Should Read This Book?

The goal of this book is to introduce UNIX's powerful tools to beginning and experienced computer users who are first-time UNIX or Linux users in an office or college environment.

The tools that we've chosen to present are those most needed for work in an electronic office. We also provide those skills needed to write and run simple programs in various computer languages such as C. Whether your interest in UNIX is at the professional or hobbyist level, you will find the clear details and examples to become a skilled UNIX user. We hope you will enjoy learning UNIX as much as we have enjoyed writing this book.

What You Need to Know Before Reading This Book

You don't need to know much about computers in general, although you need to know what a computer is. Any experience you have will be helpful. Most importantly, you should have time available to experiment with book examples.

You also won't need any software to use this book. It's assumed that you have access to a UNIX account.

How This Book Is Organized

The chapters of this book are ordered so that you can become productive almost immediately. By glancing through the first four chapters, you will see that these chapters contain the *basic* ideas and commands that you will need. We furnish analogies, pictures, and stories to provide mental hooks on which you can hang these concepts. If you are a casual UNIX user, you may not need to read beyond these chapters.

After you are introduced to UNIX and its basic structure, you learn about two text editors—`vi` and `emacs`—in Chapters 5, "The `vi` Screen Editor," and 6, "The `emacs` Editor."

The later chapters explore a variety of the more interesting and powerful UNIX commands and features. You may want to just browse through them, picking up on those commands and usage that most interest you. In Chapter 7, "Manipulating Files and Directories: `mv`, `cp`, and `mkdir`," Chapter 8, "The UNIX Shell: Command Lines, Redirection, and Shell Scripts," and Chapter 9, "File-Management Commands and Others: `wc`, `sort`, `lpr`, and `chmod`," you build your skills by learning advanced UNIX file and shell commands, such as `mkdir`, `chmod`, and `lpr`. Chapters 10, "More Text Processing: `join`, `sed`, and `nroff`," and 11, "Information Processing: `grep`, `find` and `awk`," add to your knowledge by showing you information-processing commands such as `join`, `nroff`, `grep`, and `awk`. The last chapter helps you hone the text-editing skills you gained in Chapters 5 and 6.

Try the Review and the Exercises at the end of each chapter. They should give you more confidence in your new skills and they may clarify a point or two for you.

At the end of this book are seven appendixes that provide reference information as well as a glossary of terms and answers to the Chapter Review questions.

Conventions Used in This Book

The following typographic conventions are used in this book:

- Code lines, commands, statements, variables, and any text you type or see onscreen appears in a `mono` typeface.

- Anything you type or enter at a screen prompt appears in **`mono bold`**.

- Placeholders in syntax descriptions appear in an *italic mono* typeface. Replace the placeholder with the actual filename, parameter, or whatever value it represents.

- *Italics* highlight technical terms when they're being defined.

- The book also contains notes, tips, and cautions designed to help you quickly spot important or useful information and shortcuts to enable you to work more efficiently.

CHAPTER 1

INTRODUCTION TO UNIX

You will learn about the following in this chapter:

- What an operating system is
- The history of UNIX
- The UNIX philosophy

- How UNIX works as an electronic office
- UNIX's support tools for programmers

D id you know that today more than 750,000 UNIX installations around the world are supporting million's of users? The recent introduction of relatively inexpensive ($3,000–$25,000) computer systems capable of running UNIX means that in the next few years, more and more people will become members of the UNIX Information Age.

This book will help you take that step toward membership. It's designed to introduce newcomers to the powerful magic of one of the world's most successful operating systems.

An Overview of UNIX

A computer needs special programming called *software* to make it work. UNIX systems have two kinds of software: the operating system software and the *application* or *utility* software (see Figure 1.1). The operating system software is what breathes life into the computer. It behaves somewhat like our subconscious, taking care of myriad everyday housekeeping details. If the operating system is doing its job, you can do your tasks without ever needing to worry about the computer's inner workings.

FIGURE 1.1

An overview of UNIX.

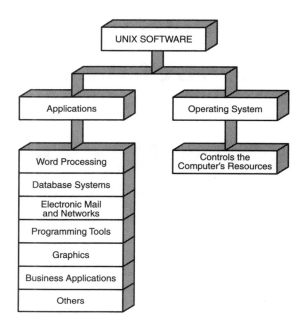

The other kind of software, the utilities or application software, does *your* work.. This software might include an *editor* (a program that lets you write, change, and store text and data), electronic mail programs, business applications, and languages for programming (such as C++).

UNIX consists of both kinds of software. The term *UNIX*, then, refers both to the operating system and to a host of useful application programs. This book only briefly describes the operating system part of UNIX. We'll spend most of our time on how to use the powerful UNIX utilities.

What Is an Operating System?

If you are new to computers and computing, you may find such terms as *operating system, utilities,* and *multiuser* to be confusing when you first encounter them. We will digress briefly here to explain these and other terms. We will discuss what an operating system is, why it's necessary, and what it does. If you are already familiar with operating systems, you may want to skip to the next section.

In a broad sense, an operating system is like a teacher in a classroom. The teacher gives out assignments, schedules use of equipment, and, in general, coordinates student activities. In a more restricted sense, the operating system coordinates the inner workings of the computer (see Figure 1.2). The operating system relies on an internal clock within the computer to help make simple scheduling decisions, such as when to send information to the printer or when to load and execute user programs. Operating systems themselves are just programs created to reduce the amount of programming required of the user, especially programming required to take care of routine, repeated tasks.

FIGURE 1.2
The operating system.

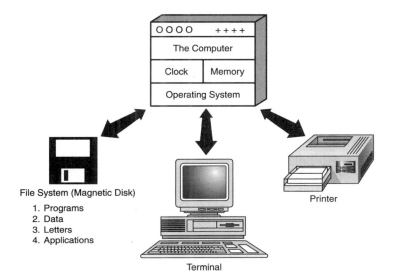

You also can define an operating system as the link between the computer and the computer user. Its purpose is to provide the user with a flexible and manageable means of control over the resources of the computer. All operating systems fulfill a number of primary functions:

- *They provide a filing system*—A *file* is a block of information stored in the computer. Files can hold letters, programs, budgets, schedules, and anything else that you can type on a typewriter. In UNIX, you can write new files, add to old files, copy files, rename them, or move them elsewhere, all by giving rather simple commands.

- *They provide for the loading and executing of user programs*—*Loading* a program consists of placing the program instructions into the proper locations. *Executing* a program means to run the program. In providing these services, the operating system lets you run programs that might be written in a high-level language, such as C++, as well as run programs already written and stored in the filing system. Again, the purpose of the operating system is to make these tasks as simple as possible.

- *They provide a communication link between the computer and its accessories*—The accessories, sometimes called *peripheral* devices or *input-output* devices, include terminals, printers, and information storage devices, such as magnetic tapes and disks.

- *Multiuser time-sharing*—This means that several people at different terminals can use the computer at the same time. This process resembles the activities of a restaurant staff. The staff divides its time preparing and serving several customers simultaneously, sending out the soups, salads, main courses, and so on. An efficient staff will give each patron the feeling of being waited on as if he or she is the only customer. An efficient timesharing computer will give you the same sensation.

- *Multitasking*—This feature allows one user to run several computing jobs simultaneously, such as printing one program while editing a second one. The user can assign different priorities to each job as appropriate.

Besides the five basic housekeeping operations just mentioned, UNIX has a library of application and utility software that has grown over the years to provide essential services to thousands of users. There is a seemingly endless supply of new services available, so you should be prepared to adapt to new programs. Before we discuss this software, let's look at how UNIX has evolved into what it is today.

The History of UNIX

During the early 1960s, computers were expensive and had little memory. For example, one middle-priced workhorse of that day, the IBM-1620, had only 24KB of memory and could store about 40,000 numbers. The primary design criteria for all software—languages, programs, and operating systems—was to use memory efficiently and make programs simple for the computer. This was usually at the cost of being unwieldy for the programmer and other users.

UNIX grew out of the frustrations that programmers faced when working with this early time-consuming software. UNIX was born in 1969 at Bell Labs, the prestigious research arm of the American Telephone & Telegraph Company. Surprisingly, it began when one man, Ken Thompson, decided to try to create a less expensive and more hospitable programming environment.

Thompson was working on a program called Space Travel that simulated the motion of the planets in the solar system. The program was being run on a large computer made by General Electric, the GE645, which was using an operating system called Multics. Developed at MIT, Multics was one of the first operating systems designed to handle several users simultaneously. However, its use on the GE computer was expensive and awkward. Each run of the Space Travel program cost more than $70. (Remember, these were 1969 dollars!) Thompson found a little-used smaller computer made by Digital Equipment Corporation called the PDP-7. He began the burden of transferring his Space Travel program to run on the smaller computer. To use the PDP-7 conveniently, Thompson created a new operating system that he christened UNIX, as an offshoot of Multics. Thompson was successful enough in this effort to attract the attention of Dennis Ritchie and others at Bell Labs, where they continued the process of creating a useful environment. UNIX became operational on the Bell Labs system in 1971.

During the early 1970s, UNIX ran primarily on computers manufactured by Digital Equipment—first on the PDP-7, and then on the PDP-11/40 and /45, and finally blossoming on the PDP-11/70 where it achieved widespread acceptance throughout Bell Labs. During the same time, universities and colleges, many of whom were using the PDP-11/70 computers, were given license to run UNIX at minimal cost. This shrewd move by AT&T eventually led to UNIX being run at more than 80 percent of all university computer science departments in the United States. Each year, thousands of computer students graduate with some experience in running and modifying UNIX. This is still the case, despite the growth of personal computers running newer systems.

UNIX, like most operating systems, was originally written in what is called *assembly language*, a primitive set of instructions that controls the computer's internal actions. Because each computer model has its own particular set of internal instructions, moving UNIX to another computer involved significant programming effort. The solution to this problem, and perhaps the key to UNIX's popularity today, was Thompson's decision to rewrite the operating system in a higher-level language—one less primitive than assembly language.

The language was called B. Soon it was modified extensively by Ritchie and, in 1973, rechristened C. As a general-purpose language featuring modern commands, C is much easier to understand and use than assembly language. Although not as efficient as assembly language in terms of the speed with which the computer carries out its manipulations, C is much more convenient. This convenience has encouraged users to modify and improve UNIX. Thus, a tremendous amount of additional UNIX software has been created, especially in the areas of word processing and programming support.

The use of C makes UNIX easily portable to other computer systems. Only a tiny fraction of UNIX is still written in assembly language. Probably more important (for computer users) is that C *compilers* (which translate C into the host computer's internal language) are now available for every major 32-bit microprocessor on the market.

Today, UNIX can be run on many other computers, including computers made by HP, Unisys, Digital Equipment, NCR, IBM, Cray Research, Apple, and Sun. This has resulted in several slightly different versions of UNIX produced by different companies (vendors). These differences apply more to highly experienced UNIX users than to beginners because the basic commands (described in this book) are similar across most UNIX platforms.

Microprocessors form the brains of microcomputers. One significant fact about microprocessors is that their sophisticated, complex, electronic circuits are all contained in a single small package called a *chip*. The first microprocessor was a 4-bit chip made by Intel in 1970. It was followed by the 8-bit chip, which launched the microcomputer revolution of the late 1970s. Today, 32-bit microprocessors promise even greater computing power at lower cost.

The net result of these advances in hardware is that UNIX can now run on newer, relatively inexpensive microprocessor-based computer systems. For example, in the late 1970s, a PDP-11/70 time-sharing system with 15 terminals might have cost $150,000. In the 1980s, a microprocessor-based system with 15 terminals could have been installed for about $35,000. Single-user UNIX systems could cost as little as $5,000. In the late 1990s, a moderately powerful workstation can be had for just under $3,000. This has caused some people to opt for a UNIX workstation rather than spend about the same price for a nice PC.

Like computer hardware, the UNIX operating system has gone through several iterations. In the early 1980s, UNIX and UNIX lookalikes multiplied like rabbits, with such names as Cromix, Idris, Ultrix, XENIX, Coherent, Version 7, BSD, and so on. By 1990, however, only two versions of UNIX dominated: Berkeley UNIX and System V UNIX (with its variations, XENIX, Vp/ix, and so on).

Berkeley UNIX

Almost from the start, the University of California at Berkeley was a focal point of UNIX development. Its computer science department has been the major distributor of UNIX to several hundred colleges, universities, and organizations. As a research and development center, UC-Berkeley created a host of features, such as the C shell with alias, history and job control, the vi editor, and improved file handling and communication programs.

The final version of Berkeley UNIX is known as UNIX 4.4 BSD (Berkeley Standard Distribution). This final version was released in 1993. Since then, Berkeley ceased developing a separate version of UNIX.

UNIX System V

The biggest change for UNIX occurred in 1983 when AT&T announced that it was licensing a new "standard" version of UNIX for the commercial OEM (original equipment manufacturer) marketplace. This version, called UNIX System V, was based on the UNIX that AT&T was using internally. It added many of the best features of Berkeley UNIX. AT&T became a software supplier, offering full support for UNIX developers. The licensing fee for UNIX System V also was much more reasonable than for previous versions.

In June 1986, AT&T introduced UNIX System V, release 3.0. The major features of release 3.0 were improved network file sharing and greater portability of UNIX application software from one UNIX machine to another. Both features were designed to improve standardization of UNIX System V for software developers and users.

UNIX System V Release 4 (SVR4) shipped in 1989. This last major release from AT&T attempted to combine some of the features of other popular UNIX flavors.

OSF Versus UI

In 1988, AT&T shocked the UNIX community by combining forces with fast-rising Sun Microsystems. Together, they planned to completely rewrite the UNIX operating system software by producing a new ultimate standard, UNIX System V, release 4.0.

Several major computer companies, including IBM, Hewlett Packard, and Digital Equipment reacted quickly by forming a competing group called Open Software Foundation (OSF). They immediately raised more than $90 million to start development of a new UNIX standard.

Meanwhile, the AT&T–Sun group backed off slightly and—with Unisys, Data General, and others—founded UNIX International (UI). This open consortium of companies agreed to oversee the development of System V standards. SVR4 emerged as the surviving standard for UNIX. BSD released its final version and now lives on mostly in what other versions have incorporated from it.

Part of the early competition between and within these groups revolved around creating a graphical interface. A *graphical interface* is what you see onscreen. In the past, the interface or screen consisted mostly of characters. Today, graphical interfaces have not only characters and lines but also small pictures (icons) representing files, programs, and so on, like those used on Apple Macintosh or in Windows.

X-Windows and Linux

Possibly one of the most important developments for the survival of UNIX occurred in 1989 when OSF and UI became members of X/Open, a consortium of companies developing and supporting the X-Windows standard.

X-Windows acts like a language translator, except that it includes a graphics language. If the computer wants to draw a square or menu onscreen, it doesn't have to send detailed instructions keyed to each type of terminal. It can send a generalized set of instructions to the X-Windows translator residing at the terminal.

For programmers, system administrators, institutions, and companies, other issues involving the operating system are important, too. Such issues include openness, flexibility, multiprocessor use, development tools, file security, and networking. Here, the UNIX operating system excels and has done well in the 1990s.

The recent rage in the UNIX world has been the growth of Linux, a UNIX-looking operating system designed to run on Intel processors. To run, Linux needs only a 386 processor. Linux is distributed free over the Internet but can be purchased with additional options from multiple vendors. The net result is that people with virtually any PC (386 and above) can have their own UNIX-like system for little or no cost. This has provided a great way for new people to get involved with UNIX via Linux without the higher costs of a real UNIX workstation. The basic commands covered in this book will also apply to most Linux installations, so feel free to experiment with Linux if you have the means.

The UNIX Philosophy

The major design factors behind UNIX were to create a simple, elegant, and easy-to-use operating system and supporting software. *Elegant*, in this context, generally means good programming style and thrifty memory management. These design characteristics led to the following maxims among UNIX builders:

- Make each program do one thing well. These simple programs often are called *tools*.

- Expect the output of every program to become the input to another, yet unknown, program. This means that simple tools can be connected to do complex jobs.

- Don't hesitate to build new programs to do a job. The library of tools keeps increasing.

The net result of these maxims is that UNIX systems are sometimes said to embody Schumacher's dictum that "small is beautiful." Each UNIX program is a compact, easily used tool that does its job well.

Thousands of students, teachers, engineers, programmers, secretaries, managers, and office workers have found that UNIX's friendly environment and quality software have become time-saving tools that improve their productivity and employ their creativity.

What Can UNIX Do for You?

Earlier, we explained that UNIX has two kinds of software: the UNIX operating system, which manages the internal workings of the computer system, and built-in application or utility software, which provides a range of useful services. An easy way to get an overview of these UNIX services is to divide this software into two major categories. These software categories could be called Electronic Office and the Programming Support areas. Most of the UNIX software discussed here concerns services that can be categorized under the Electronic Office.

The Electronic Office

Most discussions of what an electronic office involves center around four interrelated functions:

- Word processing
- Electronic filing
- Electronic mail and networking
- Electronic databases

Word Processing

UNIX has dozens of tools to help you do word processing. These tools have such names as editors, text formatters, spellers, and grammar checkers. With these tools, you can throw away the liquid correction fluid, correction tape, scissors, erasers, paper clips, cellophane tape, and all other paraphernalia you used to use when dealing with printed words on paper. You now manipulate words inside an electronic memory. They can be moved and changed easily, quickly, and efficiently, allowing you to type your words without thinking about the appearance of your finished product.

With a text-formatting program, you can turn a ragged-right margin into a beautiful, professional-looking typeset format just by using a few keystrokes. Or, suppose that you want to add a new sentence in the middle of your 10-page document. No problem! Simply enter the editor's insert mode and start typing away. Because the editor has an electronic brain, it can instantly shift all the text in its memory to make room for new words and do it without losing its paragraph structure. Or, suppose that you spelled the same word incorrectly in 157 places. Merely use the search-and-replace command to have the computer automatically change all occurrences of the misspelled word as you sit back and relax. With simple key operations, you can move paragraphs and blocks of text, boldface your text, underline, and make superscripts and subscripts.

These UNIX tools allow you to accomplish tasks that would require days of work using a standard typewriter. Examples of such tasks are converting a long double-spaced document to a narrow column width, single-spacing a document so that it's suitable for publication, printing individually addressed copies of the same letter, sorting and merging mailing labels, proofreading large documents for spelling and syntax errors, and generating an index.

This kind of power will alter your writing experience drastically. The ability to change words quickly and easily gives them a new malleability. Words become like wet clay—you can rework the same sentence over and over, deleting old words with hardly a care until the words say exactly what you mean. Because of the fluid nature of the work, you become braver. You can be more creative because you're not concerned with how the typing looks. Neither are you hampered by the fear of putting an idea in the wrong place because you can easily move the words around later. You create the words—let the machine manage them.

Electronic Filing

Supporting the word processing function and providing even more services is the electronic filing system. To visualize the filing system, imagine that all the written information you now store in a filing cabinet or on shelves is placed in an electronic filing cabinet.

A file can contain anywhere from one to several thousand words or numbers. Anything you can type on a typewriter can be placed in a file. Each file has a name that you give it, and each file contains whatever information you put in it, as discussed in Chapter 4, "Files and Directories: `ls`, `cat`, `more`, and `pr`," and Chapter 7, "Manipulating Files and Directories: `mv`, `cp`, and `mkdir`."

When you have a filing system set up and your information is stored there, here's what you can do. By using simple commands, you can get a list of the titles of every document or file, or you can read any one file in its entirety. You can scan (search) the first (or last) 10 lines of a number of files looking for specific information. Better still, suppose that you want to find a certain letter that was sent to you about a specific product. You can let "UNIX do the walking." One command will scan one or more files searching for the product name. Phone listings, product listings, bills, and bookkeeping can all be kept on file and scanned in the UNIX filing system. And the best part about the UNIX filing system is that the files can be organized the same way that you would arrange them in a cabinet.

You can build categories of files. For example, you might place all your travel files in one drawer (called a *directory* in UNIX), insurance records in another drawer, clients' accounts in a third drawer, and so on. Files can be easily moved from one drawer to another, copies can be placed in several drawers, or files can be cross-referenced. Files can be combined, cut in two, or merged alphabetically. In fact, all the word processing functions described earlier can be applied to any of your files, even though you may not have originated them.

Electronic Mail and Networking

Another related, necessary, and very useful function of the electronic office is electronic mail and networking (see Figure 1.3). As you might suppose, electronic communication is the glue that holds together the electronic office. With electronic mail, you can turn paperwork shuffling into the more rewarding task of information processing. For example, in writing letters, you have all the advantages of word processing that were described earlier, and you can send copies instantly to anyone on the UNIX system or the Internet.

One valuable use of electronic mail occurs when two or more people collaborate on a letter, report, or other typewritten document while using the word processor/mail system. Each person can write his or her part of the document, mail it to someone else for changes or additions, and then receive a new copy back. These documents, as well as any UNIX file containing any kind of written information, can be mailed (transmitted) easily with just a few keystrokes.

Another useful and related feature of UNIX mail is the *reminder service*. If you keep a diary of your important dates in a file named calendar, the UNIX operating system will send you mail each day, reminding you of your day's schedule.

FIGURE 1.3
Electronic mail and net-
working.

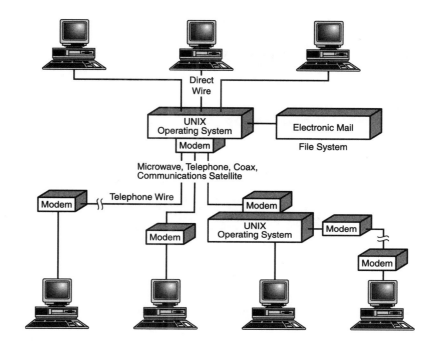

In addition to sending *local mail* to people connected to your computer, the UNIX mail system can send mail to other computer systems anywhere in the world.

Sending electronic signals over telephone wires can be relatively slow. Other types of net-
works, such as Ethernet, allow several computers to be connected, sharing resources at very
high speeds.

No matter which network you use or what kind of computer you have, if your computer is
running UNIX, you can communicate with other systems. And, in doing so, you will have
available all the UNIX services just described—word processing, electronic filing system, and
electronic mail.

Electronic Databases

An electronic database is essentially an extension of an electronic filing system. In fact, the
UNIX filing system already has the features of a very simple database. For example, if you
placed all the phone numbers you use (or even a whole telephone book full of numbers) into
one or more UNIX files, you could search those files for a particular name and number with
just a single command. Or you could pull out all the names beginning with "John" and place
them in a new file.

An *electronic database* is a collection of information that you can add to, delete from, or sort in
various ways. It can be searched by using keywords, and specific information can be copied
and printed. The UNIX filing system can do all of this easily, as you will see in later chapters.

More powerful database systems, such as Oracle, are available for running under UNIX. These systems have more sophisticated searching and storing techniques. For example (using the telephone book example again), you might want to find all the phone numbers listed under "John" living on "Beachside Avenue," but *not* all those starting with the numbers 454. The beauty of a database system like Oracle is that you can pull out specific information and then create a new database from it quickly and easily.

Electronic databases are essential for many businesses. Payroll, sales, employee records, inventories, clients' records, and economic data can all be easily accessed within a database. However, for maximum use, databases must be tied into the electronic office. The services of word processing, electronic filing, and electronic mail give the database user additional powers. For example, as the inventory control manager, you could extract specific information about an inventory, add a few remarks, and mail the result to your staff.

The Sum Is Greater Than the Parts

In UNIX, all four services of the electronic office are ready to go. These services combine synergistically so that the total is much greater than the sum of the parts. You could purchase computer systems and software that would do two or three of these functions or that would provide these services to just a few people. However, when all these services are provided to most office workers in a company, the nature of their work can change radically. Research shows that these services improve productivity and communications, save money, and improve people's attitudes toward work. That's why organizations large and small, local and national, have adopted UNIX as their software standard.

A key element in the widespread adoption of UNIX is its user-friendliness. How easy is it to use UNIX? Is it worthwhile to spend time learning to use UNIX's services? We believe the answer is an overwhelming *yes*. Thousands of employees at Bell Labs and AT&T, at colleges and universities, and in other businesses and industries would agree.

Besides the electronic office services offered by UNIX, another major service is to help programmers solve programming problems. This is the topic of the next section.

Programmer's Support Tools

UNIX was originally developed to make life easier for programmers. However, it turned out that programmers wanted the electronic office services just as much as everyone else. Thus, both types of UNIX software have evolved side by side and are widely used. The programmer's tools can be classified into four major areas:

- *Programming languages and compilers*—All the major languages (C, C++, COBOL, and so on) can be run under UNIX. This means that if UNIX has a standardized form of a language, any programs in that language written anywhere in the country (and there are thousands) can be run on your system and vice versa.

  Of course, since UNIX is written in C, that language is available and widely used to write programs. A *compiler* translates programs written in the high-level languages into the primitive instructions that the machine can understand.

- *Command-line interpreter* (called the *shell*)[md]The shell is a program that forms the link between most users and the computer. The shell accepts commands that you type into the computer, and then executes them. The shell contains more than 100 built-in commands for your use. Actually, there's more than one version of the shell. The shell provided with the standard Bell Labs version of UNIX is called the *Bourne shell* after its developer. The other widely used current shell is the *C shell* developed at the University of California, Berkeley. A newer shell, *Korn* (named after its developer, David Korn), is also popular. The Korn shell combines the best features of C shells with compatibility with Bourne shells. Several other shells are now in wide use, thanks to popularity of Linux. These public domain shells are available free of charge to anyone who wants them. The most widely used shells under Linux are the Bourne Again shell (based on the Bourne shell), `tcsh` (based on the C shell), and `pdksh` (based on the Korn shell). Most features discussed in this book are common to all shell versions, but some are exclusive to one version. In this book, we will explain more than 60 shell commands and what they can do for you.

  The shell can be used as a programming language that has many features of C. The programmability of the shell—a feature that few other systems offer—plus the large number of built-in commands that the shell already knows gives programmers exceptional flexibility and power. The *pipe*, a UNIX concept that has since been widely copied, enhances this power. Pipes, as you will learn later, allow programs or commands to be coupled together. The output of one program becomes the input to another, and so on.

- *Programmer debugging tools*—The first time a program is written it rarely runs correctly. Usually the program has errors or "bugs" that need fixing. UNIX, like most systems, has built-in programs that help locate these errors. However, we will not be discussing these programming aids in this book.

- *The Programmers Workbench*—This package of UNIX tools is especially valuable for team-oriented programming projects. These software tools maintain a complete record of all changes made to a program as it's written. They also allow programs to be tested in part as they're developed and simplify the task of transferring programs to other computer systems. We won't discuss the Programmer's Workbench in this book.

The electronic office, along with the programmer's support tools, new applications, and the adaptability of the UNIX software in general are the main reasons that UNIX has gained such wide popularity today.

CHAPTER 2

GETTING STARTED: LOGIN, PASSWD, AND WHO

You will learn about the following in this chapter:

- The login procedure used by UNIX
- How to change your password
- How case is used by UNIX

- How to use options and arguments with UNIX commands
- Some basic UNIX commands, such as `cal`

Frederick Porteous Ramshead III answered the door. Outside stood a small, white-haired woman with rosy cheeks, a merry grin, and an avaricious glint in her eyes.

"Freddie Pet, let me in!"

Frederick made way, noting the small suitcase in her hand.

"Grandma! You haven't left Grandpa again! And my name is Frederick, not Freddie Pet."

"Of course I haven't, and of course it is, deary. Now offer your dear Granny a seat and a pitcher of lemonade."

"Yes, yes, please make yourself comfortable. But why…, I mean, to what do I owe the honor of this visit?"

"Freddie, I am here to make you a wonderful offer, one that will change your life for the better—and you certainly can use that!"

"That's wonderful, Grandma," beamed Frederick, while inwardly groaning. He recalled the 20 newspaper subscriptions she sold him last year so she could win that trip to Disneyland.

"You have a computer terminal, right?"

"Right, Grandma." She had sold him one last Christmas.

"Well, I'm going to give you access to a UNIX system."

"A UNIX system?"

"You're sure quick on the uptake, Pet. Yes, a UNIX system." Grandma spilled open the suitcase, liberating a mass of documents, brochures, and contracts. She fixed Frederick with a steely gaze. "Now pay attention to what I am going to tell you."

An hour later, a triumphant Grandma left with a signed check, and a dazed Frederick Porteous Ramshead III sat down at his terminal, wondering what he had gotten into this time. He attached the modem and dialed the number Grandma had given him. Soon the following display appeared on his screen:

```
Grandma's Old-Fashioned UNIX
Login:
```

He typed the *login name* Grandma had given him: `freddie` (someone already had taken "frederick"). The terminal responded with

```
password:
```

He typed the *password* Grandma had given him: `pet`. The system responded with

```
WELCOME TO GRANDMA'S OLD-FASHIONED UNIX, WHERE
VALUE AND QUALITY ARE NEVER COMPROMISED.
%
```

What did that `%` mean? Did it indicate that Grandma was getting a percentage of his computer payment? Oh, now I remember, he thought. It was the signal that UNIX was ready for his next command. Grandma called it the UNIX *prompt*. The first thing he wanted to do was change the password Grandma had given him. He typed the `passwd` command and then changed his password to `hotdog6`. Ah, that was better.

What next? He tried `date`, and the system displayed today's date and time. Frederick set his calendar watch by it. Next, he typed `cal 11 1912` to find out on which day of the week Grandma was born. The UNIX system showed the month of November for 1912. Ah yes, she was born on Tuesday. Then he typed `who` to find out who else was logged in. Hmmm, was `pierre` his brother? He looked at the nice book that Grandma had left him and found the command `finger`, which gives more detail on users. He typed `finger pierre` and found that `pierre` was, in fact, his brother, Pierre Robustus Ramshead. Yes, Grandma had hit him up, too. Well, he'd better learn more about UNIX. He typed `learn`, a command used to access a built-in UNIX tutorial.

An hour later, and much more knowledgeable about the UNIX filing system, he sat back, typed `logout`, and gave a sigh of relief. *This* time, Grandma really had done him a favor. UNIX *was* going to improve the quality of his life.

Getting Started

How do you get involved with UNIX (aside from the obvious method of being hustled into it by your grandmother)? For many, it's a matter of circumstances.

UNIX is by far the leading computer operating system on college and university campuses, and it's gaining significant ground in the corporate world. Many students acquire their first knowledge of computing on UNIX systems, even though Windows is much more common. Now, increasing numbers of college graduates are entering business and industry and are demanding access to UNIX and UNIX-like (Linux) systems. Computer manufacturers are responding with a large range of microcomputer and minicomputer systems.

Suppose that, by choice or fate, you now are involved with UNIX, so let's begin our study of UNIX. First, we'll show you how to get started on a UNIX system and describe the major characteristics of a typical terminal that you might use to communicate with UNIX. It's increasingly common to access UNIX through a personal computer running `telnet` or an X Windows–like interface, or through a PC running Linux. However, old-fashioned terminals are still widely used because they allow access to mainframe and minicomputers running UNIX applications that haven't been ported over to Windows or similar operating systems. If you can learn on a terminal, the other interfaces will seem easy (or at least modern). Next, we'll discuss the login and password process in detail. Finally, we'll look at the first of many simple, yet powerful, commands in the UNIX shell.

Establishing Contact with the System

Lured by the wonders of UNIX, you want to unleash its powers. But how do you get in touch with the system? The precise details will vary from system to system, but the following general features are necessary:

- You need a means of communicating with the system. Normally, the means will be a keyboard and a screen display (terminal or monitor), and that is what we will assume you have.

- You have to tell the system who you are by *logging in*. Computers that handle multiple users are usually selective with whom they deal. Logging in involves your *username*, which often consists of your first initial and your last name. Your professor or systems administrator (SA) will likely give this username to you.

- You may have to give the system a password so that the computer will know it's really you who is logged in. This password is for *your* protection; *don't* let *anyone* know what it is, no matter how much you trust them. There is no *valid* reason for anyone except you to know your password. If you give it out, you probably deserve the failing grade or work termination you'll get if/when that password is misused.

- When you are done, you need to *log out* to tell UNIX that you are finished. Otherwise, the system will just sit there waiting for your next instruction. Or, worse yet, someone will sit down at your logged-in computer (still logged in as you) and do nasty things like delete all your files or send email telling your professor/boss how much you dislike them. There would be no way to prove it wasn't you who did these things, so it's in your best interest to log out when done.

Now we will explain how these features are implemented.

The Keyboard

The keyboard of most computers resembles, at a minimum, that of a typewriter. It will have keys bearing letters of the English alphabet such as D and U. Other keys have symbols on them, such as #, *, ~, @, and ^, which may not be found on all typewriters. Some keys contain short words such as Return (Enter or C/R on some keyboards), Ctrl (for control), Break, Shift, and Esc (for escape). Many of these keys are special keys, not found on the standard type-writer, that have been added to the keyboard to make life easier for computer users. We will discuss some of these special keys and their meaning to UNIX later in this chapter.

Some Keyboard Conventions

In this book, we capitalize the name of a key—for example, the Return key or the Backspace key. When a key is used in a screen display, it will be enclosed in angle brackets (`<Return>`) to distinguish it from user input. In other words, when you see `<Return>` at the end of text that you type, simply press the Return key—don't type "<Return>".

In addition, we use lowercase letters to refer to an alphabet key—for example, the *a* key—even though many keyboards use capital letters on the face of the key. Our reason for doing this is simple. When you press the *a* key (or any other alphabet key), the screen will show the lower-case version, not the uppercase. Of course, if you want an uppercase letter, you must hold down the Shift key while you type the letter, or use the Caps Lock key, which we will explain soon.

You may have noticed that we use a special typeface to simulate what you see onscreen. In case you've missed it, it looks like the following:

```
Grandma's Old-Fashioned UNIX
Login:
```

Whenever you are to type something on the keyboard, such as a command or other informa-tion, we use this same typeface. For example, the text might read, "To find out the current date and time, type **date** and press Return."

Sometimes we use an italic version of this typeface. The italic font means that you that you must substitute an actual value, filename, command, or some other appropriate information for the italicized word. For example, the text might say, "The format for using the calendar command is `cal` *year*." This means that to use the calendar command, you must type `cal` and then an actual year, such as 1942, for *year*. Your command would be

```
cal 1942
```

The ASCII Character Set

It would be nice if there was a standard keyboard layout, but not all keyboards are identical. Fortunately, there is a standard *character set* that most keyboards carry. It's called the ASCII (pronounced "as-kee") character set. ASCII stands for American Standard Code for Information Interchange. You can find a copy of this character set in Appendix A, "ASCII Table." Although terminal manufacturers agree on where to place the alphabet and the numbers, they go their separate ways when it comes to the placement of other ASCII characters. Thus, if you want to learn the placement of keys on one terminal, be aware that some keys may be in a different location on a different terminal. The same goes for PCs acting as UNIX terminals. Also, many have special keys not found in the ASCII character set, such as keys with editing or graphics uses.

Using the Keyboard

Using the keyboard is a straightforward procedure. Simply press the key with the symbol you want to appear onscreen. Sometimes you may need to press a combination of keys to get the desired symbol. You may be given a message to enter a value for which several correct keys could be used. For example, to reply "Yes" to a question, either a capital *Y* or a lowercase *y* could be used, depending on your system. In this case, choose whichever is easiest for you.

Tip

There is no such thing as the *any key*. If you see the message `Press Any Key to Continue`, you simply press whatever key you want on the keyboard.

You should know a few additional facts about keyboards:

- Some keys have two symbols on the face of the key. Ordinarily, the lower of the two characters is sent when the key is pressed. To send the upper character, press one of the Shift keys at the same time you press the character key. Some examples are

Key Pressed	Result
5	Sends the number 5
Shift-5	Sends the percent sign, %
a	Sends a lowercase *a*
Shift-a	Sends an uppercase *A*

- Pressing the Caps Lock key is like permanently holding down a Shift key. However, Caps Lock affects only letters. Some terminals have a signal light on the Caps Lock key to show you that it's engaged. Other terminals will lock down the Caps Lock key when it's engaged. Some examples are

Key Pressed	Result
Caps Lock	Turns on capital letters
a	Sends an uppercase *A*
5	Still sends a 5
Caps Lock	Turns off capital letters

Note

The actual keys on the terminal are usually labeled with uppercase letters, but because they normally transmit lowercase letters, we will use lowercase letters like a rather than *A* to stand for the key. UNIX is case-sensitive; the letters *A* and *a* are two different letters to UNIX. Almost all UNIX commands are lowercase.

Caution

Don't do most of your work with the Caps Lock key on. This can send some strange commands to the computer when you are using UNIX or some editors. These strange commands could cause errors for the computer and headaches for you. It's also considered rude to use all uppercase on email messages.

- Additional characters are produced by pressing the Ctrl (or Control) key and then pressing a regular key. Such characters are known as *control characters*. Some examples are

Key to Be Pressed	Procedure
Ctrl-d	Hold down the Ctrl key and then press d once
Ctrl-c	Hold down the Ctrl key and then press c once

Control characters aren't always displayed onscreen, but when they are, they usually appear as ^d, for example. ^d is truly one character, although it takes two symbols to represent it onscreen. Such control characters are often used for special purposes in computer systems.

- The keyboard has special keys to correct typing errors. Because all terminals aren't the same, here are several possibilities:

Key Pressed	Result
Backspace	Backs up and erases the last character you typed
Left Arrow	If not part of arrow set, works the same as Backspace
Rub	Usually works the same as Backspace
Ctrl-h	An older version of Backspace
Del (or Delete)	Deletes the character under the cursor
Ctrl-u	Deletes the entire line

These keys are described later in the chapter. For now, understand that because not all UNIX systems are configured the same way, some of these keys might not work the way stated here. We advise you to experiment with your own system to find what really works well.

- On many typewriters, the lowercase *l* and the numeral 1 are interchangeable. This isn't true on a computer keyboard. If, in your typing, you have used the letter *l* for the number 1, you must break that habit. The same situation holds true for the uppercase letter *O* and the digit 0 (zero). They aren't interchangeable, and UNIX will give you errors if you try to misuse them.

- Develop a good touch. Many keyboards will repeat a letter if you hold down a key too long. You may find yours typing lines like "Myy ssincereest apoloogiees.." if your terminal is sensitive and your fingers aren't.

Note
Try not to press the keys on the keyboard with all your strength. Although many people "type hard" and can be heard typing from across the room, don't be one of them. This is hard on the keyboard and could (if done over many years) cause problems for you.

The Return Key

The Return key is also known as the C/R (carriage return) or Enter key. On an electric typewriter, pressing this key advances the paper a line and returns the typewriter to the left-hand margin of the page. The Return key performs a similar function on a computer terminal. More important, pressing the Return key tells the system that you have finished that line. Suppose that you are on the system and want to enter the UNIX command who. If you merely type the letters *w h o* and nothing else, nothing will happen. Is who a useless command? No—the

problem is that UNIX doesn't know you are finished. You could be a slow typist working on
`who`, `whoami`, `who is this`, and so on. After entering your command, you must press the
Return key. Pressing Return tells the system, "Okay, I'm done; take it from here." Thus, the
correct way to use the `who` command is to type

who `<Return>`

where `<Return>` stands for the Return key. At first, we will remind you to press Return after
each new line command, but later we won't bother—we have confidence that you will soon be
pressing Return automatically.

Logging In

The first step in using a UNIX system is to log in. The word *log* comes from the shipping era
when the captain filled out the daily log with a record of activities. In this context, you are
signing into the "log" of the UNIX system. We will assume that the screen display on your
computer is turned on and you are raring to go. The first key you should press is Return.
UNIX should respond with something like the following:

`UNIX(r) System V Release 4.0`

`Login:`▯

Don't be alarmed if the first line doesn't look the same on your screen. There are many different versions of UNIX and each is configured differently. Although the message may be different, the login prompt and login process will remain the same.

The ▯ after the `Login:` prompt is the UNIX *cursor*. On some systems, you might see an underscore instead (blinking on some terminals). The cursor is your guiding light; it shows where
your next letter will be placed onscreen.

Now type your login name. Your *login name* is the name by which you are known to the UNIX
system. This name is usually assigned by the system administrator. Let's assume your login
name is `sneezy`. Don't put a space before or after your name. A space is a character, just like *a*
or 7. Thus, adding a space would make your login name different. Login names are normally
in lowercase letters only, so type **sneezy**, not "Sneezy" Or "SNEEZY." Finish with a Return as
shown in the following:

`Login:` **sneezy** `<Return>`

The Prompt Character

If your account has been set up without a password, and if the system recognizes **sneezy** as a
valid name, there will be a pause while the system sets up things for you. It may give you some
messages, and then it will display a prompt, a special symbol at the left of the screen telling
you that UNIX is in operation and waiting for your next command. Each time you give UNIX
an instruction, it will give you a new prompt when it has finished and is ready for the next
instruction. The standard prompt is usually **%** or **$**. We will assume the prompt is **%**. With a lit-
tle experience, you will learn how to change this prompt.

The Password

What happens if you have a password or if the system doesn't recognize **sneezy** as a login name? In either case, the system responds to the previous line with the following:

`password:`

You then type your password. The letters you type won't appear onscreen as you type them. After all, what good is a password if someone can look over your shoulder and read it off the screen? Also be careful that no one is watching what your fingers type. Again, press Return (Enter) when you're done typing your password. (Your password to use the account may be set up so that you neither have nor need a password to use the system.) If you have no password and still get this message asking for one, you do need a password. The system doesn't recognize you but, being a bit cagey, it asks you for a password anyway. The login procedure won't continue unless you give some password—anything—at this point, so fake one. The fake password won't get you on the system, but it will cause the system to ask for your login name again. At this point, you may notice that you mistyped your login name. For example, suppose in answer to password, you (**sneezy**) typed

snowwhite

for your password. UNIX then compares the password you typed with its record of **sneezy**'s password. If the two agree, you are welcomed to the system and presented with the system prompt. If you typed either word incorrectly, the system responds with

```
Login incorrect
Login:
```

and you get to try again. You can repeat this as many times as necessary unless the system administrator has set a limit on the number of attempts to log in. This would be to guard against someone trying to break into the system by trying to guess your password. Most systems allow you at least three attempts to login.

Setting Up and Changing Passwords

It's a simple matter to give yourself a password if you lack one. When you are logged in and have the UNIX prompt, type the following command:

`% `**`passwd`**` <Return>`

Notice that **passwd** is in lowercase letters. The UNIX commands you enter will always be in lowercase letters; you can't substitute uppercase letters. Also, note that the command is **passwd**, not **password**. (This dubious shortcut saves you time in typing a command that you may use once a season, if that often. For some people, these UNIX abbreviations are a system foible because the abbreviations are harder to remember than the full word!) After you type **passwd**, UNIX responds with the following:

```
changing password for sneezy
Old password:
New password:
```

At the `Old password:` prompt, type your current password; at the `New password:` prompt, type your choice of new password. It won't appear onscreen. Press Return and UNIX responds with

```
Retype new password:
```

This is a check to make sure that you and UNIX both have the same word in mind. Because you don't see what you type, this check is valuable. If the two words you typed disagree, UNIX responds with

```
Mismatch - Password unchanged.
%
```

The return of the prompt means that UNIX is finished with the `passwd` command. If you want to continue, you have to start over again by typing `passwd` and pressing Return. Get used to UNIX not saying "good" or "correct" when it does something successfully; it just gives you the old prompt.

If the words you typed did agree, UNIX will accept the new password and you will have to use it the next time you log in. Don't forget your password once you have entered it. Don't write it down anywhere it could be seen. Preferably, don't write it down at all.

What sort of passwords can you use? Generally, a password should contain at least one nonnumeric character and a mix of letters. Don't use simple words without numbers or other special characters. Unacceptable passwords are `007007`, `pipe`, and `dog`. Some acceptable examples are `TO52LIFE`, `747F22`, and `rock69`. Don't use your username as your password. Although this is easy to remember, it's also easy for someone to guess. Secure passwords shouldn't be in the dictionary or be any other common name. The reason is that some people try to illegally access systems by entering a username and then (using an automated process) trying every word in the dictionary! If the system administrator hasn't limited number of login attempts, your secret password may be the only defense for your system. Try to use a password that you can remember without having to write it down. If you forget it, your system administrator can help you.

Logging Out

The process of signing off when you are done is called *logging out*. To log out, the UNIX prompt must be showing. Thus, you can't log out in the middle of the `passwd` process. If the prompt is showing, just type

```
% logout <Return>
```

You will now be logged out, and the screen should show your system's standard welcome message:

```
UNIX(r) System V Release 4.0

Login:
```

You can walk away knowing that you have said goodbye properly to UNIX and that the terminal is ready for the next user.

Certain procedures will cause the system to delay logging you out after you give the logout command. We assume that you don't know how to do these things yet. Later, we will give some examples (such as background jobs running) and tell you what to do.

Correcting Typing Errors

Even the most talented fingers sometimes stumble as they sweep across the keyboard, and even the most brilliant minds sometimes have second thoughts about commands they have typed. One major advantage of an interactive system such as UNIX is that it gives you the opportunity to see and correct errors immediately.

The mechanics of making corrections depend on the terminal you use and on how your particular system has been set up. Therefore, the methods we describe here may work differently on your system. You have to check out your particular system.

Erasing Characters

Erasing a character usually means to move the cursor back one space and remove the offending character. The key most commonly used to do this is Backspace. For example, if you mistakenly type

passqr

and then press Backspace twice, the cursor will back up (move left) over the last two letters, erasing them and leaving the word

pass

You then can correctly complete the command by typing **w** and **d** to produce

passwd

Another common way to erase characters is to use Ctrl-h. Press the Ctrl key and press the *h* key once.

Canceling Lines and Interrupting a Command

A character that cancels a whole line instead of just one letter is called a *kill* character. For example, on our system, the kill character is Ctrl-u. (Note that Ctrl-u is considered a single character, even though it involves pressing two keys—*Ctrl* and *u*—simultaneously.) Thus, the following sequence,

% passwd<Ctrl-u>

produces a blank line; **passwd** is deleted. (Some systems use the Ctrl-x sequence to accomplish the same thing.) Notice that in this case (when using the Ctrl key), it's not necessary to press Return for UNIX to acknowledge your command because whatever you typed is never sent to UNIX; instead, it's removed from the keyboard buffer before it goes anywhere.

Some systems use @ as a kill character. In this case, the line is usually not erased from the screen, just from what is transmitted. For example, the following sequence will transmit `passwd` because the @ voided the letters `osddef`:

`osddef@passwd`

Another special character is the *interrupt* character, which usually is generated by Ctrl-c or the Del key. This causes the system to "interrupt" what it's doing. The interrupt character not only erases lines but also halts many programs after they start running. It's the common way to stop the computer from doing something and to return to the shell (%).

Note

The Break key can sometimes be used like an interrupt. However, on some systems, pressing Break locks up a terminal, interrupting not only UNIX but also the user. We suggest that you *don't* use Break.

Some Simple Shell Commands

Suppose that you've logged in successfully by answering the login and password questions properly. The prompt appears onscreen, telling you that UNIX is ready to obey your every command. After your first flush of joy and power, you may wonder, "What do I tell it to do?" There are literally thousands of legitimate possible answers to that question and, in this section, we will look at four of the simplest: the commands `date`, `cal`, `who`, and `finger`. These are examples of *shell commands,* which are standard commands recognized by the shell program. We chose these four commands because they are useful and easy to understand.

Chapter 1, "Introduction to UNIX," explained that the shell is the liaison between you and the computer. Let's see how that works in the context of shell commands. After you log in, the shell provides you with a prompt (%, we assume), signifying that it's ready for your move. You give it a command, such as `date`, and press Return. The shell then identifies this command as something it knows and executes the command, usually giving you output onscreen. Whether or not it gives you an output, you will know when it's finished because the shell will send another prompt to the screen to let you know it's your turn again. If you enter a command that the shell doesn't recognize—`getlost`, for example—it lets you know with a response like the following:

```
% getlost <Return>
getlost: not found
```

Now, let's try one of the commands that does work—the `date` command.

The Bourne, C, and Korn Shells

The *shell* is the part of the UNIX operating system that acts as an intermediary between you and the computer. It relays your commands to the computer and returns its responses to you. Two main shells are in widespread use:

- The Bourne shell, named after the man who developed it. It's the shell that comes with the standard Bell Labs release. (It may vary slightly from older to newer releases.) Recent shells, such as the Bourne Again shell, are based on the original Bourne shell but have some new features.

- The C shell, developed at the University of California at Berkeley and included as part of Berkeley Software Distribution (BSD) packages.

Most of what we say in this book applies equally to both shells, but there are differences. This book is written for the C shell. (For the Bourne shell, see *The Waite Group's UNIX System V Primer*, by Mitchell Waite, Stephen W. Prata, and Donald Martin.)

How can you tell which shell you have? You can ask. You can try using a C-shell–only feature and see if it works. Usually you can tell by the prompt. The Bourne shell normally uses $\underline{\$}$ as the main prompt, and the C shell normally uses **%** as the main prompt.

Another shell, Korn, is widely available because it's distributed with UNIX System V Release 4. Over time, many of its features are being added to the Bourne shell. The Korn shell uses the same prompt as the Bourne shell.

The date Command

The `date` command displays the current date and time onscreen. To use it, type **date** after the prompt and press Return, as follows:

```
% date <Return>
```

UNIX provides the %; you provide the word **date**. (Don't forget that you have to press Return.) This line of instruction is known technically as the *command line*. The result of giving this command is that UNIX prints the date. It will look something like the following:

```
Tue Aug 8 14:49:10 PST 2000
```

UNIX uses a 24-hour clock and gives the time to the second. The full sequence of command and response would look like the following:

```
% date <Return>
Tue Aug 8 14:49:10 PST 2000
%
```

You can then give another command after the last prompt.

Throughout this book, after each new command is presented, you will find a summary of that command. The following is the summary for **date**:

date: Displays Date and Time		
Name	Options	Arguments
date	None	None

Description: When you type **date**, UNIX displays the date and time of day.

In the preceding summary of the **date** command, notice the two categories Options and Arguments. Although these categories are empty for **date**, we will explain their meaning here.

Some commands perform operations such as printing or listing information. These types of commands often need something on which to operate. The name of the thing operated on is called the *argument*. Many commands aren't complete without an argument, and some commands can have more than one argument. For example, to print two files one after the other, you would use a printing command and the names of the two files. These two filenames would be two arguments. The **cal** command, described next, is an example of a command requiring an argument.

Options generally are variations on the command. For example, a printing command may have an option to double-space the output. In Figure 2.1, you can see commands, options, and arguments onscreen.

FIGURE 2.1
Commands, options, and
arguments.

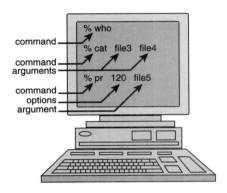

Figure 2.1 uses two different UNIX commands (don't worry what they are, you will learn more later) with arguments and options. UNIX provides a great many commands, with each command usually having many possible options and arguments. Memorizing all these commands and their options might seem difficult. Take comfort in knowing that no one ever *memorizes* all the commands and their options. If you need to use a command but don't know what it is, look it up through the online help facility. From the command line simply type **man command**. For example, if you forgot what the **passwd** command did, you could type

% man passwd

and UNIX will provide you with a quick description of the command and instructions on how to use it. You will likely find the man (for manual) command very useful. We do, however, recommend that you become familiar with all the common commands and their usage to improve your productivity.

The cal Command

You might want to use the **cal** command next. It doesn't give information about California, but it will print a calendar. This command is more sophisticated than the **date** command because it requires an argument. Recall that an argument provides additional information needed by the command. In this case, the **cal** command needs to know the year for which you want the calendar. Thus, to produce a calendar for the year 1776, enter the following command line:

% cal 1776

Here, the command is `cal` and the argument is **1776**. When you press Return, the display shows the first part of the page:

```
                            1776
          Jan                 Feb                 Mar
  S  M Tu  W Th  F  S   S  M Tu  W Th  F  S   S  M Tu  W Th  F  S
     1  2  3  4  5  6            1  2  3               1  2
  7  8  9 10 11 12 13   4  5  6  7  8  9 10   3  4  5  6  7  8  9
 14 15 16 17 18 19 20  11 12 13 14 15 16 17  10 11 12 13 14 15 16
 21 22 23 24 25 26 27  18 19 20 21 22 23 24  17 18 19 20 21 22 23
 28 29 30 31           25 26 27 28 29        24 25 26 27 28 29 30
                                             31
```

To save space, this display shows only the first three months. However, you will see all 12 months onscreen. If the full calendar doesn't fit onscreen, press Ctrl-s to stop the display before January rolls off the screen and then press Ctrl-q to restart it. (Some systems use different keys for this.)

To get the calendar for a single month, type the number of the month before the year. You can use a one- or two-digit number for the month. Thus, May is 05 or 5. The following is the command line to get the calendar for July 1872:

```
cal 7 1872
```

The format for this command is

```
cal [month] [year]
```

The square brackets around *month* indicate that the month is an *optional argument*, meaning it can be omitted. The year is also optional, but if you don't want to refer to the current year only, you must give it. You don't actually type the brackets when you use the command. The italic typeface indicates that you don't literally type the word; rather, you type a value in place of the word.

You call use `cal` for future calendars (up to the year 9999) as well as for the present and the past.

---

cal: Provides a Calendar

Name	Option	Arguments
cal	None	*[month] year*

Description: The `cal` command provides a calendar for whatever year you type after the command. There must be at least one space between the command and the year. The year should be in the range of 1-9999 A.D. You can get the calendar for just one month by preceding the year with the number of the month, numbered from 1 to 12.

Example: To see the calendar for May 1942, type

`cal 05 1942`

The who Command

Recall that UNIX is a time-sharing system. This means that several people can use the system at the same time. In recognition of the inquisitiveness of human nature, UNIX has a who command. When you give this command, UNIX responds with the list of people logged in to the system at that moment. The command and its result might look something like the following:

```
% who
bob        tty04     Aug 23      8:27
nerkie     tty07     Aug 23      8:16
catfish    tty11     Aug 23      8:36
sneezy     tty15     Aug 23      8:52
granny     tty21     Aug 23     23:13
boss1776   tty24     Aug 23      9:33
%
```

The first column gives the user's login name. The second column identifies the terminal being used. The label `tty` is a throwback to the days when most terminals were Teletype machines that printed on paper rather than onscreen. The `tty` number can provide a clue to the person's location if you know the rooms where specific terminals are placed. The remaining columns give the date and time that each user logged in, using the 24-hour clock.

From the display, it looks as though `granny` has been on the system all night, or maybe she forgot to log out again. But who is `catfish`? (On a large system or one where people don't use identifying usernames, you won't know everyone.) Your system may have some commands that tell you more about your comrades in computing. An example is the `finger` command, which we will discuss next.

who: Who's on the System		
Name	Options	Arguments
who	Several	[am I]

Description: The who command, when typed without an argument, tells you who's now on the system. It gives you the user's login name, the terminal name, and the time that the user logged in. If you ask who am I, it gives you this information about yourself, and it may also tell you which UNIX system you are on.

Options: The options for the who command aren't important here. If you want more information about them, check the online manual, as described in Chapter 3, "Electronic Mail and Online Help: mail, talk, and man."

Example: To find out who is on the system, type who.

The finger Command

The finger command can be used with or without an argument. It's used to gather information about a user. Without an argument, it works like who but also gives users' full names, idle time, and office numbers. The idle time is the time, in minutes, since the user last gave UNIX a command. The finger command might give the following display:

```
% finger
Login          Name          TTY   Idle    When          Office
bob        Robert Sniggle    04            Tue 9:27      SC256
nerkie     Nercules Pigrow   07     7      Tue 10:16     BH019
catfish    Kitty Trout       11            Tue 9:38      WD40
sneezy     U. R. R. Reader   15            Tue 10:52     WD38
granny     Henrietta Goose   22     15     Mon 23:13     ZX280
boss       V.I. Parsons      26            Tue 11:59     Penthouse
%
```

Aha! The mystery is explained: catfish is the new person in the next office. To learn more about her, use finger with an argument. In this case, the argument is her name: login or first or last. For example, typing the following using the login name:

```
% finger catfish
```

will return the following:

```
Login name: catfish              In Real Life: Kitty Trout
Directory: /usr/catfish          Shell: /bin/csh
Last Login: Tue Aug 23 9:38 on tty11
Plan: To utterly master Java
%
```

Here you learn her home directory (more about home directories in the next chapter), and you learn that she uses the C shell (/bin/csh is the C shell and /bin/sh is the Bourne shell). You also learn her current intentions in using UNIX. This full printout of information is called the *long form*. Yes, there is also a *short form*; it's the one-line-per-user form that you saw in the first example.

If you had used finger Kitty as a command, you would have obtained a similar listing for all persons named Kitty who have accounts on the system, whether or not they were currently logged in. The command finger Kitty Trout would provide information about all persons named Kitty or Trout.

The finger command is useful if you need to know someone's login name (to send mail, for example), but you know only that person's real name. The finger command also has what are known as *flag options* (simply *options*, for short). Such options come after the command and before the argument and usually are in the form of a hyphen followed by a letter. The following is an example:

```
finger -s catfish
```

The -s option stands for *short form*. Note that there's no space between the hyphen and the s, but that there are spaces on either side of the option. The following shows the result of giving this command:

```
catfish  Kitty Trout    11    Tue 9:38    WD40
```

You can use more than one flag option in a command. An example would be finger -m -s catfish. Some commands allow options to be strung together in any order. For example, the following commands would all give the same results:

```
finger -m-s John
finger -ms John
finger -sm John
```

Note

Rearranging option flags is usually, but not always, possible.

In the following command summary and in future summaries, we will include descriptions of the most important options available. After you become familiar with your particular system, you should probably research the command options further to find ways to better do your job.

`finger`: Provides Information about Users

Name	Options Arguments	
finger	[-m, -l, -s]	[*name*...]

Description: When used without an argument, the `finger` command provides a list of all users on the system, giving the login name, the real name, the terminal, the idle time, the login time, and the office (if known) for each user. (This list of information constitutes the *short form.*)

When used with one or more names, `finger` provides the previous information plus information about the home directory and the shell of the named users. (This argument list of information constitutes the *long form.*) The `finger` program will search for all users whose login names or real names match the given name.

Options:

-m   Causes `finger` to search only the login names that match the argument name(s). Thus, `finger -m john` gives information only about a person whose login name is `john` and will ignore people named John who have a different login name.

-l   Forces `finger` to display the long form.

-s   Forces `finger` to display the short form.

Example: To find out the login names of every user named `john` and to print just the one-line summary, type

```
finger -s john
```

The result might look like the following:

```
Login       Name            TTY  Idle       When      Office
jonny       John Grock      5               12:13     ACH000
buny0234    John Bunyon     17         <Jul 4 14:14>
daffy       John Duck       18         <Aug 2 06:02>   CB122
suzie       Susan John      19         <Aug 8 15:23>
john        Johannes Brahms 22         <Aug 9 09:42>   MU244
```

Notice that `finger` finds all users named `john`, whether that's the user's first, last, or login name. This could be cumbersome on a system with hundreds of users. The angle brackets indicate that the user isn't currently logged in (the date and time indicate when that user logged out). In searching for names, `finger` ignores capitalization. It will find both `john` and `John`. The command

```
finger -s -m john
```

would produce just the last line of this listing because the -m option restricts the `finger` command to searching only login names.

Although your system may not have `finger`, the information that `finger` uses is stored somewhere in the system. Much of the information is kept in a file named `/etc/passwd`, and we will discuss this file in Chapter 11, "Information Processing: `grep`, `find`, and `awk`."

In Chapter 3, you will learn how to communicate with your fellow computer users by using electronic mail.

Summary

In this chapter you've seen a lot of the basic commands used by UNIX, as well as the login procedure. You now know how to change your password, which you should do regularly, as well as how to make sure your password isn't easily guessed by a hacker. The next few chapters start building on the basic knowledge you've gained in this chapter.

Review Questions

Matching Commands and Descriptions

Match the command in the left column to the corresponding description in the right column.

1. `who`   a. Gives the date and time

2. `passwd`   b. Tells who's logged in

3. `date`   c. Produces a calendar

4. `cal`   d. Lets you choose a password

5. `finger`   e. Gives information about users

Questions

1. Which of the following commands include arguments? Identify the arguments, if any.

    a. `cal 1984`

    b. `cal 09 2025`

    c. `who`

    d. `finger don`

2. What is the difference between `passwd` and `password`?

3. Which of the following is the basic purpose of the UNIX prompt (%)?

    a. To demonstrate UNIX's ability to produce unusual symbols

    b. To tell you that UNIX is ready to accept a command

    c. To tell UNIX that you are finished

4. What happens when you fail to press Return?

5. What does the phrase "press Ctrl-s" mean?

6. How do you correct a typing error on the same line as the cursor?

7. Which keystroke combination interrupts the current job and returns the prompt?

8. What happens if you hold down a key?

9. How do you stop the screen from scrolling? How do you restart it?

10. What is a kill character?

Exercises

1. Log in to your UNIX system.

2. Type **whp** and correct it to who.

3. Type **fenger** and correct it to finger.

4. If you don't have a password, give yourself one now. If you do have one, change it to a new one.

5. Find out how many people are logged in and who has been logged in the longest.

6. Find the time of day.

7. Find out on which day of the week you were born.

8. Find out which day of the week is January 1, 1991.

9. Type a command and then use Ctrl-u to kill the whole line.

CHAPTER 3

ELECTRONIC MAIL AND ONLINE HELP: MAIL, TALK, AND MAN

You will learn about the following in this chapter:

- Sending and reading mail
- Saving and printing mail you want to keep
- Deleting mail you want to get rid of
- Modifying the mail environment
- Using the man system to get help

T he term *electronic mail* (or *email*) refers to a mail delivery system that replaces conventional mail delivery with an electronic computer-based service. Electronic mail can also replace some types of telephone calls and interoffice memos. The form of electronic mail used with UNIX is sometimes called a *mailbox system*. Each user with a login account has a mailbox file to which other users can send mail.

This chapter also looks at the way you can get help on your UNIX system using the man command. This is often the most convenient and fastest way to look up an option or syntax that you've forgotten.

Working with Email

An electronic mail system has several major benefits:

- Correspondence can be conveniently created on a keyboard or terminal, and word-processing capabilities make entry and corrections easy.

- You can print paper copies and even have them typeset.

- The mailing process is much faster than postal letters; a message reaches its destination almost instantaneously.

- You can mail identical copies to several users simultaneously.

- Electronic mail doesn't interrupt the recipient the way a phone call does, allowing people to use their time more efficiently.

- Electronic mail can be electronically filed with all the inherent advantages of that process.

- No paper, envelopes, or stamps are required, and no trips to the post office are needed.

- Electronic mail can be mailed locally, such as in a local UNIX time-share system, or it can be routed through many computers, traveling thousands of miles electronically in just moments (see Figure 3.1).

FIGURE 3.1
A hypothetical UNIX net-
work.

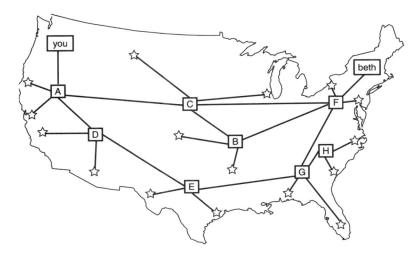

Using Either `mail` or `mailx`

Email goes through several stages of processing much like conventional mail does. You, as the author of an email letter, must first create your message by using some form of a mail user agent (MUA), such as UNIX `mail` or `mailx`. Without an MUA, you can't begin the electronic mail process—it would be like trying to send a handwritten letter without using pen and paper. This chapter focuses on text-based MUAs such as `mail` or `mailx`.

When your message is composed, it's given to the UNIX system to begin the delivery and routing process. To do this, UNIX uses a mail transfer agent (MTA), such as Sendmail. Sendmail is like the post office itself. It receives your messages, figures out where they need to go based on addressing, and initiates a connection to other computers to begin the delivery of your mail. After your mail messages are delivered, the recipient again uses an MUA, such as `mail` or `mailx`, to read their mail.

UNIX uses the command `mail` (or `mailx` on some systems) to initiate the sending and receiving of mail. The mail system actually contains several options for preparing, delivering, reading, and disposing of mail, as briefly described later in this chapter. However, most new users can get along very nicely with the command sequence described next.

Sending Mail to Yourself

The UNIX mail system provides a handy way to send mail to yourself. Suppose that your login name is `fred` and that you want to send yourself a memo about an upcoming meeting. When the shell prompt appears onscreen, type `mail fred` and press Return. You may see the prompt `Subject :`. Enter a subject and begin typing your memo. Press Return whenever you want to start a new line, just as you would press the carriage return on a typewriter.

When your memo is complete, press Ctrl-d at the beginning of a new line. Your memo might look like the following:

```
% mail fred <Return>
Subject: Meeting with Susan <Return>

Just a reminder of our meeting <Return>
With Susan at the Admin Bldg. <Return>
Fred <Return>
```

The <Return> items indicate where you need to press Return.

At this point, you can press Ctrl-d or use a period (.). UNIX will respond with the following:

```
EOT
%
```

The next time you log in, or a few minutes later if you stay logged in, the screen greeting will include the happy announcement **you have mail** (see Figure 3.2).

FIGURE 3.2
Sending mail to others.

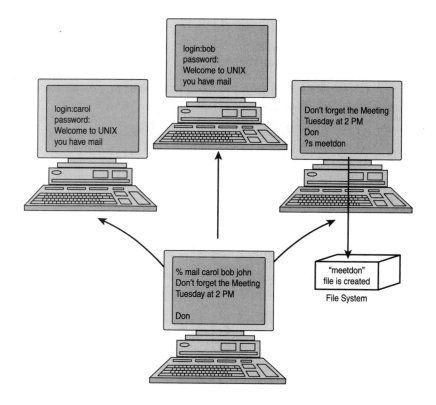

Reading Your Mail

To read electronic mail, give the single command mail from the shell. The system responds by displaying a summary of the messages received. Assume that you've received several letters. You begin by issuing the command to read your mail (**mail** or **mailx**). You will see something like the following:

```
"/var/spool/mail/wesley": 5 messages 5 unread [Read only]
>U  1  Billi Joe    Wed Jul 07  11:30  33/579  Your new Car
 U  2  Bob Hess     Wed Jul 07  13:34  11/357  Files and Dirs
 N  3  Martin       Fri Jul 09  12:00  12/423  Colts Games
        Daniels
 N  4  Kodi Dane    Fri Jul 09  14:15  10/256  Late Lunch
 N  5  Poe          Sun Jul 11  13:40  45/898  News Article
        Robertson
 N  6  Susan        Sun Jul 11  13:55  11/357  Internet Access
        Packard
&
```

This example shows how helpful it is to enter a subject when sending mail. Subjects appear as part of the incoming mail header listing the messages to be read. In addition to giving the subjects, the header tells whether the letter is new (N) or unread (U), the date and time the letter was sent, and the letter's length in terms of lines and characters. The & (ampersand) is the mail prompt, similar to the UNIX prompt %. Remember that with the many different flavors of UNIX (Solaris, AIX, HP, and Linux, just to mention a few) now available, you might see some minor variations in the way that mail is presented to you, but the preceding example is a good starting point.

To read the newest message, simply press Return. If you would prefer finding out about the Colts games, you can skip directly to message 3 by typing **3** and pressing Return.

To quit the current mail session, type **quit** or **q** and press Return.

After you read a letter, it's automatically placed in the mbox file in your home directory. (Your UNIX system administrator might set up mail so that the already read letters remain in your mailbox where you will see them each time you read mail. This is a clever way of encouraging you to get rid of old letters and save disk space.) Ideally, you will take matters into your own hands and make use of mail's many tools for handling letters. The simplest choices for disposing of mail are as follows:

- Delete the current letter from your mail file .

- Save the current letter to any new or old file (s).

.eply to the author (**R**).

Leave the letter in the **mbox** file.

:lect a choice, give the appropriate command (**d**, **s**, or **R**) right after reading the letter, or ₒ the command followed by the letter's number (**d4**, **s3**, **R1**, and so on). For example, after reading the first letter, you can type **d** to delete it.

If you want to save letter 2 in a file called **bobstuff**, just give the following command

& s2 bobstuff

Because the disposition of each letter takes place immediately after reading the letter, you can easily return to (and dispose of) previously read mail by using the **-** command (a minus sign) to display the previous letter. To continue back through other letters, just type another minus sign (**-**). To step forward through each letter, type a plus sign command (**+**) or, easier yet, just press Return.

When you're reading your mail, the **mail** application is in command mode. The **&** prompt means that mail is waiting for you to give it a command. More than 30 commands are available for reading mail. If you are a beginning user, the **-** and **+** commands are all you need to start using mail. However, if you like to explore or play with new gadgets, a quick way to see what mail has to offer is to ask for help.

Getting Help in `mail`

When sending or receiving messages, you can get a partial listing of the mail commands by using the **help** command. Type **~?** (a tilde and a question mark) at the beginning of a new line while sending mail or type **?** at the **&** prompt while receiving mail. These commands will display help screens.

For Advanced Users: Sending Mail

Some feature referred to in this discussion assume that you have advanced UNIX experience. If you are unfamiliar with these features, you can read about them in later chapters. The **vi** screen editor, for example, is described in Chapter 5, "The **vi** Screen Editor." Other advanced features connected with the filing system are described in Chapter 4, "Files and Directories: **ls**, **cat**, **more**, and **pr**," and Chapter 8, "The UNIX Shell: Command Lines, Redirection, and Shell Scripts."

When you enter **mail** to send a letter, **mail** is in input mode (as opposed to command mode). This starts up the basic mail editor, which supports basic editing commands, such as cursor movement and back spacing capabilities.

While you are in input mode, additional commands are available, the most important being **~v**, which invokes a UNIX editor. This command must be given at the beginning of a new line. The default editor is **vi**, but that can be changed in the **.mailrc** startup file in your home directory.

When you finish editing and leave an editor such as **vi** in the normal fashion, you're returned to **mail**'s input mode. This means that you have the primitive editor back to add anything else or to give the command to send your letter (Ctrl-d).

To see a screen display of other commands available in send-mail (input) mode, use the help command, ~?. This command, like all tilde commands, must be given at the start of a new line. Table 3.1 shows the commands for sending mail that you would see on a typical help screen.

TABLE 3.1   Commands for Sending Mail in Input Mode

Tilde Command	Result
~b *users*	Adds users to Blind Cc list
~c *users*	Adds users to Cc list
~d	Inserts *dead.letter*
~e	Edits the message buffer
~h	Prompts for the To list, Subject, and Cc list
~r *file*	Reads a file into the message buffer
~P	Prints the message buffer
~m *messages*	Inserts messages, right-shifted by a tab. (This command can be given only when replying to incoming mail.)
~s *subject*	Sets the Subject
~t *users*	Adds users to the To list
~v	Invokes display editor on message
~W *file*	Writes message to file
~p	Prints this message
~! *command*	Invokes the shell
~¦ *command*	Pipes the message through the command

Note

In the first column, you must substitute an actual filename, message number, and so on for the word in italics. For example, in the ~r command, *file* must be replaced by an actual filename (~r bob-stuff).

The commands in Table 3.1 give you full control of the message headers, provide advanced editing capabilities, offer interaction with the UNIX file system, and allow commands to be run in the UNIX shell. For example, typing **~c name** and pressing Return adds **name** to the carbon copy list; entering **~w filename** places a copy of the letter in a file named **filename**; and entering **~m 3** reads message number 3 into your letter.

Tip
The ~m feature is often used when responding to an incoming letter. It reminds the other person of the message he or she sent to you. The inserted message is offset by a tab space to make it clear that it's not your writing but the sender's. However, ~m can be used only when responding to incoming mail, as described next. (You can change this setting, if you want.)

For Advanced Users: Reading Mail

When you give the command **mail** at the UNIX prompt, you're placed in **mail**'s command mode (rather than input mode). The **mail** command displays a summary of incoming letters and the **&** command prompt.

A host of commands are available for reading or disposing of mail. The most important of these are listed in the help screen. To see the help screen, type a question mark at the **&** prompt. Table 3.2 shows the commands for reading mail that you would see on a typical help screen.

TABLE 3.2 Commands for Reading Mail in Command Mode

Command	Result
t *message_list*	Types messages
n	Go to and type next message
e *message_list*	Edits messages
f *message_list*	Gives headlines of messages
d *message_list*	Deletes messages
s *message_list file*	Appends messages to the named file
u *message_list*	Undeletes messages
R *message_list*	Replies to message senders
r *message_list*	Replies to message senders and all recipients and puts a copy in your mailbox
pre *message_list*	Returns messages to /usr/spool/mail
m *user_list*	Sends mail to specific users
q	Quits, saving unresolved messages in mbox
x	Quits, doesn't remove system mailbox
h	Prints active message headers
!	Shell escape

Command	Result
cd [*directory*]	Changes to named directory or to home directory if none given
a	List aliases defined in .mailrc file in your home directory

The format for using **mail** commands is

command [*message_list*] [*arguments*]

Square brackets enclose optional parts of the command line. As mentioned earlier, you must replace italicized words with an actual command name, a message number, and so on. The following are some sample command lines and what they do:

& t 1-3	Type message numbers 1 through 3
& s 1 2 file	Save message numbers 1 and 2 in file
& 3	Read message number 3: no command given
& r3	Reply to message number 3
& d3	Delete message number 3
& u3	Undelete message number 3

Notice how **mail** accepts variations on numbering. You can use either **s 1 2 file** or **s1-2 file** to save messages in **file**. However, the commands **s1 2** and **s 1 2** both save message number 1 to a file named **2**.

You can see how helpful **mail** tries to be in the following examples using the delete and undelete (u) commands. These commands work with message numbers, names, or even parts of the subject.

& d 1-3	Delete messages 1 through 3
& d fred	Delete all messages from **fred**
& d /Meeting	Delete all messages with **Meeting** in the subject
& u /Meeting	Undelete all messages with **Meeting** in the subject
& u	Undelete all messages
& R3	Reply to the senders of message 3

ne last command shown is the most useful one of all. The **R** command lets you reply to incoming messages simply and conveniently. Actually, there are two versions of the reply command: `reply` and `Reply`. The difference between the two is worth noting:

- To respond to everyone who received a copy of the letter, use `reply` or r.

- To respond to the author(s) only, use `Reply` or R.

Note
Be careful with the r command. If someone sends you a letter and sends copies to a half dozen others, r will send your reply to everyone. To avoid polluting mailboxes, use the R command whenever possible.

For Advanced Users: Adjusting the `mail` Environment

The `mail` program has more than 40 options, called *environmental variables*, that you can set to change its behavior. Options include such features as creating an abbreviation or autograph for your signature, changing the escape character (~), or creating a special folder for saving incoming messages.

Options can be set temporarily by using the **set** command while receiving mail. Or, options can be created semi-permanently by placing them in the `.mailrc` file in your home directory. If you want to see which options are now set, type **set**.

In addition to options, certain other commands are helpful for customizing the mail environment. One of the most important of these is the **alias** command. It can be used to create an alias for login names, as shown in the last line of the next example.

A typical `.mailrc` file might look like the following:

```
ask
hold
folder=PathName
crt=Lines
dot
alias Newalias [address]
```

`.mailrc` Command	Description
ask	Asks for a subject when sending mail
hold	Keeps messages in the system mailbox rather than your personal mailbox.
folder=*PathName*	Gives the pathname of a directory in which to store mail folders.
crt=*Lines*	Sets the number of lines to the integer failure of *Lines*
dot	Allows a dot to substitute a Ctrl-d

.mailrc Command	Description
alias *Newalias [address]*	Creates an alias called *Newalias* or distribution group called *Newalias*. To have multiple persons in a distribution group, separate several addresses by spaces.

Notice that the `folder=PathName` line specifies the directory in which to store mail folders. The mail can be stored in several ways: by a person's name, by subject matter, or by job title. For the folder to work, however, you must first set up a directory for storing mail. Then, as you read mail, you can use a new version of the save (**s**) command like the following:

```
s4 + susan
```

This command stores or appends letter 4 in the file **susan** located in the **Mail** subdirectory.

Note

Most UNIX systems use a default `.mailrc` file in `/usr/share/lib/Mail.rc`. If you create your own personal `.mailrc` file in your home directory, your settings will take precedence over `/etc/mail/mailx.rc`.

To see a description of all **mail** options, check your online manual or the **mail** reference manual.

Making Electronic Chit-Chat with `talk`

Many UNIX systems have a second form of electronic communication that lets you hold conversations with other users. This method can work only if the person you want to talk to is logged in and wants to talk back. First, see who is on the system by using the **who** command. Suppose that you spot your friend Hortense (login name **hortense**). Then you (**abner**) would give the following command:

```
talk hortense
```

Hortense would receive an audible beep and see the following message onscreen:

```
Message from Talk_Daemon@sterling at 1:30 ...
talk: connection requested by abner@sterling.
talk: respond with: talk abner
```

Your screen is divided horizontally into two parts by a dashed line. While you await a response, you see

```
[ Waiting for your party to respond ]
[Ringing your party again]
[Ringing your party again]
```

If Hortense decides to talk back and complete the connection, whatever you type appears on the top half of your screen, and whatever she types appears on the bottom half of your screen. If you are fast talkers (or typists), the cursor flies back and forth printing your letters. After you talk enough and want to quit, both of you should press Ctrl-c to end the program.

Chapter 9, "File-Management Commands and Others: `wc`, `sort`, `lpr`, and `chmod`," shows how to block `talk` messages by using the `mesg` command if you want to work undisturbed.

talk: Talk to Another User		
Name	Options	Arguments
talk	None	user login name

Description: The `talk` command transmits lines from your terminal to the other user's terminal. To terminate transmission, press Ctrl-c. This sends `EOT` to the other user.

Note: To block incoming messages, use the `mesg` command described in Chapter 9.

Getting More Information with `help` and `man`

Two commands may or may not be installed on your UNIX system: `help` and `man`.

The help command doesn't behave the way you might expect on all systems, as UNIX supports two help commands. The first is true `help` about UNIX commands—similar to using the `man` command but with simpler output. The second and most common form of `help` doesn't have anything to do with basic UNIX commands; instead, it deals only with the Source Code Control System (SCCS) and provides help about that subject only. Because most current versions of UNIX and Linux don't use the `help` command for anything but SCCS, you may want to use the `man` command instead. Some older versions of UNIX will support both properly.

The `help` command varies greatly from one UNIX vendor to another. The command is used by typing `help` at the shell prompt. UNIX then provides a series of menus or questions that lead to a description of the most commonly used commands.

Note
This isn't the same `help` command described earlier in the electronic mail discussion. This is a "queried" `help` command used for the shell.

In addition to the `help` command, you can refer to a large document called the UNIX Reference Manual, available in bound printed form. Part of the manual may also be stored online in a file. All UNIX commands and utilities are documented in this manual, and, if it's available, you can easily summon this information to your terminal screen. Sound great? It is, except that the manual is written for experienced UNIX programmers, not for beginners. (That's one reason we wrote this book!) This may not be a problem if the command you want to study is a simple one such as `date`. But other commands may require a lot of trial-and-error work on your part.

To tap into this fountain of knowledge, simply type **man** followed by the name of the command you want to study. For example, to learn all there is to know about `date`, type

man date

Don't forget the space between `man` and `date` and remember to press Return.

To learn more about the `man` command itself, type

man man

Be prepared to wait a bit—sometimes the system takes a while to find the desired entry. Let's look at an example of using the `man` command (edited for brevity):

```
% man who
who(1)                          User Commands                          who(1)
NAME
     who - who is on the system

SYNOPSIS
     /usr/bin/who [ -abdHlmpqrstTu ] [ file ]
     /usr/bin/who -q [ -n x ] [ file ]
     /usr/bin/who am i
     /usr/bin/who am I

     /usr/xpg4/bin/who [ -abdHlmpqrtTu ] [ file ]
     /usr/xpg4/bin/who -q [ -n x ] [ file ]
     /usr/xpg4/bin/who -s [ -bdHlmpqrtu ] [ file ]
     /usr/xpg4/bin/who am i
     /usr/xpg4/bin/who am I

AVAILABILITY
/usr/bin/who
     SUNWcsu
/usr/xpg4/bin/who
     SUNWxcu4

DESCRIPTION
The who command can list the user's name, terminal line, login time, elapsed
time since activity occurred on the line, and the process-ID of the command
interpreter (shell) for each current UNIX system user. It examines the
/var/adm/utmp file to obtain its information. If file is given, that file
(which must be in utmp(4) format) is examined. Usually, file will be
/var/adm/wtmp, which contains a history of all the logins since the file was
last created.

The general format for output is:
     name [state] line time [idle] [pid] [comment] [exit]
where:
     name            user's login name.
     state           capability of writing to the terminal.
     line            name of the line found in /dev.
     time            time since user's login.
     idle            time elapsed since the user's last activity.
     pid             user's process id.
     comment         comment line in inittab(4).
     exit            exit status for dead processes.
```

```
OPTIONS
The following options are supported:
     -a          Process /var/adm/utmp or the named file with -b,
                 -d, -l, -p, -r, -t, -T, and -u options turned on.

 ...

FILES
     /sbin/inittab          script for init.
     /var/adm/utmp          current user and accounting information
     /var/adm/wtmp          historic user and accounting information

SEE ALSO
     date(1),  login(1),  mesg(1),  init(1M),  su(1M),  wait(3B),
     inittab(4), utmp(4), environ(5)

NOTES
Super-user: After a shutdown to the single-user state, who returns a prompt;
since /var/adm/utmp is updated at login time and there is no login in
single-user state, who cannot report accurately on this state. who am i,
however, returns the correct information.

SunOS 5.5.1          Last change: 1 Feb 1995   4
```

Let's look more closely at the example. First, under the NAME heading is the command name and a brief description of the command. Next, SYNOPSIS shows how the command is used:

```
/usr/bin/who [ -abdHlmpqrstTu ] [ file ]
/usr/bin/who -q [ -n x ] [ file ]
/usr/bin/who am i
/usr/bin/who am I
 ...
```

The command is shown with its many options. You can use one option at a time or combine several together. The best way to become comfortable with UNIX is to try it out. As mentioned earlier in the chapter, options contained between square brackets are optional. More detailed information of what the options do is located in the OPTIONS section located further into the man page.

Note

The command is shown with /usr/bin/ preceding the actual command—this is considered the path to the command. UNIX online manual pages usually show the full path to a command. Your login account to the UNIX system handles the path for you. As you become more familiar with UNIX, you may want to further investigate the path and how you can modify it to meet more advanced needs.

The AVAILABILITY area shows you which versions of the command are included in the UNIX release you are using.

Next, the **DESCRIPTION** area of an online man page gives a more detailed analysis of what the command you're investigating will do and how it affects or uses the UNIX system to carry out its task. If the command has output, its format is described in this section. As you can see, the **DESCRIPTION** section presupposes knowledge about the system (such as what /var/adm/ wtmp is).

Next comes the **OPTIONS** section, which provides users with an explanation of what each option does and how to invoke it. More often than not, you will find a command that does almost exactly what you want it do. In the **OPTIONS** section, you can find out how to get more than the default output from a command.

Next comes the **FILES** section, which lists the files used by UNIX to run this particular command.

The **SEE ALSO** section lists some related commands and utilities. The numbers in parentheses tell which section of the manual contains the description.

For most UNIX systems, the first section of the user's manual describes general-purpose commands; sections 2 through 5 usually describe programmers' commands. Table 3.3 gives more detailed information on the manual's different sections.

TABLE 3.3 • Sections and Their Descriptions from the User's Manual

Section Number	Description
1	User commands who, cd, pwd, and ls
2	System calls to the UNIX system
3	C Library functions such as fprintf, qsort, and atof
4	Special files
5	File formats
6	Games (we've rarely seen games loaded onto systems—good luck!)
7	Miscellaneous feature such as troff macro packages
8	System maintenance commands

Note

AT&T documentation uses two terms to distinguish between the manual pages and any other material. Any document titled "Manual" contains manual pages consisting of UNIX commands; any document titled "Guide" contains text describing some aspect of the UNIX environment (such as using an editor).

Other specialized reference manuals are available that describe graphics commands and other utilities. Generally, each topic that has its own reference manual will also have a guide.

Now that you have a list of commands that deal with directories, you can examine the `man` page for the commands that appear to be along the lines of what you're looking for.

man: Find Manual Information by Keywords			
Name	Options	Arguments	Keyword
man	-k	[*Sections*]	Descriptive word

Description: When used with the -k (minus k) flag, the `man` command searches the entire online manual for the section containing the keyword. It then displays a description of the command similar to the printed version of the manual.

Example: This command displays the online manual explanation of the commands available that may have to do with the keyword `directory`:

```
man -k directory
```

Summary

The UNIX mail system is one of the most complex applications ever written. We have only touched the surface of this complex system. The system's administrator is well advised to gain additional in-depth knowledge of the UNIX mail system because it is often one of the more difficult areas to manage. The Internet is made up mostly of UNIX systems. Because email is a huge part of any Internet server, you can see the importance of learning and managing this complex environment. Every site we have worked at has always devoted a large portion of their system's administrative resources to ensuring that their mail systems was running at peak performance. We are sure that you will attach the same level of importance at your site.

Review Questions

1. What are the two modes of mail and when are they used?

2. Which command is used to send a letter?

3. Give a command that saves letter number 2 to a file called `jobs`.

4. If you see the ampersand prompt (&), are you in command mode or input mode of `mail`?

5. After you finish reading your mail, how do you leave the program?

6. When you're sending mail, which command calls the `vi` editor? How do you leave the editor? When you leave the editor, what happens?

7. Why is it important to enter a subject when you're prompted by `mail`?

8. How do you send mail to more than one person at a time?

9. What is the help command for input mode? for command mode?

10. When reading mail, why is **Reply** (**R**) often preferred to `reply` (r)?

Exercises

1. Send yourself mail, perhaps some reminders of things to do today. When the message that you have mail arrives at your terminal, read it and save it in a file called **today**.

2. Try the **who** command to see who is on the system. Choose someone from the list of login names and send that person electronic mail.

3. Send yourself three separate letters. (Each letter could be a short sentence about someone you know.) When the mail arrives at your terminal (maybe 10 minutes), use the **s** command to save each letter as a file. (You will use these files in the next chapter.)

4. Send mail to someone you know (or perhaps would like to know).

5. Try the **who** command to see if anyone you know is using a terminal right now. If so, use the **talk** command to ask him or her if you can practice sending some mail.

6. Try out the online manual. Select a command you already know about. Then experiment using the manual (you can't hurt it). Note that some systems may not have the **man** command.

CHAPTER 4

FILES AND DIRECTORIES: LS, CAT, MORE, AND PR

You will learn about the following in this chapter:

- How UNIX handles files and direc-tories

- The UNIX directory hierarchy

- How to name files and directories

- The ls command and its options

- How to use redirection to increase the power of UNIX commands

The UNIX file and directory system is wonderfully simple but versatile. The best way to learn its features is to use them, so we strongly urge you to experiment with the commands presented in this chapter, even if you don't need them yet. When you have a solid working knowledge of the basics, you can learn the more advanced options. We think you'll be amazed with the power and flexibility of the UNIX operating system after you have it mastered.

You need to know three things to use the UNIX file and directory system with ease:

- *Know the system's structure*—That will be the first topic of this chapter.

- *Find out which files you have*—The ls command will help you there.

- *See what's in the files*—The commands cat and more will handle that necessity.

These three commands—ls, cat, and more—form the core of your relationship with files.

Of course, it would be nice to have a way to create files, and that will be the subject of Chapters 5, 6, and 8. However, this chapter gives you a head start by showing you a quick and easy way to produce files. (Actually, you've already learned one way—sending mail to your-self!) The chapter will end by describing how to format and print files.

That's what's coming up, so let's begin by seeing how UNIX organizes files.

Files and the UNIX Directory System

Files are the heart of the UNIX system. All the UNIX programs as well as the programs you create, the text you write and edit, and the data you acquire are stored in files. When you want UNIX to remember something created by you, you must save it in a file. One very important skill to acquire, then, is the ability to create files. But unless you can keep track of your files, it doesn't do much good to create them. A little planning and care when you create files will save you big headaches later. The UNIX directory system is designed to help you with this important task.

Just as a telephone directory contains a list of subscribers, a UNIX directory contains a list of files and subdirectories, each of which can contain lists of more files and subdirectories.

Now look at the most basic example of a directory—the home directory. When you are given an account on the system, you're assigned a home directory. When you log in, you can think of yourself as being "in" your home directory. (Later you will learn to change directories but, for now, stay confined to your home directory.)

Now, suppose that you create a file. You have to give it a name, such as **ogre**. (See the later section "File and Directory Names.") This name is then added to the list of files in your home directory and, in future instructions, you may refer to the file as **ogre**. After you create a few files, you can visualize your home directory looking like the sketch in Figure 4.1. (We'll explain the "branches" and "leaves" in a minute.) Your home directory may contain zero, one, or many files that you create. You will also learn later that it can contain files placed there belonging to other users. As an illustration, you can think of your directory as being your personal filing cabinet with the files being individual papers.

FIGURE 4.1
A home directory.

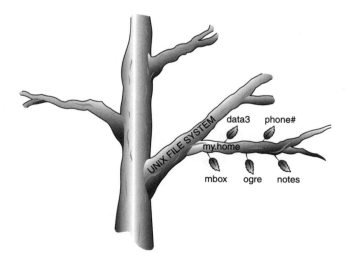

Of course, every other user has a home directory, too. Thus, UNIX needs a way to tell home directories apart. UNIX accomplishes this by giving your home directory a name—often, your login name. Next, UNIX needs a way of keeping track of all these home directories. It does this with a new directory that contains other directories. Typically, this directory is called usr, and the home directories are termed subdirectories of usr.

Think of the usr directory as being the single parent of multiple children (the subdirectories). Just as in real life, the parent may have one or more children (the subdirectories). Also resembling real life, the number of children (subdirectories) may increase or decrease. The subdirectories themselves can contain subdirectories of their own, thus creating grandchildren-like directories. Keep in mind that each subdirectory can contain zero, one, or many files. A home (parent) directory might have one subdirectory (child) that contains another subdirectory (a grandchild directory). Or, a home (parent) directory could be fortunate enough to have "twins"—that is, two subdirectories at the same level. Also, within different subdirectories, multiple files can exist with the same name but contain completely different data. Pretend that you have a home directory named melissa with two separate subdirectories called work_stuff and social_stuff. A file named phone_list could exist in both subdirectories but would contain very different information. In this example, it's easy to see why a logical structure with meaningful names is important.

It's entirely possible, and likely, to have a directory tree going several layers deep with multiple branches. Figure 4.2 will help you visualize this with a simple example. Notice that the usr directory in this example contains some files (leaves) as well as directories (branches). In general, any directory can contain files and subdirectories.

FIGURE 4.2
The usr directory.

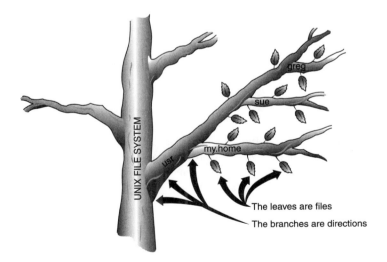

Is usr the ultimate directory? No, that distinction goes to a directory known informally as *root* and formally as /. (Computers usually insist on the name /; however, *root* is easier to say, so we'll use that name.) All other directories stem directly or indirectly from root, which, of course, is why it's called root. Incidentally, root is also referred to as *super-user*—that is, the user with total control over the UNIX machine. (The role of the root user is a systems administration issue and, therefore, outside the scope of this book.) Figure 4.3 represents a complete directory system.

FIGURE 4.3
The directory system.

As you can see, Figure 4.3 looks like a tree. The directories are the trunk and the branches, and the files are the leaves. For this reason, the UNIX directory system is often described as having a *tree structure*. (Here the metaphors become a bit confusing because the root directory is actually the trunk of the tree.)

A different analogy (see Figure 4.4) portrays the system as a hierarchy. At the top is the root directory. Serving under root is the next rank of directories: bin, lib, usr, and so on. Each of these, in turn, commands a group of lower-ranking directories, and so on.

FIGURE 4.4
The UNIX hierarchy.

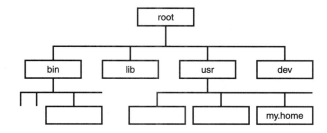

The directory system, then, provides a structure for file organization. It also provides a clear way of specifying a file's location, as will be explored in Chapter 8, "The UNIX Shell: Command Lines, Redirection, and Shell Scripts."

What can you do in the UNIX directory system? You can expand it by adding subdirectories (children) to your home directory and subdirectories (grandchildren) to those subdirectories. You can change directories, moving to one of your subdirectories. Therefore, you move from subdirectory to subdirectory. If you want to use the tree analogy, you can move up and down branches and even jump from one branch to another. You also can place files (leaves) in any directory or subdirectory that you control.

The words *file* and *directory* are sometimes used with two different meanings and can create confusion at first. We often talk about the *filing system* or the *directory system*, where both terms refer to the entire system of files and directories. On the other hand, we say that a file can contain only data (such as employee names or phone numbers); it can't have subdirectories coming from within it. The analogy of the files being like individual paper documents and the directories being like folders (containing files) in a filing cabinet keeps the proper relationship.

Listing Directories: `ls`

As its name suggests, the `ls` (list) command lists the contents of a directory. For example, Sammy Spade is a new student enrolled in a computer science course (called cs1) at a large university. His UNIX login name is Sammy, and his instructor has identified his account in the UNIX hierarchy as shown in Figure 4.5. In this case, a directory other than `/usr` is being used to house the student accounts.

Assume that Sammy is properly logged in and has established contact with the shell as indicated by the `%` prompt. At this point, the shell is ready to execute his every command. Suppose that Sammy types

`ls`

The system will respond with

`1999    English    birthdate    mar.99        mbox`

FIGURE 4.5
Sammy's directory.

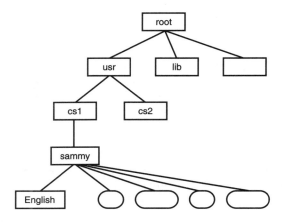

Note

We list the file and directory names horizontally. Your system might list them vertically.

These are the names of the four files and one subdirectory in Sammy's account. The directory is **English**, and it's listed with the files. You can't tell that it's a directory just by looking at this list. You either have to remember from Figure 4.5 that it's a subdirectory, or use the **-F** option (described later), which puts a slash in front of directory names.

That first command was pretty simple, but there's more to **ls** than what you've seen. For example, you can list the contents of almost any directory, not just your own. And, in the words of one version of the online manual, "There is an unbelievable number of options." Before looking at some options, you need to familiarize yourself with file and directory names. If you want to skip ahead, that's okay, but remember to return to these pages later so you will be familiar with the naming conventions.

File and Directory Names

UNIX gives you a lot of freedom in naming your files and directories. The name can be more than 200 characters long, and you can use almost any character you want. However, avoid using characters that have a special meaning to UNIX. In particular, avoid using the characters /, \, ", `, *, ;, -, ?, [,], (,), ~, !, $, {, }, <, and >. (It's not impossible to use these characters, just inconvenient because the characters must be *escaped*, or prevented from being interpreted literally.) You can use numbers as part of a filename with no difficulty. In fact, you can have names such as **22** if you want. However, try to make the names as descriptive as possible. Most UNIX systems allow names up to 255 characters long, but only the first 32 or so are significant.

UNIX uses spaces to tell where one command or filename ends and another begins, so you should avoid spaces in names. The usual convention is to use a period or underscore where you normally would use a space. For example, if you wanted to give the name `read me` to a file, you could call it `read.me` or `read_me`.

Uppercase letters are distinguished from lowercase letters. Thus, `fort`, `Fort`, `forT`, and `FORT` are considered four distinct names.

UNIX makes no distinction between names that can be assigned to files and those that can be assigned to directories. Thus, it's possible to have a file and a directory with the same name. The `snort` directory could contain a file called `snort`. This doesn't confuse UNIX, but it might confuse you. Some users adopt the convention of beginning directory names with a capital letter and beginning filenames with a lowercase letter.

File and Directory Naming Conventions

A naming convention is nothing more than an agreed-on naming standard developed by people (not machines). There are no official UNIX-defined rules governing naming conventions that will cause errors if they aren't followed. There are, however, syntax rules concerning names. The user-defined convention of beginning directory names with a capital letter (or all capitals) and filenames with a lowercase letter can help prevent confusion. Another convention is to end subdirectory names with the `_dir` suffix. For example, if the suffix convention was used and capitalization was dropped, `English` would become `english_dir`. If Sammy knows he won't be keeping a set of files around for long, he could move them to a directory called `Sammy_tmp` (`tmp` meaning temporary).

Just as there are several conventions to use with directory names, there are several ways to name files. Try to use a meaningful and descriptive filename. Remember that you may need to come back and use that file sometime later, perhaps after a vacation. You may not quite recognize the cute little three-character name you gave it when you were in a hurry in the afternoon before that vacation. On the flip side, typing 30-character filenames over and over can be a hassle, so find a happy medium. Suffixes of `.tmp` (for temporary files), `.lst` (for file listings), or `.txt` (for text files) can be useful. Adding a date to the end of a filename can also be a time saver. Yes, it's true that the `ls` command has options to tell when a file was created/modified, but a suffix of *YYYYMMDD* can be helpful. For example, `phone_numbers-19990712.txt` can quickly show a creation date. Authors have also used the suffix convention `.bk` (backup) or `.old` many times when dealing with programming files. This convention has saved authors from modifying or erasing the wrong file more than once.

The specific type of naming convention used is less important than consistently using a convention. Most companies and many schools have "official" naming conventions (often with long lists of naming standards). While it's very easy to go overboard with zealously followed standards, it's important to have some logic or reason for the way you name files and directories.

Listing Other Directories

If you type `ls` with no options, you get a listing of your current working directory. (You can always find out what directory you are in by using the `pwd` command.) Right now, that would be your login directory but, later, when you learn how to change directories, it will be a listing of whatever directory you're working in (just like the name says!). To get a listing of files and directories in some other directory, just follow `ls` with the name of the directory you want to see. For instance, the following command will show what's in the directory `English` (assuming it's under the current directory):

```
ls English
```

Note

There must be a space between `ls` and the directory name. Some directory names are more involved than this example, and you will learn more about directories in Chapter 8.

Some ls Options

Option flags tell UNIX which options you want. (Remember the option flags used with **who** in Chapter 2, "Getting Started: **login**, **passwd**, and **who**"?) Use spaces to separate the flag from the command name and from any following arguments. Suppose that Sammy types

```
ls -s
```

The `-s` option gives the size of the file in blocks. (In the example, the blocks have a size of 1,024 bytes.) The UNIX response would look like the following:

```
total  17    1  English        1 mar.99

1 1999     13 birthdate        1 mbox
```

Thus, the file **birthdate** contains 13 blocks, or 26×1024 = 26,624 bytes.

The bulkiest and most informative option is `-l` (long). For Sammy, this option would produce the following listing:

```
total 17
-rw-r--r--  1  sammy       231  Aug  18  12:34  1999
drwxr-xr-x  2  sammy       112  Aug  19  10:15  English
-rw-r--r--  1  sammy     13312  Jul  22  16:05  birthdate
-rw-r--r--  1  sammy        52  Aug  01  17:45  mar.99
-rw-r--r--  1  sammy       315  Aug  28  09:24  mbox
```

On the first line, **total** shows the number of blocks used. After that is one line for each file or directory. The first character in each line indicates whether the entry is a file (shown by -) or a directory (shown by **d**). Following the file or directory character are several letters and hyphens. These describe permissions to read and use files: you'll learn about these when we discuss **chmod** in Chapter 11, "Information Processing: **grep**, **find**, and **awk**." Then comes a numeral that gives the number of links; you find out about links when we examine the **ln** command in Chapter 8. Next is Sammy's login name. This column tells who "owns" the file. The fourth column gives the actual length of the file in bytes. Then come the date and time that the file was last changed. Finally, there is the filename.

You can use more than one option with the **ls** command by stringing together the option letters. For example, the following command produces a long listing (the `-l` option) of all the files revealed by the `-a` option:

```
ls -la
```

ls: List Contents of Directory

Name	Options	Arguments
ls	-a, -c, -l, -F, -r, -s, -t,	[*directory*...] -R, and others

Description: The ls command lists the contents of each directory named in the argument. The alphabetical output can list both files and subdirectories. When no argument is given, the current directory is listed. You'll see the term *dot entries* several times. A dot entry is a file starting with a period.

Option	Description
-a	Lists all entries, including dot entries
-c	Lists by time of last file change
-l	Lists in long format, giving links, owner, size in bytes, and time of last file change
-F	Marks directories with a /
-r	Reverses the order of the listing
-s	Gives the size in blocks of 1,024 bytes (this number may vary)
-t	Lists entries in order of modification time
-R	Also lists each subdirectory found

Comments: Some versions of UNIX use the same commands for different things, and sometimes option combinations must be used to achieve the output you want. The best way to check what the options do with your version of UNIX is to look at the man page.

Also, remember that directories contain only the names of files and subdirectories. To read information contained in a file, use cat. As is true for many UNIX command options, the option letters for ls can vary from system to system.

Reading Files: cat

The cat command con*cat*enates and displays files. *Concatenate* means to link together. Some people prefer to think of cat as meaning *catalog*. cat can display the contents of one or more files onscreen. To display the mar.99 file in Sammy's account, you would type

`cat mar.99`

The system would then print the contents of the file `mar.99`. Assume that it looks like the following:

```
     March 1999
 S  M Tu  W Th  F  S
    1  2  3  4  5  6
 7  8  9 10 11 12 13
14 15 16 17 18 19 20
21 22 23 24 25 26 27
28 29 30 31
```

As you can see, this file contains a calendar for the month of March. Apparently, Sammy has mastered the `cal` command (Chapter 2) and learned how to save the output.

To read the `mbox` file, you would type

cat mbox

If you make a mistake and type

cat box

UNIX will respond

cat: No such file or directory.

---

cat: Concatenate and Display

Name	Options	Arguments
cat	Several	[*file...*]

Description: The `cat` command reads each file in sequence and writes it on the standard output (terminal). If no filename is given or if - (a hyphen) is given as a filename, `cat` reads the standard input (the keyboard). Ctrl-d terminates keyboard input. If the file is too large for a single screen, press Ctrl-s and Ctrl-q to control the file information appearing onscreen, or use the `more` command described next. If you are on a fast machine, the Ctrl-s and Ctrl-q keys usually can't be pressed fast enough. On slower terminals or on those using a modem to connect to a UNIX system, they will work properly.

Options: Several; not important here.

Example: This command will display `file2`:

cat file2

Note: If no input file is given, `cat` takes its input from the terminal keyboard. Note that the redirection operator uses the symbol >. You can use **cat > file5** to create a new file called `file`, and you can enter text into that file. You call use **cat file2 file3 > > file4** to append `file2` and `file3` to the end of `file4`.

Reading Files with more

The major problem with **cat** is that it won't wait for you. If we assume that the file **1999** is a full 12-month calendar, there won't be enough room to fit it onscreen. The **cat** command doesn't care. It will fill the screen and then continue adding more information at the bottom of the screen, scrolling the screen upward. The first few months go by too fast to read, let alone reminisce. Because almost everyone will own files longer than a screen, this common problem needs a solution.

There are two ways to handle the problem of screen scrolling. If you have too much information for one screen, press Ctrl-s to stop the scrolling and Ctrl-q to restart it. This tricky and amateur way to view a file requires super-quick reflexes (or luck) to find the spot in a file you want. The second and preferred way to handle large amounts of information is to use the **more** command.

The **more** command is designed to make it easier to look through long files. With it, you can look through a file one screen at a time. If you like, you also can back up and review material that you read earlier. To use **more** to read a file, follow the command name with a space and the filename. For example,

```
more mbox
```

lets you scan the **mbox** file. When you give this command, you see the beginning of the **mbox** file onscreen. You also see the words **more ... 42%** at the bottom of the screen. Pressing the spacebar causes **more** to show the next screen of text. By pressing the spacebar repeatedly, you can scan the whole text. When you reach the end of the file, **more** returns to the UNIX shell. If, after reviewing a few screens of data, you decide you want get back to the command prompt, simply press Ctrl-d or the Delete key to break you out of the **more** process and return you to your normal prompt.

Some other commands can be used with **more** to control screen flow:

Key/Command	Result
Return	Advances the screen 1 line
d	Advances the screen 11 lines
Spacebar	Advances a full screen (usually 22 lines)
b	Scrolls back one screen

All these commands act instantaneously. You don't have to press Return after entering the command.

To see other commands available with **more**, try the help (**h**) command.

more: Displays a File One Screen at a Time

Name	Options	Arguments
more	Several	[*filenames*]

Description: The **more** command displays the named file or files one screen at a time. Commands can be typed on a command line at the bottom of the screen to control which part of the file to display. The following is a partial list of commands:

Key Pressed	Result
Spacebar	Advances one screen
Return	Advances one line
d	Advances 11 lines
b	Backs up one screen
h	Displays help screen
q	Quits

Options: Several.

Example: This command displays the contents of the **myths** file:

```
more myths
```

System V Users: If you don't have **more**, try using the similar **pg** command.

Formatting and Printing Files: pr and lpr

The next two commands can be used to format and print files: pr for print (or format) and lpr for line printer. (There's a possibility for confusion here because the pr command stands for "print" when it really is a formatting command, whereas the lpr command sends a file to the printer for producing a paper copy.) Look at the lpr command first.

Suppose that you want to print a copy of a file on a printer. It can be any kind of printer: dot-matrix, laser, line, or whatever is connected to your UNIX computer. The format for the lpr command is

```
% lpr filename
```

where *filename* is the name of a file in your directory. Usually, the printer must be turned on before you give the command. The lpr command has options for selecting different printers, checking printer status, making multiple copies, and so on, as described in Chapter 11.

If you're printing a file that's longer than a single page, printing will continue right off the bottom of the first page onto the second page and so on (assuming that you're using continuous form paper). For long files, you can improve the appearance of the printed output by formatting it before printing it.

The pr command was created primarily to prepare file information for printing with a line printer. When used with no options, the pr command formats text to fit on a page 66 lines long. At the top of the page, it puts a five-line heading consisting of two blank lines, an identifying line, and two more blank lines. At the bottom of the page, it puts five blank lines. For example, the command

```
pr mbox
```

produces the following output:

(two blank lines)

```
Jul 27 19:34 1999 mbox Page 1
```
(two more blank lines)

```
Hi, Beth
How about...
```
(56 lines of text, then 5 blank lines)

The problem with pr is that it formats and displays the file onscreen, not to the printer. For example, you have a long file called **mbox** and use the following commands:

% pr mbox	Formats inbox, but the output is onscreen
% lpr mbox	Prints inbox on paper, but not in formatted form

To get formatted files to the line printer, use a UNIX feature called a *pipe*. Pipes direct the output of one command to the input of a second command. The pipe command is a vertical line, either solid (|) or dashed (¦). You can use a pipe to direct the output of pr to lpr:

```
$ pr mbox ¦ lpr
```

Note
You must use a space after `pr`, but you don't need to use a space before or after the pipe. Pipes are discussed in more detail in Chapter 10, "More Text Processing: `join`, `sed`, and `nroff`."

pr: Prints Partially Formatted File onto Standard Output

Name	Options	Arguments
pr	-l and others	[*filename(s)*]

Description: The `pr` command prints the named file or files onto the standard output. It divides the text into 66-line pages, placing five blank lines at the bottom of the page and a five-line heading at the top. The heading consists of two blank lines; a line bearing the date, filename, and page number; and two more blank lines.

Option:

-l*k*	Sets the page length to *k* lines

Examples: This command prints the file `myths`. The heading would include a line such as `May 1 12:29 1999 myths Page 1`:

```
pr myths
```

The file `myths` is formatted, and the output is piped to the printer rather than displayed onscreen:

```
pr myths ¦ lpr
```

Creating Files with cat and Redirection

Now that you can list files and display the contents of text files, you undoubtedly are eager to create files of your own. After all, that's where the action is! The best way to create files is to use one of the UNIX editors discussed later. However, using the UNIX editors requires some practice. Luckily, we know an easy way to create files without using an editor—you can use `cat` (a versatile animal) to produce your files.

Suppose that you want to create a file called `poem`. Type the following:

```
cat > poem
A bunch of officers
Sat in their tunics
Hoping to learn
more about UNIX
<Ctrl-d>
```

When you press Ctrl-d, your words are funneled into the file **poem**. To make sure that the procedure worked, type **cat poem**. Your glorious work will shine again onscreen.

How does this command work? Two tricks are involved:

- If you *don't* tell **cat** which file to look at (that is, if you type **cat** and press Return without providing a filename), it will look at whatever you type next on the terminal (see Figures 4.6 and 4.7). Indeed, it considers your input to be a file. You can have as many lines and Returns in your file as you like. Pressing Ctrl-d tells UNIX that you are done pretending to be a file and to close the new file.

- Use the magic of *redirection*, a UNIX ability that's discussed fully in Chapter 10. > is a redirection operator. It takes information that ordinarily would be sent to the screen and channels it to the following file instead. (By thinking of > as a funnel, you can easily remember that the redirection proceeds to the right.)

FIGURE 4.6
Using **cat** to read a file.

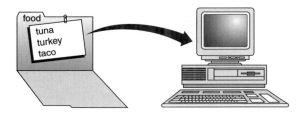

FIGURE 4.7
Using **cat** to read a file but redirecting the output into form.

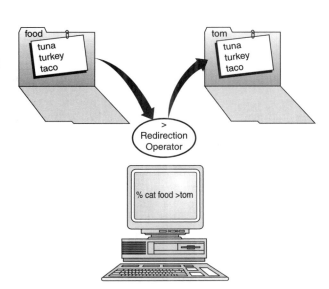

Any command that normally sends output to the screen can be followed by the operator `>` and a filename. This causes the output to be sent to a file instead of to the screen. For example, the following command places all the users who are logged in to the system into a file called `users_on_system`:

```
who > users_on_system
```

Where does this file come from? It's created on the spot! As soon as UNIX sees the redirection operator, it looks at the name following the operator and creates a file by that name.

Caution

If you already have a file by that name, it's wiped out and replaced by the new version. As you can see, be very careful in this area. For example, the preceding command would wipe out any previously existing `users_on_system` file. (Chapter 11 outlines ways to protect your files.)

Look back at the earlier example of the poem. Notice how the command line `cat > poem` contains all the necessary instructions: where to get the material (the keyboard), what to do with it (`cat` it), and where to put the results (into the file `poem`). Of course, this method of creating files doesn't allow you to make corrections to the file. To gain that ability, you really do need to learn about editors.

Input and Output

Creating files by using the `cat` command and the redirection operator involves the concepts of input and output. Let's look briefly at these concepts. UNIX deals with at least three different levels of input and output:

- First are input and output devices such as terminals, printers, and disk storage units.

- Second is the information transmitted through these devices. Depending on its destination, the information is termed either "input" or "output." An interactive system such as UNIX normally accepts input from the keyboard (the characters you type) and sends its output (the characters it produces) to the screen. The keyboard and the screen are termed the *standard input* and *output* devices.

- A *command* also can have input and output. For example, `cat` takes its input from the filename following it and, normally, sends its output to the output device (the screen). On the other hand, you don't have to supply `date` with an input, but it does give you an output. The redirection operators deal with the input to and output from commands. It would be beneficial to master redirection because it's a powerful way to manipulate the UNIX system.

More on Redirection

The `>` operator is a very useful tool. It can be used with any command or program that normally sends output to the screen. For example, the following command first creates the file `mar.99` and then executes the `cal` command:

```
cal 03 1999 > mar.99
```

The output of `cal`, which is the calendar for March 1999, is placed in the `mar.99` file.

Note
The > operator redirects output from a command to a file, not to other commands or programs. For example,

`poem > cat`

doesn't work because `poem` isn't a command.

The command `pr poem > lpr` wouldn't redirect `poem` to the line printer. It would create a file called `lpr` and put a formatted version of `poem` there. Notice that you can use `pr` and redirection and the line printer as follows:

`% pr mbox > mbox.pr`	Formats the mbox file and stores in `mbox.pr`
`% lpr mbox.pr`	Sends a copy of `mbox.pr` to the printer

The advantage of redirecting the formatted file before printing is that you can proofread the formatted file first.

Look at one more example of `cat` and redirection. Assume that you have the files `bigbucks` and `morebucks`. What will the following command do?

`cat bigbucks morebucks > money_bank`

Let's answer this question piece by piece:

- The input is the files `bigbucks` and `morebucks`.

- The operation is `cat`, or concatenate.

- The output of the operation is the input files printed in succession.

- The output destination is the file `money_bank`.

- For the final result, the file `money_bank` contains combined copies of the files `bigbucks` and `morebucks` with `bigbucks` first.

Caution

Don't try a command of the form

`cat bigbucks morebucks > bigbucks`

You might think this command would result in adding the contents of `morebucks` to what was in `bigbucks`. However, the right side of the command begins by erasing `bigbucks` before any concatenating is done. When UNIX gets to the `cat` part, `bigbucks` is already empty!

All in all, `cat` is a pretty useful command. You can use it to see the contents of a file, to create new files, and to make copies of one or more files. You may find it useful for generating temporary files (with a `.tmp` suffix) while you work. Just remember to be cautious when you work with `cat` so you don't overwrite anything you need.

Redirection and Electronic Mail

Redirection doesn't always have to point to the right (>). In some cases, left-pointing redirection is not only possible but also very desirable. Electronic mail is a good example.

Normally, to send mail, you give the command `mail` *`login_name`* and enter the mail editor to draft the letter. But suppose that you want to mail an existing file. Do you have to retype it? No—use redirection. The following is an example:

```
mail michael < schedule
```

This command says to send mail to `michael`, but take the input from the file schedule.

UNIX provides two kinds of redirection: one dealing with output (>) and the other dealing with input (<). Let's compare these two operations:

- `who > users_on_system` says to funnel the output of `who` to the file `users_on_system`. Most commands send information to the standard output, the screen. The greater-than symbol, >, redirects this output usually *to* a file.

- `mail michael < schedule` says to funnel the file `schedule` into the `mail` command. Some commands take information from the standard input, the keyboard. The less-than symbol, <, redirects the source of input, usually *from* a file. You'll learn more about redirecting input and output later in Chapter 10.

Removing Files with `rm`

In creating files with redirection, you may have created files that you don't want to keep. How do you remove files? Use the remove (`rm`) command as follows:

```
% rm money_bank
% rm poem mbox.pr
```

Caution

The remove command is irreversible. Make sure that you know what's in the file before removing it. The `rm` command is described in more detail with other file-handling commands in Chapter 8.

Summary

The basic commands of this chapter will become second nature as you begin to depend on the UNIX filing system to help you handle information. You've seen all the basic file-handling commands you need, including the options used by the `ls` command. You've also delved into more advanced material using the redirection operators.

Review Questions

Match the functions shown on the left to the commands shown on the right.

1. `cat dearsue`
2. `more butter`
3. `cat story.1 story.2`
4. `ls`
5. `who >userlist`
6. `lpr dearsue`
7. `pr userlist ¦ lpr`

a. Prints the contents of a file one page at a time

b. Lists the contents of the present directory

c. Prints the contents of `story.1` and `story.2` onscreen

d. Displays the contents of the file `dearsue`

e. Places a copy of the users now logged in to the system into the file `userlist`

f. Formats a file and sends it to the printer

g. Produces a printed copy of the file `dearsue`

Exercises

1. List the contents of your home directory.

2. Use `cat` and `more` on each file (assuming that you have only three or four files to look at).

3. After using a command that works as you expect, try the command again but with an error in it to see what happens. For example, try `lss` or `cat date` or `dates`.

4. Use `cat` and redirection to place a copy of all your files into a new file. *Hint:* Try `cat a b c d > e`

5. Try to read the file(s) you created in exercise 4, using `cat` and `more`.

6. Send mail to yourself using the method shown in Chapter 3, "Electronic Mail and Online Help: `mail`, `talk`, and `man`."

7. Read your mail and then save any letters in a new file, perhaps calling it `letters1`.

8. Create a file using `cat` and call it `today`. Put in a list of some of the things you have to do today.

9. Make a printed copy of one of your files.

10. Use the **pr** command to format a file and pipe it to the printer.

11. Print a list of all people now logged in to your system.

CHAPTER 5

THE VI SCREEN EDITOR

You will learn about the following in this chapter:

- How the vi editor works
- How to add and delete text from files
- How to change modes in vi

- Some of the search and replace options vi offers
- How to save, update, and abandon your editing

T he UNIX editors are the keys to creative use of the computer. These editors allow you to create and alter text files that might contain shell scripts, form letters, sales data, interactive programs, programs in C++ or other languages, and much more. This chapter will introduce the major features of the vi editor, which is in the ex family of editors. The ex family consists of four editors:

Editor	Description
ex	A line editor (replaces ed)
edit	A slimmed-down version of ex, useful for beginners
vi	A visual editor, great for everyday editing
ed	The original standard line editor (still available on some UNIX systems)

A *visual* editor displays a screen of text and has a cursor that can be moved anywhere in the text. It's much easier to start using than a line editor. A *line* editor doesn't have a movable cursor; thus, changes to text must be made by specifying lines and text.

Many other editors are available on UNIX in addition to the **ex** editors. The most popular and widely used editor (because it's on every UNIX system) is **vi**. The **ex** editor isn't widely used anymore because vi offers more power. These can include some of the more popular editors normally found on PCs, but they have been ported to UNIX. This is especially the case with Linux. Chapter 6 discusses another editor, the emacs editor.

Introduction to Editing

In the UNIX operating system, everything is stored in files, even UNIX itself. In Chapters 3 and 4, you learned to place text, data, or programs into files by using `mail` or redirection (>). The chief problem with those two methods is that the only way to make changes or corrections to a file is to erase the entire file and start over.

The UNIX editors overcome this problem. They let you alter files efficiently and easily, providing you with the basic support you need for most UNIX tasks. This chapter will give an overview of how editors and editor buffers work, and will describe `vi`'s major features.

The Memory Buffer

Files are stored in the system's memory. When you use an editor to work on a file, it leaves the original file undisturbed. The editor creates a copy of the file for you to work with. This copy is kept in a temporary workspace called the *buffer*. The changes you make are made in this copy, not in the original file. If you want to keep the changes you've made, you must replace the original file with your altered copy. This is easy to do. Just give the `w` (write) command, and the original file will be replaced by the updated version.

This buffered approach has a big advantage. If you really botch your editing job (accidentally deleting a page, for example), you haven't damaged the original file. Just quit the editor by using the `q` (quit) command without using the `w` command. All evidence and results of your error(s) will disappear, leaving the original file unchanged.

There is, we confess, a disadvantage to this method of operation. Your changes aren't saved automatically. *You must remember to write your changes* with the `w` command! If you quit without doing so, your changes are discarded. Most versions of UNIX editors try to jog your memory if you try to quit without writing your changes, but some don't. The failure to save editing changes has led to many an anguished cry and slapped forehead across this great nation. It may even happen to you, but you've been forewarned.

Although no editor (or computer system) is perfect, the average UNIX user has probably benefited more from *not* having their changes saved automatically than if the editor automatically saved files. This is yet another example of how UNIX gives the power to make decisions (such as saving) to the user rather than make choices for the user (like some operating systems). The power UNIX gives you is great, but *you* really need to know how to use each tool rather than rely on the operating system to do all the work.

Two Modes of Operation

The `vi` editor has two basic modes of operation: text input mode and command (or editing) mode. Figure 5.1 shows an overview of these two modes.

FIGURE 5.1

Two modes of operation.

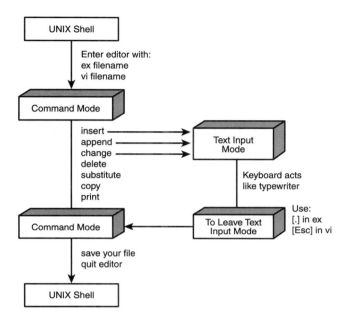

When you first enter an editor, you are placed in command mode. This means that any keyboard entry is interpreted to be a command. In this mode, you can delete a word or line or change a spelling error. To enter text input mode, use the **a** (append) command. Now any key entry will be interpreted as text to be stored in the buffer, not as a command. You can enter text representing C++ programs, sales data, chapters in a book, and so on. For each editor there is only one way to leave (exit) text input mode. Use the Esc key to leave **vi**'s input mode and return to command mode.

If you like what you've written in text input mode, or what you've modified in command mode, you can save it in memory by using the **w** (write) command. The **w** command is quite versatile. You can save the entire buffer or a portion of the buffer by using line numbers. You can also save or write to the existing file (created when you first went into the editor), or you can write to a new file (creating the new file in the process). These techniques will be discussed in detail later in this chapter.

Working with the vi Editor

The **vi** editor is an interactive text editor designed to be used with a CRT terminal. It provides a *window* into the file you're editing. This window lets you see about 20 lines of the file at a time, and you can move the window up and down through the file. You can move to any part of any line onscreen and can make changes there. The additions and changes you make to the file are reflected in what you see onscreen. The **vi** stands for *visual*, and experienced users refer to it as "vee-eye."

> **Note**
>
> Those who know and use this editor often hold a special status among those in the computer field. vi is considered by some to be "old-school," but it's respected by most people. Most computer professionals (who use UNIX) know at least some vi, even if they choose another editor such as emacs.

The vi editor has approximately 100 commands. Because a complete description of so many commands would overwhelm beginning vi users, our presentation of vi commands is divided into three parts. Each part represents a different level of expertise:

I. *Basic Commands to Start Using* vi

- Commands to position the cursor: h, j, k, l, and Return

- Commands to enter text input mode: a, i, o, O

- Command to leave text input mode: Esc

- Commands that delete or replace: x, dd, r

- Commands that undo changes: u, U

- Commands to save and quit the editor: ZZ, :w, :q!, :wq

- Commands from the shell for erasing: Del, Ctrl-h, #, or Rub, depending on your terminal

II. *Additional* vi *Commands to Enhance Your Skill*

- Commands to position the cursor including scrolling, paging, and searching: Ctrl-d, Ctrl-f, Ctrl-b, Ctrl-u, e, b, G, nG, Ctrl-g, /pattern, $, 0

- Commands that will operate on words, sentences, lines, or paragraphs: c, d, y

- Abbreviations for words, sentences, lines, or paragraphs: w, b, e, <, >, 0, $, {, }

- Commands to print storage buffers: p, P

- Command for joining lines: J

III. *Advanced Editing Techniques*

- Chapter 12 explains 60 or so additional commands that do more of the same kinds of editing as that described previously. Chapter 12 also explains how to use special vi features, such as mapping, editing multiple files, and customizing vi.

Starting vi

Although vi is a very sophisticated editor with an enormous number of commands, its basic structure is simple. As explained earlier, it has two modes of operation: command mode and text input mode, as shown in Figure 5.2.

FIGURE 5.2
Starting and exiting the
vi editor.

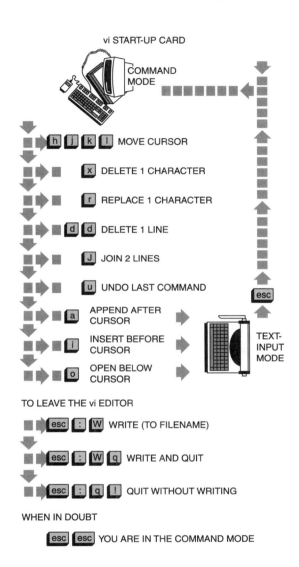

vi START-UP CARD

COMMAND MODE

h j k l MOVE CURSOR

x DELETE 1 CHARACTER

r REPLACE 1 CHARACTER

d d DELETE 1 LINE

J JOIN 2 LINES

u UNDO LAST COMMAND

esc

a APPEND AFTER CURSOR

i INSERT BEFORE CURSOR

o OPEN BELOW CURSOR

TEXT-INPUT MODE

TO LEAVE THE vi EDITOR

esc : W WRITE (TO FILENAME)

esc : W q WRITE AND QUIT

esc : q ! QUIT WITHOUT WRITING

WHEN IN DOUBT

esc esc YOU ARE IN THE COMMAND MODE

This section will cover only the minimum number of commands that you need to start using vi. Even though these commands are only a few of the many available in vi, they can handle most of the major editing tasks:

- Starting the editor: vi filename

- Cursor positioning: h, j, k, l, and Return

- Text insertion: a, i, o, O

- Deletions and changes: x, dd, r

- Permanent storage of information: :wq, Return

> ### Note
>
> For most commands in **vi**, you don't have to press Return to complete the command. The major exceptions to this rule are commands beginning with a colon (**:**), a slash (**/**), or a question mark (**?**).

The first example shows you how to get into and out of the **vi** editor. You must be in the UNIX shell, as indicated by the shell prompt (**%**). Give the command

```
% vi filename <Return>
```

where *filename* is the name of the file that you want to edit. The *filename* may be a file already in your directory, in which case, the file contents are copied into a temporary buffer for editing. If you don't have a file by that name, a new file is created.

When you call the **vi** editor, it responds by displaying onscreen the contents of the file, followed by a series of tildes (~)—only if the file is less than a screen long—and, at the bottom of the screen, the name of the file. The editor is now in command mode and the cursor is positioned in the upper left corner of the screen.

To leave **vi**, press the Esc (Escape) key and enter the command

```
<Esc>:wq <Return>
```

Remember that **:wq** stands for **write** and **quit**. Note that the colon is actually a prompt and will show up at the bottom of the screen.

In using the **vi** editor, any changes, deletions, or additions must be made with reference to the cursor position. So the next question is, "How do you move the cursor?"

Moving the Cursor

The **vi** editor has more than 40 commands to help you position the cursor in the buffer file. In this section we will show you how to get anywhere onscreen (and, therefore, in a text file) by using the five basic keys shown in Figure 5.3. A later section, "Cursor-Positioning Commands," demonstrates many more cursor commands.

FIGURE 5.3
Basic cursor-positioning keys.

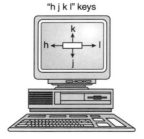

"h j k l" keys   "Return" key

Most terminals have arrow keys to move the cursor. Be careful using the arrow keys, however—they can sometimes (though rarely) lock up your terminal. Most experienced typists prefer the h, j, k, and l keys because they're easier to reach. The Return key is similar to the j key in that it moves the cursor down one line. However, the Return key always positions the cursor at the *beginning* of the next line down, whereas the j key moves the cursor straight down from its present position, which could be in the middle of a line.

If you've never tried moving the cursor, try it now. It's fun and easy to do. Make sure that you practice moving the cursor on an existing file because the cursor can't be moved in a new file that doesn't contain any text. That is, these keys will move the cursor over only lines or characters of text that already exists in a file. Figure 5.4 illustrates this.

FIGURE 5.4

Positioning the cursor.

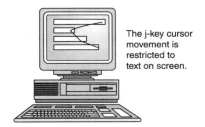

The j-key cursor movement is restricted to text on screen.

Here's an exercise to give you practice in moving the cursor. We'll begin by listing the contents of our directory in order to find a file to practice on. Let's assume that we're logged in and showing the prompt. Here is what we'll see:

% **ls** <Return>	List the files in our directory
mbox notes today	Typical listing
% **vi mbox** <Return>	We'll edit this file

The screen now fills with the contents of the mbox file or with tildes (~). Try the following suggestions for moving the cursor:

- Use the j and k keys several times to move the cursor up and down the file.

- Now use the h and l keys to go left and right on the same line.

Experiment as long as you want. When you are finished practicing with the cursor, press Esc and enter this next command to quit vi:

<Esc>**:q** <Return>

Notice that you used :q to quit (not :wq) to make sure that you didn't write any unwanted changes. (If changes were made to the buffer, the editor won't quit without warning you. Use :q! to force the editor to quit without writing.)

Text Input Mode

How do you turn the keyboard into a typewriter? Any one of the following four commands will do that:

a	Append
i	Insert
o and O	Open

The usual way to start a new file is to type `vi` and follow it with a space and the filename that you want to use. When the editor is ready, position the cursor to where you want to insert text and type `i`. Then start typing as though you were using an electric typewriter. Press Return to start a new line. If you make a typing error, you can use Backspace or your regular erase key to back up and correct your error. On some terminals, the erased letters don't disappear from the screen until you type over them, but they're erased from the buffer regardless.

Line Lengths and Wraparound

There is an interesting point about line lengths that may not be obvious to you: The length of a line onscreen may not correspond to its actual length in the editor. When you type text, the screen will start a new line when you exceed 80 characters or press Return (whichever comes first), but the editor will start a new line in your file only when you press Return. Thus, you could type a line of, say, 150 characters before pressing Return. This line would "wrap around" onscreen and would look like two lines. However, the editor would count it as just one line. Not only would this throw you off if you were counting lines, but it could produce surprising results when you sent the file to a line printer.

There are three solutions to the problem of lines being too long. The simplest is to use the Return key as it's used on a typewriter. As you near the end of a line onscreen, press Return to start a new line.

The second approach to setting line lengths is to ignore them until you finish using `vi`. Then use a text formatter such as `pr` or `nroff` to set the line lengths.

Another solution is to use the **wrapmargin** command to let the editor insert Returns automatically. Suppose that you want the right margin to be set 15 spaces from the end of the screen. While in command mode, give the command

```
:set wrapmargin=15
```

or

```
:set wm=15
```

(Don't insert any spaces in the command wm=15.) Now enter text input mode and try typing some text. When you reach column 65 (that's 80–15), the editor will start a new line, just as though you had pressed the Return key. Actually, the editor is even cleverer than that. If you are in the middle of a word that would take you past column 65, `vi` will move the whole word to the next line. This means that your right margin may not be even, but your lines won't end with broken-off words.

The **wrapmargin** command stays in effect until you quit the editor. This command can also be set semi-permanently by placing it in the `.exrc` file as described in Chapter 12.

In this next example, we begin a new file and use the **i** (insert) command to insert text in it:

% vi ohio **<Return>**	Invoke the editor
i	Go into insert mode (this command doesn't show onscreen)
What is the capital of Ohio?	Type this
Columbus	
<Esc>	Leave text input mode
<Esc> :wq <Return>	Leave the editor with a save

Now that you have a file called **ohio**, let's look at ways to add text to it. The following example assumes that you've gone into **vi** and have moved the cursor to the **o** in the word of:

```
What is the capital of Ohio?
Columbus
```

What happens when you use the four text input commands?

Each command puts you in text input mode for entering text. You can enter one letter or dozens of lines of text. The major difference between the commands is *where* the new text is entered. For example

a	Enters whatever you type *after* the cursor, pushing the rest of the line to the right. (On many terminals, you don't see the words pushed over until after you press Esc to leave text input mode. The new text will appear to obliterate the old text while you type, but the old text reappears when you press Esc. See the upcoming sidebar, "Dumb Terminals and Smart Terminals.")
i	Enters whatever you type *before* the cursor, again pushing the rest of the line to the right.
o	Opens a line *below* the cursor, places the cursor at the beginning of the new line, and enters whatever you type.
O	Like o, except that it opens a line *above* the present cursor position.

Dumb Terminals and Smart Terminals

A *dumb terminal* consists of only a keyboard and a monitor. It has no computing power of its own and allows you only to type information into the main computer and display information presented by the computer. Dumb terminals aren't as widely used as they once were but still can be found. If you're using a dumb terminal to append and insert text in the middle of a line, the new text may appear to write over the old text. However, when you finish inserting or appending with the Esc command, the old text reappears in the right place.

A *smart terminal*—one with its own computing power—doesn't have this problem. As text is inserted or appended in the middle of a line, the screen shows the correct location of each character at all times. Smart terminals, for purposes of this discussion, include workstations and PCs running

UNIX or Linux. These are much more popular than dumb terminals because of their increased power and shrinking purchase price.

The **vi** editor can make a dumb terminal appear somewhat smarter by setting the **redraw** option. Go into command mode and give the command

:set redraw

The **redraw** option, like other options, can be set semi-permanently as described in Chapter 12.

Suppose that you try each of the commands just described and enter **33333** from the keyboard. Here is what each command would do to the text:

`What is the capital of Ohio?` `Columbus`	Cursor is on the o in of
a	Enter append mode (this command doesn't show onscreen)
33333	Type this
`<Esc>`	Leave text input mode
`What is the capital o33333f Ohio?`	Here is the result
`Columbus`	
`What is the capital of Ohio?` `Columbus`	Start with cursor on o in of
i	Enter insert mode (this command doesn't show onscreen)
33333	Type this
`<Esc>`	Leave text input mode
`What is the capital 33333of Ohio?` `Columbus`	Here is the result
`What is the capital of Ohio?` `Columbus`	Start with cursor on o in of
o	Enter open mode (this command doesn't show onscreen)
33333	Type this
`<Esc>`	Leave text input mode
`What is the capital of Ohio?` `33333`	Here is the final result
`Columbus`	

If you had used the O (Open) command instead of the o (open) command, the 33333 would have appeared before the first sentence.

Now that you have a changed version of ohio, how can you "clean" it up? *Clean up* is a commonly used expression in a computer environment. It means to make the text or program right; to remove all unnecessary garbage. Unfortunately, there always seems to be a lot of cleaning up to do. This leads to our next set of commands for deleting and changing words and lines.

Deleting and Changing Text

You will find that the next three commands are handy for making small changes to the contents of a file. These commands are x for erasing one character, r for replacing one character, and dd for deleting one line. All three commands are made from command mode, and all three leave you in command mode after using them. Of course, all three commands use the cursor onscreen as the reference point for making changes.

The following example uses the old ohio file to illustrate these commands. Begin by typing

vi ohio

The vi editor responds by displaying

```
What is the capital o33333f Ohio?
33333
Columbus
~
~
~
~
~
"ohio" 3 lines, 49 characters
```

The cursor is in the upper-left corner on the letter W. Let's eliminate the 3's in o33333f. First use the lowercase l key to move the cursor to the first number 3. Then type

x

This deletes the first 3 and very conveniently moves the rest of the line to the left. Repeat the process four more times. That is, type

xxxx

or

4x

to delete the remaining 3's. The screen should look like this:

```
What is the capital of Ohio?
33333
Columbus
```

The cursor is on the letter f in of. Now, to get rid of the remaining 3's, move the cursor down one line by using the j or the Return key. The j key moves the cursor straight down. However, because there's no text below the f, the closest point is the last number 3 in the next line.

The Return key would position the cursor at the beginning of the line, on the first **3**. Actually, when you want to delete a line, it doesn't matter where in the line the cursor is located. Just type

dd

and the line is deleted. On some terminals, the editor places an **@** symbol on the deleted line and moves the cursor down to the next line. It looks like

```
What is the capital of Ohio?
@
Columbus
```

The **@** symbol means that the line doesn't exist in the buffer even though you still see the space it left behind onscreen. Some terminals are "smart" enough to actually remove the line onscreen right after you delete it. The screen is redrawn with the remaining text moved up line by line to replace the deleted line.

Suppose that you wanted to make one last change—you wanted to capitalize each letter in **Ohio**. First, move the cursor up to the letter **h** by pressing the **k** key to move up one line and then the **l** key to move to the right. When you are on the letter **h**, type the following sequence:

rH

The first letter you typed was **r**, the replace command. This replaced whatever was under the cursor with the next keystroke—in this case, a capital **H**. The cursor remains on **H**.

To replace **i** with **I**, move the cursor one letter to the right by using the **l** key and type

rI

Repeat the process and type

rO

You may think that there ought to be a better way to make these changes. There is. In fact, there are two slightly easier ways, but to keep this introduction to **vi** simple, we've postponed discussion of these until later in the chapter.

Undoing Changes: u and U

Sometimes you will make a change and suddenly wish that you hadn't made it. When that time comes, you will bless the undo commands. As the name implies, these commands undo what you've just done. The **u** command, which can be given only in command mode, negates the preceding command. If you delete a line with a **dd**, typing **u** will restore it. As another example, if you use the **i** command to insert the word **mush** in a line, **u** will remove it. (You must return to command mode to undo.)

The **U** command is more general. It will undo *all* changes you've made on the current line. For instance, consider the earlier example in which you used the **r** command to change **Ohio** to **OHIO**. Pressing the **u** key would undo the last command (replacing **o** with **O**), restoring **OHIO** to **OHIo**. But the **U** key would undo all the changes, restoring **OHIO** to **Ohio**.

The undo command is nice to have around. With it, you can practice changing a line and then restore the line to its original pristine condition.

Leaving the vi Editor

Probably the single most frustrating experience you can have with a computer is to lose several hours worth of work. When you're leaving an editor, a single careless command can wipe out your work. Before you leave the editor, ask yourself this question: "Do I want to save the changes made during this editing session?" There are three possible answers: yes, no, and maybe.

There are several ways to save information and leave the vi editor. Here is a summary:

Command	What It Does
<Esc> **ZZ**	Writes contents of temporary buffer onto disk for permanent storage. Uses the filename that you used to enter vi. Puts you in the shell. *Caution:* ZZ stands for capital Z's. You must press Shift-z (press Shift and type z) twice. However, if you accidentally press Ctrl-z, the editing process will probably stop and you will be returned to the UNIX shell. To restart the editor where you left off, type **fg**.
<Esc> **:wq** <Return>	The same as ZZ; w stands for write, q stands for quit.
<Esc> **:w** <Return>,	Writes the buffer contents to memory and then quits the editor.
<Esc> **:q** <Return>	A two-step version of :wq.
<Esc> **:q!** <Return>	Quits the editor and abandons the temporary buffer contents. No changes are made.

All these commands must be made from command mode. Each will return you to the shell as indicated by the prompt (%). Remember to press Return after entering your command.

To leave the vi editor and save any changes made, it's best to use :wq while in command mode. You could also leave the editor by entering either **ZZ** or **:w** <Return> **:q** <Return>.

To leave the editor *without* saving changes, use the **:q!** command. Normally, you might use this command if you started to edit a file and didn't like the way the changes were shaping up. The **:q!** leaves the original file unchanged and lets you abandon the editor's temporary buffer. Another way to accomplish the same task is to use the **:e!** command, which refreshes the vi buffer.

If you're not sure about saving changes, the best step is to save both versions of the file, the original and the changed version. To do this, use the write command with a new filename—for example,

`:w ohio.new`

or

`:w ohio2`

Thus, if you're editing `ohio` and make some changes, this command creates a new file under the new name. Here are two common ways to create similar names: add either `.new` or `2` to the existing name. After creating your new file, the `vi` editor will provide confirmation:

`"ohio.new" [New file] 2 lines, 39 characters`

You can now safely leave the editor with `:q` or with `:q!`. The difference between: `q!` and `:q` is that `:q` will leave the editor only if no changes have been made since the last `w` command. Thus, it provides some protection against accidentally quitting the editor. The command `:q!` leaves the editor in one step.

Actually, when you are involved in long editing sessions, it's advisable to use the write command every 15 to 20 minutes to update your permanent file copy. Some users use `cp` to make a copy of a file before editing. This allows them to update their copy every 15 to 20 minutes and still retain the original version. All these comments about saving text apply equally to all file types, whether they are programs, data, or text files. No one ever thinks they really need to save a file until it's too late and the file is lost; don't let that happen to you (save often!).

If you've been trying out these commands, you now have the basic skills needed to edit a file. You can create a file with the `vi` command and insert text with the `a`, `i`, `o`, and `O` commands. You can delete letters and lines with `x` and `dd` and replace letters with `r`. Rash changes can be undone with `u` and `U`. When you are finished, you can save your results and exit the editor. With these basic commands, you are equipped to edit or create short files. Try to practice them, if at all possible, before beginning the next section on additional commands. For your convenience, a tearout reference card at the back of the book summarizes the structure of `vi` and lists the `vi` commands.

Additional `vi` Commands

If you need to edit or create short text files once or twice a week, the basic `vi` command list, discussed in the previous section, will probably be satisfactory for most of your work. However, if you must edit long texts, you may want greater editing power, and `vi` has plenty of power. In this section, we will further explore the magic of the `vi` editor.

Because cursor positioning in the text buffer is so important, especially in medium-size and long files, we will show you how to place the cursor anywhere in the file with just a few keystrokes. Then we will explore three commands known as *operators* that can make changes to words, lines, sentences, or paragraphs. Two of these operators actually provide you with temporary storage buffers that make relocating lines and paragraphs within a text file very easy to do.

Cursor-Positioning Commands

You've already used five basic keys to position the cursor—the h, j, k, 1, and Return keys. Now we will add nine more keys and a searching function that will position the cursor easily over any size text file. We will start by considering four keys (b, e, $, 0) that are useful in short text files. Then we add four keystrokes (Ctrl-d, Ctrl-u, Ctrl-f, Ctrl-b) that are handy for medium (2 to 10 screen pages) text files. At this point, we will also explain scrolling and paging. Then, we will complete our cursor-positioning repertoire by looking at two commands used to position the cursor in large (10 to 100 or more screen pages) text files. These are the nG and /**pattern** commands.

The b, e, $, and 0 keys have a certain symmetry in their operation. Let's look at them:

b	Moves the cursor to the beginning of a word. Each time you press the b key, the cursor moves left or back to the first letter of the preceding word.
e	Moves the cursor to the end of a word. Each time you press the e key, the cursor moves right to the last letter of the next word.

Both the b and e keys will move to the next line, unlike the h and 1 keys, which can move the cursor back and forth only to the end of the line. Figure 5.5 shows the b and e key operations.

FIGURE 5.5

Using the b and e keys to move the cursor.

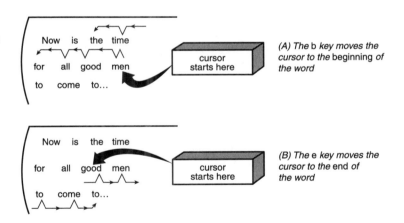

(A) The b key moves the cursor to the beginning of the word

(B) The e key moves the cursor to the end of the word

The 0 (zero) and $ keys move the cursor to the beginning and end of a line (rather than a word) as follows:

0(Zero)	Moves the cursor to the beginning of the line.
$	Moves the cursor to the end of the line.

These two keys can be used only on the line containing the cursor. The cursor doesn't jump to the next line as it does with the **b** and **e** key commands. Recall that Return will jump lines and is similar to the sequence **j**, **0**. Figure 5.6 shows the **0** and **$** operations.

FIGURE 5.6

Using the **0** and **$** keys to move the cursor.

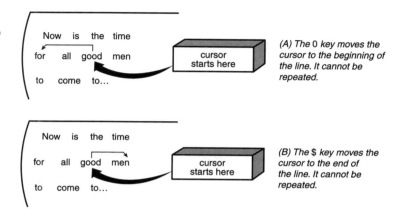

(A) The 0 key moves the cursor to the beginning of the line. It cannot be repeated.

(B) The $ key moves the cursor to the end of the line. It cannot be repeated.

Screen Scrolling and Paging

Sometimes there's more text in the buffer than can fit onscreen at one time. When this happens, you may have noticed that you can bring more text into view by trying to move the cursor past the bottom (or top) of the screen. The cursor stays put, but a new line moves up (or down) into view. This is called *scrolling*. Until now you've accomplished scrolling by using five cursor-positioning keys: **b**, **e**, **j**, **k**, and Return. These keys scroll the screen only one line at a time. Soon we will introduce four new keys that scroll multiple lines.

To visualize scrolling, imagine that the text is arranged on one long continuous page (like a scroll) and that only a portion of it appears onscreen at any particular time. Your CRT screen, then, is like a window into the text, usually showing 24 text lines with 80 characters per line (see Figure 5.7). Imagine that the window moves while the text remains fixed.

The direction of scrolling usually refers to the direction that the window moves past the text. For example, when you give the command to scroll down, the window moves downward and the text below the original window comes into view. When you scroll up, you "push" the window up, revealing portions of the text that precede the text in the original window location.

Different terminals will behave differently, even though the same **vi** commands are used. Some terminals can scroll down but not up. If a terminal can't scroll up, it must page up. *Paging* means that the screen is completely erased and redrawn in a new position. Paging has the same end effect as scrolling 24 lines, but the process is different.

The cursor-positioning keys **b**, **e**, **j**, **k**, and Return generally page or scroll the screen one line at a time. However, because a screen usually contains 24 lines, moving the text one line at a time in a large text file is unnecessary and time-consuming. The **vi** editor has four handy scrolling (or paging) commands that solve this problem: Ctrl-u, Ctrl-f, Ctrl-b, and Ctrl-d. (Recall that to perform a Ctrl-d, you hold down the Ctrl key and press the **d** key once.)

FIGURE 5.7

Screen scrolling.

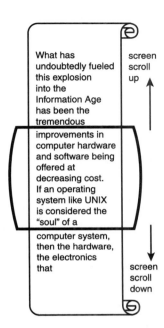

Here is a summary of these four cursor-positioning keys:

Ctrl-d	Scrolls or pages the cursor *down*, usually 12 lines at a time.
Ctrl-f	Scrolls or pages the cursor *forward*, usually 24 lines at a time.
Ctrl-u	Scrolls or pages the cursor *up*, usually 12 lines at a time.
Ctrl-b	Scrolls or pages the cursor *back*, usually 24 lines at a time.

Most users generally prefer scrolling to paging because it's easier to follow the positioning of the cursor in the text file as the file moves up or down. Recall that paging erases the screen and redraws it, so you can't follow the cursor to its final position.

If you have really long text files, even several Ctrl-f key presses can take too long. For example, this chapter contains about 1,400 lines of text. You would have to press Ctrl-f more than 50 times to reach the end of the file. Fortunately, there is an easier way—the command

*n*G

where *n* is an integer number that will place the cursor on the line number *n*. Thus, to move to line 1400, type

1400G

A similar command is the G command, which moves the cursor to the end of the file. Thus, if you type

G

while in command mode, the cursor is positioned at the end of the file. To get to the beginning of the file, tell the editor that you want the first line—that is, type

1G

One very useful command related to the nG command is Ctrl-g, which tells you the line number that the cursor is now on. This is valuable in two ways. First, if you remember the number or write it down, you can come back to the spot later. Second, if you want to copy a portion of a file, Ctrl-g can be used to get the beginning and ending line numbers of the section. You can then save the section by using the write command with line numbers. The write command would look like this:

:120,230w chapter4.2b <Return>

This command copies lines 120 through 230 and places them in a newly created file called chapter4.2b. If a file already exists with that name, the w command either destroys the file or doesn't work, depending on your particular version of vi.

Pattern Searches

Another way to position the cursor in the file is to give the editor a word or string of characters to search for. If you are in vi's command mode, you can type the character /, followed by a string of characters terminated by a Return. The editor will position the cursor at the first occurrence of this string after the cursor. For example, if you want to find the words happy day, just give the command

/happy day <Return>

If the first occurrence of happy day wasn't the one you wanted, you can move to the next occurrence by typing n (for next). These searches will wrap around the end of the file and return to the beginning, continuing the process as long as you type n.

If you prefer to search backward through the file instead of forward, use the ? command. Thus, the following command will start from the current cursor location and search backward through your file for the word malodorous:

?malodorous <Return>

Again, the ? command will continue the search for the next preceding example. The search will wrap around to the end of the file when you reach the top. To repeat backward searches, use the n command.

When you have the cursor where you want it, you are ready to make changes, move text around, or add new text to the file. We will look at these activities next.

Operators That Delete, Duplicate, Change, and Rearrange Text

In the discussion of basic **vi** commands, you learned how to delete a line by using the command **dd**. This delete command is actually made up of two parts: the delete operator and the operator's *scope* (the *line* to be deleted is symbolized by another d). The command **dw** uses the delete operator **d** but has as its scope a *word* as defined by the cursor and symbolized by w. We can represent these types of commands as follows:

```
Operator + Scope = Command
```

In this section, we will discuss three operators and nine scopes. The operators are the *delete*, *change*, and *yank* operators. They can operate with the following scopes: words, lines, sentences, and paragraphs. We will then use the commands formed by these operators to delete, duplicate, change, and rearrange text. Sometimes, these kinds of changes are referred to as "cut and paste," describing the old-fashioned changes made with scissors and glue. This electronic version of cut and paste is more powerful, however, because you can "cut" more precisely and can make multiple copies for pasting.

Tables 5.1 and 5.2 summarize the three operators and their scopes. (The put command is included because it teams up with the yank and the delete commands.)

TABLE 5.1   The vi Operators

Operator	Description
d	Delete operator. Deletes text but stores a copy in a temporary memory buffer. The copy can be recovered by using the put command, p.
y	Yank operator. Places a copy of text (word, sentence, line, and paragraph) into a temporary memory storage buffer for positioning elsewhere. The original text is left unchanged. The copy is "pasted" relative to the cursor position using the put command, p.
p	Put command. Works with the yank and delete commands. Puts whatever was last deleted or yanked in place after or below the cursor.
c	Change operator. Equivalent to a delete operation and an insert command. Deletes a word, sentence, and so on, and enters text input mode to allow changes to be typed in. You must end the command with an Esc.

TABLE 5.2   Scopes of the vi Operators

Scope	Description
e	From the cursor to the end of the current word. For example, if the cursor is on the *u* in *current* and you type *de*, *urrent* is deleted.
w	From the cursor to the beginning of the next word, including the space.
b	From the letter before the cursor backward or the beginning of the word.
$	From the cursor to the end of the line.
0	From just before the cursor to the beginning of the line.
)	From the cursor to the beginning of the next sentence. A sentence is ended by ., !, or ? followed by either an "end of line" (provided by Return) or two spaces.
(	From just before the cursor back to the beginning of the sentence containing the cursor.
}	From the cursor to the end of a paragraph. A paragraph begins after an empty line.
{	From just before the cursor back to the beginning of a paragraph.

In Table 5.2 notice that there's no symbol for a whole line. The creators of vi decided that because an operation on a whole line is done so often, the easiest way to do it would be to press the operator key twice. Thus, **dd**, **cc**, and **yy** are commands affecting the whole line.

Of course, to appreciate the commands formed by these operators and their scopes, you need to practice them. The next three sections give you practice in using the delete, change, and yank operators and the put command.

The Delete Operator, d

The delete operator is easiest to visualize because it's a one-step process. Consider the following short line:

```
The sky opened up. Morning awoke.
```

Assume that the cursor is on the **n** in **opened**. Using various scopes, practice the following deletions, as shown.

To delete to the end of the word, type

de

The letters **ned** are deleted, leaving the result:

```
The sky ope up. Morning awoke.
```

To delete the next word, type

dw

The letters **ned** and the following space are deleted, leaving the result:

`The sky opeup. Morning awoke.`

To delete two words, type

2dw

The letters **ned**, a space, and the letters **up** are deleted, leaving the result:

`The sky ope. Morning awoke.`

To delete backward to the beginning of the word, type

db

The letters **ope** are deleted, leaving the result:

`The sky ned up. Morning awoke.`

To delete to the beginning of the line, type

d0

The words `The sky ope` are deleted, leaving the result:

`ned up. Morning awoke.`

To delete to the end of the sentence, type

d)

The letters **ned**, a space, **up.**, and a space are deleted, leaving the result:

`The sky opeMorning awoke.`

To delete the whole line, type

dd

The entire line will disappear.

A fun way to practice these deletions is to use the undo command, u. Because the u command *undoes* the last command, you can easily try one of the deletions just described and then use u to return to the starting point. Here is an example. Assume you have the text

`123 456 789. ABC.`

The cursor is on **5**. Type **dw** to delete **56** and the following space. Then type **u** to get back the original text. It would look like this:

Original: `123 456 789. ABC.`
After typing dw: `123 4789. ABC.`
After typing u: `123 456 789. ABC.`

For fun, you can type **u** again to undo your undo.

All delete operations and undo commands are used in command mode and they keep you in that mode. Now, let's consider the change operator.

The Change Operator, c

The change operator, **c**, can use the same scopes as the delete operator, **d**. In fact, the change operator deletes the same characters as the delete operator. The difference between the two operators is that the change operator places you in text input mode. You then can use the keyboard as a typewriter and can enter as much text as you like. Existing text moves to the right and wraps around as necessary to make room for your text insertion. You leave text input mode just as always by pressing Esc. Some versions of **vi** include a marker with the change operation. It marks the last character to be deleted using the **$** symbol.

Here is an example of a small change being made. Suppose that you are in **vi**'s command mode and have the following text onscreen with the cursor on **6**:

```
1234. 5678. 90.
```

You now type

cw

and the editor deletes to the end of the *word*, leaving the result:

```
1234. 567$. 90.
```

Notice that the final character scheduled for replacement (**8**), is replaced by **$**. The cursor is still on the **6**, the first character scheduled for replacement. Now, if you type

Helloooo! <Esc>

you will get

```
1234. 5Helloooo!. 90.
```

The **cw** command lets you change everything from the cursor to the end of the word. The other change commands (**c)**, **c}**, and so on.) operate similarly, but with different scopes. If you don't want to change or delete text but just want to make a copy elsewhere, the yank operator and put command are what you need.

Using the Yank and Delete Operators with the Put Command

You can use delete (**d**) and put (**p**) commands to move text around in a file. Yank (**y**) and put commands, on the other hand, are ideal for *copying* and moving text around. The nine scopes allow you to precisely mark various parts of words, lines, sentences, and paragraphs. The yank and delete commands store these pieces of text in a temporary buffer that can be copied onto the screen with a put command.

As usual, the commands are made with respect to the position of the cursor. As far as the put command is concerned, yank and delete work identically. The difference to you is that yank leaves the original text unchanged, whereas delete removes it.

Here is an example using **y**. Assume that you are in **vi**'s command mode with the following text onscreen and the cursor on **6**:

`1234. 56789.`

If you type

y$

you will have stored a copy of **6789.** in the temporary buffer. You can now move the cursor to another position (for example, at the end of the line) and type

p

This *puts* a copy of the buffer contents immediately after the cursor as in an append command. The result would look like this:

`1234. 56789. 6789.`

You might be wondering if the **p** command empties the buffer or whether the buffer contents can be reused. You can, in fact, use the buffer contents repeatedly to put down as many copies as you like. This means that by repeatedly pressing **p**, you can create many copies of your text. This can be quite useful when creating dummy data files for program tests. The only way to change the buffer's contents is to yank or to delete something else. The new text then replaces the old yank contents.

That the delete and yank commands have to share the same buffer seems to be a problem. Also, suppose that you wanted to save some text for longer periods of time in an editing session. How could you do it? You might think that there should be more buffers for temporary storage. In fact, there are, and this is the subject of the next section.

Deleting, Duplicating, and Rearranging Text Using Temporary Buffers

As explained earlier in the chapter, when you want to edit an existing file, a copy of that file is brought from memory to the editor buffer. The use of memory buffers is so convenient that the **vi** editor actually has more than 30 such temporary memory areas for duplicating, rearranging, and temporarily storing text. Also, if you accidentally delete lines of text, you can recover not only the last deletion made but also the eight previous ones as well. These deletions are stored in a set of temporary buffers numbered 1 to 9. You can get the *n*th previous block of deleted text back into your file by using the command "*n*p. (The double quotes alert the editor that you are about to give the name of a buffer.) This command will place text after the cursor. A similar put command is **P**, which places the buffer contents before the cursor. Thus, the command

`"1p`

recovers the last deletion made and puts it *after* the cursor, and the command

`"1P`

places the last deletion *before* the cursor.

The undo command, u, is especially helpful if you want to search any deletion buffers one through nine. For example, you can display the contents of buffer four by commanding

"4p

If you don't want to keep the buffer contents, type

u

You could repeat this procedure to take a quick look at several buffers.

Using buffers one through nine to save, duplicate, and rearrange text has a drawback: Buffer 1 always has the last deletion made. Thus, if you move some text and then make a deletion, the contents of the buffers change. If you plan to move or copy text, it's better to use a set of buffers unchanged by the ordinary delete operations. There is such a set, and the members are named with alphabetic letters from a to z. To use these buffers, you precede the delete operation with the name of the buffer in which the text is to be stored. Again, you need to use double quotes (") to inform the editor that you're using a buffer name. For example, the command

"c5dd

will delete five lines and store them in buffer c. These lines can be put back in their same place or in several places in the file by using the put commands, p and P, as follows:

"cp

This command will put the contents of buffer c after the cursor. You can move the cursor and repeat the command to place additional copies of buffer c anywhere in the file.

These alphabetically labeled buffers will also store your yank contents if you want to just copy and store information. The commands are used identically. Consider the next example. Assume that you have the following text onscreen and that the cursor is on the line Bountiful Beauties:

```
Ancient Adages
Bountiful Beauties
Credulous Cretins
Diabolic Dingos
```

Now type

"fdd

The editor deletes the line containing the cursor and stores the contents in a buffer labeled f, leaving onscreen

```
Ancient Adages
Credulous Cretins
Diabolic Dingos
```

If you then move the cursor to the bottom line and type

"fp

you will see onscreen the contents stored in buffer f:

```
Ancient Adages
Credulous Cretins
Diabolic Dingos
Bountiful Beauties
```

Now, if you were to start with the same original text but substitute **yy** for **dd**, you would see

```
Ancient Adages
Bountiful Beauties
Credulous Cretins
Diabolic Dingos
Bountiful Beauties
```

As you can see, the yank command leaves the original text (the second line) in its place while letting you place a copy elsewhere.

Just as before, the delete and yank commands share storage buffers for saving deleted or copied text. The text stored in buffer f (**"f**) will remain in the buffer until new text is placed there or until you leave the **vi** editor. Thus, these buffers are extremely helpful for rearranging text.

These delete and yank commands may be repeated by using commands such as

```
"g7yy
```

which copies seven lines of text and stores them in buffer g.

Moving Larger Blocks

You may have notice earlier that you can extend the range of these operator-scope combinations by prefixing the command with a number (as in the **"g7yy** command that you just used). The number specifies the *number* of lines, words, sentences, and paragraphs that you want affected. For example,

```
20dd
```

would delete 20 lines, and the command

```
5cw
```

would let you change five words. If you use this last command, a **$** will appear in place of the last character of the fifth word so you can see which words would be replaced. You are free, of course, to replace the five words with one, two, seven, or any number of words.

If you want to move large blocks of material, you probably will find it more convenient to use the **ex** editor's **co** and **m** commands. You don't have to change editors to do this because these commands are available from **vi**. We will show you how to get a few **ex** commands shortly, but we won't go into detail about **ex**.

Joining and Breaking Up Lines

All these cutting and pasting operations can leave the onscreen text somewhat messy looking. How can you clean it up? (That is, how can you even out the line lengths?) There are three major ways to join sentences together. The slowest way is to retype the lines leaving out the blanks. A much easier way is to use vi's J command, which joins the next line down to the current line. For example, if you are in vi and have four short sentences, each on a separate line, you can place the cursor on the top line and type

J

three times. This would join the sentences on the same line and wrap them around, if necessary, as shown below:

Start	Finish
The tall man strolls away.	The tall man strolls away. An alarm
An alarm sounds.	sounds. RUN! A dead end.
RUN!	*(Sentences joined and wrapped around.)*
A dead end.	
(Four short sentences.)	

If you wind up with lines that are too long, just press Return where you want to break the line. You can do this most easily by placing the cursor on the space where you want to make the break and then using the r command to replace the space with a Return. You can reshape your line lengths to suit yourself by using this and the J command.

The third way to clean up text is to use one of the text-formatting utilities discussed in Chapter 10, "More Text Processing: join, sed, and nroff." We will conclude this long chapter by mentioning some additional commands available in vi; a vi summary is provided in Appendix E.

Additional Commands and Features of vi

The commands you've learned so far will probably meet most of your editing needs. However, vi has some additional commands, as well as some special features that we will touch on here. (For detailed information on using these commands and features, see Chapter 12, "Advanced Editing Techniques.")

With vi's special features, you can

- Specify your terminal type.
- Adjust the screen size.
- Adjust indentation, tabs, and wrap margin settings.
- Use macros and abbreviations to simplify a complex operation or a long keystroke entry.
- Edit two or more files at the same time.
- Use ex-like commands.

The last feature deserves further mention, especially because we've already used it several times without telling you. To use an ex command, enter command mode and then press the : key. You will see the prompt : at the bottom of the screen. Now you can give ex commands. As soon as the command is executed, you are returned to the standard vi command mode.

If you prefer a longer stay in the **ex** line editor, you can give the **Q** command while in the **vi** command mode. This, too, will give you a **:** prompt at the bottom of your screen, but you will stay in **ex** mode until you type *vi* to return.

> **Note**
>
> We refrained from going into detail about **ex** because the editor has generally been replaced by **vi**, **emacs**, and some newer GUI editors. If you already know **ex**, we feel some of our information may help, but it would take a dedicated chapter to really increase your knowledge. On the other hand, if you are relatively new to UNIX, we feel your time is better spent learning **vi** and **emacs** in detail and a receiving only an overview of what **ex** is and was.

The examples used so far have involved the write commands (such as **:w** and **:120,230w chapter4.2b**) and the quit commands (**:q**, **:wq**, and **:q!**). Of the other **ex** commands available, the most useful are those that let you deal with large blocks of material. Two important examples are the copy command, **co**, and the move command, **m**. These perform the same tasks as delete-and-put and yank-and-put, respectively, but they work only on entire lines. For example, the command

`:20,300m500`

will move lines 20 through 300 to just after line 500. The command

`:20,300co500`

places a *copy* of lines 20 through 300 just after line 500, but leaves original lines 20 through 300 in place.

Another very useful **ex** command is the global search-and-replace command. For example, the command

`:g/e/s//#/g`

will find every **e** in the file and replace it with a **#**. Try it; it's visually stimulating. Just remember that you can undo this change with the **u** command.

The **vi** editor also has a read-only option called up by typing **view** instead of **vi**. This is useful if you want to use the cursor-positioning keys to read text without worrying about accidentally adding or changing the file. Of course, you can do the same thing by leaving **vi** with the **:q!** command. This command quits **vi** without writing any changes made.

Summary

The **vi** screen editor has an abundant set of commands rivaling the best word processing software in terms of flexibility and power. However, you don't have to be an expert at word processing to use **vi**. It can also be used by beginning users who limits their commands to a few basic commands. It's very important to remember that **vi** has two modes of operation: command mode and text input mode (see Figure 5.8). Remember about command mode that most of the commands are used to position the cursor or to find text. The rest of the commands either delete something or place you in text input mode.

FIGURE 5.8

The vi modes of operation.

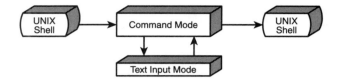

Review

Matching Commands to Functions

Match the commands on the left to the functions on the right. Assume that all the commands are given in command mode only; none are given from text input mode.

vi Editor Commands	Functions
1. 35G	a. Scrolls screen down one-half page
2. 3yw	b. Moves cursor down one line
3. r2	c. Stores four lines in buffer c
4. /fun	d. Prints line number of the current line
5. Ctrl-g	e. Moves cursor to left one character
6. 2dd	f. Replaces character under cursor with number 2
7. j	g. Yanks three words
8. "c4dd	h. Substitutes funny for fun
9. Ctrl-d	i. Deletes two lines
10. h	j. Puts cursor on line 35
	k. Finds the word fun

Questions

1. When you invoke the editor with a file—that is, when you type **vi file3**—how can you tell whether it's a new file?

2. What four commands put you into text input mode?

3. When you first enter the editor with an existing file and type **a** (the append command to add text), where is that text placed?

4. Which command is used to save the editor buffer contents?

5. Where does the insert command i place new text?

6. What's the command that will save the first three lines only of an editor buffer containing seven lines of text? Write the command.

7. How do you exit text input mode?

8. What's the command(s) needed to correct the following misspelled word?

    sometome

    Write the command(s).

9. What's the command(s) needed to delete the last five lines in 10 lines of text? Write the command.

Exercises

1. Enter the following text into a new file called **letterrec1**:

    Dear Sir:

    This is a letter of recommendation for john doe.
    john doe is a good worker.
    john doe has a find character.
    john doe is a-ok.

    sincerely
    jane doe

2. Now, do the following:

    a. Save the letter with the :w command.

    b. Correct all spelling errors.

    c. Capitalize **jane**, **john**, and **doe**.

    d. Delete the last sentence containing **a-ok**.

    e. Save the corrected letter as **letterrec2**. (Use the w command.)

    f. Leave the editor with the :q command.

    g. Use **cat** to print both copies onscreen at the same time.

3. Go into the shell; list your files with **ls** and copy one of your files—for example, **mbox**—calling it **mbox2** or something similar.

4. Invoke the editor with the copy of the file you made in exercise 3 and do the following:

    a. Insert somewhere the line **This is a test.**

    b. Move three lines using the buffer method.

    c. Find all occurrences of the word **the**, using the search operator (/).

    d. Copy two lines and place them at the beginning of the file.

    e. Use the command **cw** to change **the** to **thy**.

    f. Use the command **4dw** to delete four words.

CHAPTER 6

THE EMACS EDITOR

You will learn about the following in this chapter:

- What the emacs editor is and why you want to use it

- How to start an emacs session

- How to create a new file and add text to it

- How to delete, search, and save your file

- Some of the more advanced features emacs offers

E ditors are the workhorses of the UNIX world. In UNIX, all data, programs, and information are stored in files that are created or changed by editors.

The **emacs** editor (also known as *GNU Emacs* or *gnuernacs*) is a free-to-download editor created by Richard Stallman, formerly of the MIT Laboratory for Computer Science and now president of the Free Software Foundation. Several editors go by the name **emacs**. All are similar in general, but they may differ in their details. This chapter is based on GNU Emacs version 18, although you may use up to version 20.3 depending on your system. Searching the World Wide Web on using the keyword 'emacs' will provide a wealth of sites dedicated to this editor. For those running X, an X version of emacs, called xemacs, is readily available.

If you are new to UNIX and looking for a good editor, we recommend **emacs** rather than the standard UNIX editor (**vi**). The **emacs** editor is a modern, powerful, easy-to-use display editor. The following are some of the features that **emacs** offers for the beginning user:

- Online help facility

- Special online tutorial

- Easy text entry (to enter text, just start typing)

- Text display as you type

- An echo area providing timely prompts

- Cut and paste or search and replace using simple commands

- Automatic justification

For the advanced user, the following are some **emacs** features:

- The creation of multiple screens

- Customized command definitions

- The ability to run and capture UNIX shells in a window

- The creation of key command macros

- Special modes for C, HTML, and Lisp programming

- Programs for sending and reading electronic mail

- Formatting and outlining modes

This chapter covers all the beginning features and briefly describes the first three advanced features.

Tip
If you're interested in the advanced features, you can check either the online manuals or the well-written paper manual, which is available from Free Software Foundation, 59 Temple Place, Suite 330, Boston, MA 02111-1307, or from the **www.gnu.org** Web site.

Writing Your First Letter with emacs

The two most important questions concerning any UNIX program are, "How do I start it?" and "How do I stop it?" These questions can be answered with the following simple example:

1. Start the **emacs** editor from the UNIX shell by giving the command **emacs** *filename*, where you choose the filename (in this example, **mom**):

   ```
   % emacs mom <Return>
   ```

2. Enter the following text, pressing Return at the end of each line:

   ```
   Hi mom
   This is my first Letter using the emacs editor.
   I am fine.
   I hope you are well.
   Love, Jan
   <Ctrl-x><Ctrl-s>
   <Ctrl-x><Ctrl-c>
   %
   ```

Note

Remember that control combinations are entered by holding down the Ctrl key while typing the letter key. The preceding control combinations will be explained shortly.

This example shows you the basics of entering and leaving emacs. However, you should know about some further points. We'll begin with a comment about the Return key. In the example, you pressed Return to start a new line. Later in the chapter, we will show you how emacs can automatically enter Returns.

When you start emacs, it opens up a temporary workspace called a *buffer*. When you quit emacs, this workspace is cleared. Therefore, you have to save or write the buffer contents to a permanent file before quitting.

Several commands can be used to save your work. The emacs manual suggests using the command sequence Ctrl-x, Ctrl-s to save the buffer contents. However, on some UNIX systems, Ctrl-s can temporarily *freeze your terminal*. If this happens, either on purpose or accidentally, press Ctrl-q to resume screen display. Then see your system administrator to have this problem fixed (or check the emacs manual).

The standard way to exit emacs—Ctrl-x, Ctrl-c—can be given at any time. If any changes in the buffer have not been saved, emacs will remind you and ask if you want to quit anyway. You can answer yes or no.

When you try this example, you will see two lines of information at the bottom of your screen. These two lines are called the *echo area* (or *message line*) and the *mode line*.

The Echo Area

The echo area at the bottom line of the emacs screen displays certain commands to emacs or prompts you for input to a command. For example, if you press Ctrl-x and pause for one second or more, the symbol C-x will appear in the echo area. This is because emacs always expects another command to follow Ctrl-x; thus, it displays C-x and puts the cursor after it to remind you to complete the command.

If you give the command Ctrl-x and follow it quickly with any command, such as Ctrl-c, within one second, emacs will carry out the command without displaying it.

When the cursor is in the echo area, you can use any emacs editing tools that work on one line to change what you have typed. For example, you can use the Rub or Delete key.

To abort a command started on the echo area, press Ctrl-g. The cursor then returns to the text part of the screen, where you can enter text or start another command to emacs.

The Mode Line

Beginning users can easily ignore the mode line when doing simple text editing on single files. The information displayed is not necessary for editing.

For those of you who want to know what is happening, here is a brief explanation. The mode line sits at the bottom of the screen just above the echo area and may be displayed in inverse video. It shows status information about the **emacs** editor using the following format:

```
--CH-Emacs: BUFFER-NAME    (MAJOR MINOR)----POSITION----
```

- **CH** contains two asterisks (******) if the text in the buffer has been edited or modified and not yet saved. **CH** contains two hyphens (**- -**) if the buffer has not been changed. If **CH** is two percent signs (**%%**), the file is read-only. The symbol **%*** means the disk the file is on is write protected and the file can be opened read-only.

- **BUFFER-NAME** is the name of the chosen buffer, the window that the cursor is in, and the buffer where editing takes place. **POSITION** describes where the cursor is located in the buffer. It can read **All**, **Top**, or **Bottom**, or give a percentage.

- **MAJOR** is the name of the *major mode* for the buffer. The four possible major modes are Fundamental, Text, Lisp, and C. The default mode for normal editor use is Text mode. C and Lisp modes change the behavior of the editor slightly to simplify indention and parenthesis location. Fundamental mode is the least-specialized mode for editing files.

- **MINOR** lists several minor modes that can be turned on or off. These modes let you use abbreviations (**Abbrev**), automatic filling of text (**Fill**), overwriting of text (**Ovwrt**), and restriction of editing of text (**Narrow**).

The **emacs** editor also can display other information on the mode line. See your manual for a complete description.

Basic Cursor Moves

Now let's answer the third and most important question concerning a new editor: "How do you move the cursor?"

The cursor is usually a white line above or below a character or a white block superimposed on top of a character or space. In **emacs**, the cursor position is called *point*. Point should be thought of as lying just to the left of the cursor symbol between characters. Point will become more important later when we talk about marking blocks of text.

For now, think of the cursor as the place where new characters are added when you type. The four basic cursor-moving commands (see Figure 6.1) are

Command	Action	Mnemonic Help
Ctrl-p	Up	Previous line
Ctrl-n	Down	Next line
Ctrl-b	Left	Backward
Ctrl-f	Right	Forward

FIGURE 6.1
The basic cursor-moving
commands.

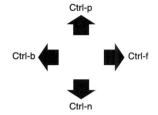

Dozens of commands can be used to move the cursor. However, these four basic commands plus one modifier and two additional cursor-positioning commands may be all that you need. Here are the two additional commands:

Command	Action
Ctrl-a	Beginning of line
Ctrl-e	End of line

Most cursor-positioning commands in **emacs** can be given a numerical argument that causes them to be repeated. To do this, precede the numerical argument with an Esc. Here are some examples:

Command	Action
Esc, 4, Ctrl-p	Move up 4 lines
Esc, 5, Ctrl-f	Move forward to the fifth character
Esc, 8, Ctrl-n	Move down 8 lines

Simple Editing: Adding and Removing Text

After you master how to move the cursor, you can easily change a file by adding or removing text. Adding text is the simplest; just move the cursor to the correct position and start typing. In **emacs**, the keyboard always acts like a typewriter, inserting text into the buffer as you type.

Because the keyboard acts like a typewriter, **emacs** requires special keystroke combinations to remove text. The following shows the most important remove commands:

Command	Action
Ctrl-d	Delete character at the cursor
Del	Delete character before the cursor
Rub	Delete character before the cursor (might not work on some systems)
Esc, Del	Kill the word before the cursor
Esc, d	Kill the word after the cursor
Ctrl-k	Kill from cursor to end of line
Ctrl-y	Yank back a previous kill

The words *delete* and *kill* have different meanings in **emacs**. Deleted characters aren't meant to be used again. Killed words or lines are temporarily stored in a *ring buffer*, and up to 30 previous kills (depending on the system) can be restored. A ring buffer has no end. However, once a ring buffer is filled, adding a new kill causes the oldest kill to be dropped. You can cycle through the ring buffer indefinitely. After reaching the 30th killed text in the buffer, one more Ctrl-y retrieves the first killed text stored in the buffer.

Kill and yank may not sound friendly, but it is the normal way to "cut and paste" in **emacs**. Yank isn't really a paste operation, but a command that uses a buffer where text is stored and copied into a file. You can do several kills in a row, and one yank will bring them all back. For example, the best way to move five lines of text would be to kill one line at a time (do this one line at a time to make sure that you get just the lines you want), and then yank back the series of kills with one Ctrl-y.

If you happen to move the cursor between kills, Ctrl-y restores only the last kill. If you want to restore a previous kill, you can cycle back through the ring buffer by entering Esc, y several times. Thirty Esc, y combinations bring you back to the last kill made. The following are some examples:

Command	Action
Esc, d	Kill one word
Ctrl-n	Move the cursor
Ctrl-k	Kill one line
Ctrl-y	Yank back the killed line
Esc, y	Replace yanked-back line with killed word
Esc, y	Replace killed word with previous kill
Esc, y	Replace previous kill with next previous kill, etc.

You must press Ctrl-y to start this process before you can use Esc, y. Remember that Esc, y means to press and release the Esc key and then press the y key. Ctrl-y means to hold down the Ctrl key while you press the y key once.

If you make a mistake and want to undo it, give the command Ctrl-x, u. If you decide to scrap all the changes made to the buffer since you started editing, you can leave **emacs** without saving your work by pressing Ctrl-x, Ctrl-c. Or you can restore the buffer to its original contents with Esc, x. The following is a summary of the undo commands:

Command	Action
Ctrl-x, u	Undo last change
Ctrl-x, Ctrl-c	Leave without saving your work (you are prompted to make sure you want to do this)
Esc, x	Restore buffer to original contents

Saving CPU Time When Adding Text

When you insert new text into the middle of existing text, **emacs** has to make room for each character by moving all the remaining characters to the right (and down). This redrawing of the screen takes considerable CPU (central processing unit) time and can be avoided by opening up two or more blank lines. While this may not seem too important, it can make a difference if you have a slower computer, or if the computer is busy running other programs.

To open up two lines, press Ctrl-o and Return. Later, extra blank lines can be killed with Ctrl-k.

Dealing with Line Lengths in emacs

A line in the **emacs** editor is limited only by the amount of memory available to the editor. In practical terms, lines can be longer than is reasonable for human beings to handle. How does **emacs** display long lines?

Suppose that you have an existing line that's 100 characters long. On most screens, **emacs** displays 79 characters and a backslash (\) at the end of the line. The \ means that the next line is not really a different line but a continuation of a line too long to fit onscreen. Instead of "continuation," long lines may also be displayed by *truncation*—characters too long to fit onscreen are not displayed at all. The remaining line stays in the buffer, temporarily invisible. The dollar sign ($) indicates that the line is truncated.

You can avoid long lines in two ways. One method is for you to press Return at the end of each line, making sure that no line is longer than 80 characters. However, the best way to limit line lengths is to use the auto-fill mode of **emacs** and limit line lengths. The following are some examples:

Command	Action
Esc, x, `auto-fill-mode`	Toggle auto-fill on or off
Esc, 64, Esc, x, `set fill-column`	Set line length to 64 characters
Esc, 64, Ctrl-x f	Alternative method of setting line length

Unfortunately, these commands apply only to your current editing session. When you leave **emacs**, the line-length setting no longer exists. You can make these commands semipermanent by placing them in a file called `.emacs` (described later in the section "For Experienced Users: Customizing **emacs**").

Ideally, new users will have both commands set in an `.emacs` file by the system administrator. If you want to check the current setting of the right margin, give the help command:

`<Ctrl-h>v fill-column`

If the `fill-column` is on, the word `fill` will be seen in the MINOR mode position.

The emacs Commands

The **emacs** editor has more than 400 commands available, ranging from `abbrev-mode` to `lowercase-region` to `yank-pop`. All **emacs** commands have such long names. However, some common **emacs** commands have an abbreviated form, such as Ctrl-n for `next-line` or Ctrl-k for `kill-to-end-of-line`.

A keyboard abbreviation such as Ctrl-n is "bound" to a command through a table called the *command dispatch table*. Experienced **emacs** users can easily change this table and redefine keys in a file named `.emacs`. Our discussion will concentrate on the unmodified **emacs** editor.

Running an emacs Command by Using Its Long Name

You can run each of the more than 400 **emacs** commands by using its long name. Just press the sequence Esc, x and then type the command name. The following are some examples of long forms of commands:

Command	Action
<Esc>**x next-line**	Move cursor down, same as Ctrl-n
<Esc>**x fill-column**	Automatically insert a Return at the right margin setting of `fill-column`
<Esc>**64**<Esc>**x set fill-column**	Set the right margin at 64 characters

Because long forms of commands are tedious, **emacs** speeds up the process in two ways:

- It provides keystroke abbreviations, such as Ctrl-n.

- It assists you with the typing. For example, if you type

  <Esc>**x next-l**<Spacebar>

  the **emacs** editor completes the line with

  next-line

  However, if you type just

  <Esc>**x next**

  emacs gets confused because there are three similar commands: next-line, next-page, and next-window. In this case, **emacs** will supply you with a list of possible completions from which to choose.

The Spacebar key can be used twice in a line. For example, if you type **nex** and press the Spacebar, **emacs** will add the **t-** and wait for you. Then you add a **p** and press the Spacebar, and **emacs** adds the **age** to get next-page.

If you are slow giving an Esc x command, **emacs** prompts you by displaying <Esc>x (actually, M-x) in the echo area.

Getting Help

There are numerous sources of help for using **emacs**, both on- and offline. These include

- A 285-page written manual

- A reference card that comes with the manual

- An online tutorial

- An extensive online help system documenting all commands

The help system is invoked by the Ctrl-h command, which is used only for help commands. The characters you type after Ctrl-h are called *help options*. One help option is Ctrl-h itself, which gives information on how to use the help system. Pressing Ctrl-h, Ctrl-h lists possible help options and then asks you to type the option. The help system prompts you with a string:

```
A, B, C, F, I, K, L, M, N, S, T, V, W, C-c, C-n, C-w
or C-h for more help:
```

You should now type one of those characters (you can enter lowercase letters).

Note

The manual uses the convention **C-n** to stand for Ctrl-n and **M-x** to stand for Esc, x. Although the conventions **C-n** and **M-x** have the same form, they have different keystroke operations. Some versions of **emacs** use different keys for Esc, such as the Alt key used by many Linux versions of **emacs**.

Pressing Ctrl-h a third time displays a description of what the options mean. However, the help system still waits for you to enter an option. To cancel any command, press Ctrl-g.

The following are examples of some of the options. You can enter them in lowercase, as shown.

Option	Action
`<Ctrl-h>t`	Run the **emacs** tutorial
`<Ctrl-h>a word`	Display a list of all commands whose names contain *word*
`<Ctrl-h>b`	Display a table of all key bindings in effect
`<Ctrl-h>k key`	Display name and information about the command *key*
`<Ctrl-h>l`	List the last 100 characters typed
`<Ctrl-h>i`	Run **info**, the program for browsing files, which includes the complete **emacs** manual

These commands are enough to get you started. Then you can use the help system itself to discover more about the help system and about **emacs**.

Searching for Text

The **emacs** editor has two commands that search for text strings:

Command	Action
`<Ctrl-s>[string]`	Incremental search forward for *string*
`<Ctrl-r>[string]`	Incremental search backward for *string*

Both commands prompt you for a string on the echo area, and both commands search only from the cursor (point) to one end of the buffer, either forward to the end of the buffer or backward to the beginning of the buffer.

Both commands start the search as soon as you begin typing the search string. For example, if you are searching for the string `Indian Ocean` and you type **I**, the command will find the first character **I** in the text. Then when you type **n** it will find **In**, and so on.

If you type something incorrectly, just use the Delete key. To end the search string, press Esc. Pressing Ctrl-s while in incremental search will move the cursor to the next occurrence of whatever you've already typed.

Caution

On some systems, the command Ctrl-s will *freeze the terminal*. If your screen appears stuck, press Ctrl-q to restart it. If Ctrl-s freezes your terminal, you have four choices in searching for text:

- You can stick with Ctrl-r.
- You can use the long form of the command: `<Esc>x isearch-forward`.
- You can redefine the keystroke abbreviation from Ctrl-s to something else.
- You and/or your system administrator can disable the Ctrl-s and Ctrl-q commands in the `.emacs` file. This solution should be your first choice.

The editor remembers the last search string used, so you can repeat a forward search by pressing Ctrl-s, Ctrl-s. A good way to search a whole file, forward and backward, is to give the command

`<Ctrl-s>[search string]<Esc>`	Search forward for string
`<Ctrl-r><Esc>`	Search backward for same string

In addition to the searching techniques already described, **emacs** can search for patterns using *regular expressions* (described in the **emacs** manual and in Chapter 12, "Advanced Editing Techniques," of this book).

Searching for and Replacing Text

Several commands search for and replace text strings, with the `query-replace` command (Esc, %) being the most common. For example, to replace the word **book** with the word **epic**, type the following:

`<Esc><`	Go to beginning of buffer
`<Esc>% book<Return>epic<Return>`	Replace, depending on next key

The following are some of the available options:

Option	Action
Spacebar	Make the change and advance to the next occurrence
Delete	Skip this change and advance to the next occurrence
Esc	Exit query-replace
!	Replace all remaining occurrences
^	Back up to previous occurrence
Ctrl-h	Display a help screen

If you type any other character, the `query-replace` command is exited and the character is executed as a command. To restart `query-replace`, press Ctrl-x, Esc. To return to where you were before the `query-replace` command, press Ctrl-x, Ctrl-x.

Defining Regions with Point and Mark

In `emacs` it's possible to select a portion of the text in the editor buffer by using the cursor to define two positions, one called *point* and the other called *mark*. The cursor itself is at point. Mark is set by using Ctrl-@ or Ctrl-Spacebar. The text between point and mark is called a *region*.

To specify a region, move the cursor to the beginning (or end) and press Ctrl-@. Then move the cursor to the other end. Now you have the region.

Because `emacs` shows you only the cursor and not the mark, you have to remember where you put it. The `emacs` editor helps you with this by providing a command to interchange the point and the mark—the command Ctrl-x, Ctrl-x. The following is the procedure for selecting a region:

1. Move the cursor to the beginning of a region.

2. Press Ctrl-@.

3. Move the cursor to the end of the region.

4. Press Ctrl-x, Ctrl-x to double-check the location of mark.

5. Do something to the region.

What can you do to a region? The following commands operate on a region. The commands are shown in their long form with key bindings where they exist.

Command	Action
`upcase-region` or Ctrl-x, Ctrl-u	Capitalize all text
`downcase-region` or Ctrl-x, Ctrl-l	Lowercase all text
`append-to-file` *[filename]*	Append region to a file
`write-region` *[filename]*	Write region to a file
`kill-region` or `Ctrl-w`	Kill the region
`copy-region-as-kill` or Esc, w	Copy region (to kill buffer)
`fill-region` or Esc, g	Justify region

As you can see, regions are useful. You might be wondering if changes to a region are reversible. The answer is yes; **emacs** does have a global *undo* command: Ctrl-x, u.

Formatting Text

UNIX provides several ways to format text. UNIX provides simple formatting commands such as **fmt** and complex formatting programs such as **nroff**. And, of course, you can always format text yourself by using an editor. The **emacs** editor has several commands to help you:

Command	Action
`auto-fill-mode`	Word wrap at right margin setting
`fill-region`	Justify region
Esc, q	Justify paragraph at right margin setting
Esc, *n*, Ctrl-x, f	Set right margin *n* characters

The following example sequence shows how to change the right margin and justify the text throughout an entire buffer:

Esc, <	Go to beginning of buffer
`Ctrl-@`	Set mark
Esc, >	Go to end of buffer (define region)
Esc, 44, Ctrl-x, f	Set right margin at 44 characters
Esc, x, `fill-region`	Justify text

To obtain paragraphs with different right margins, set the right margin at the value you want, move the cursor into the paragraph, and press Esc, q. Then reset the right margin to a new value, move the cursor into the next paragraph, and press Esc, q again.

Creating Multiple Windows

One advantage of `emacs` is its ability to split the screen into two or more windows. Windows can be used to display two parts of the same file or to display two different files.

The window containing the cursor is called the *current* window, and it is the only window active. (However, you can page or scroll the inactive window.)

The following are some of the window commands available:

Command	Action
Ctrl-x, 2	Divide current window into two windows, one above the other
Ctrl-x, 3	Divide current window into two windows, side by side
Ctrl-x, 1	Delete all windows but the Current one
Ctrl-x, 0	Delete current window and redistribute space
Ctrl-o	Switch to other window (cycle through all)
Esc, Ctrl-v	Page other window
Ctrl-x, ^	Grow current window one line, vertically
Ctrl-x, }	Grow current window horizontally

When you create a second window, the same buffer contents appear in both windows. That is, you now have two windows on the same buffer. This is handy for cutting and pasting—for example, moving a paragraph from one part of the buffer to another. Or you can use a second window as a reference, referring to previous text entered into the buffer. Of course, any changes made in one window are made to the buffer contents and will be seen in both windows when they display the same text.

You view different files in each window by putting a different buffer in each window. Before doing that, look at how to create multiple buffers.

Creating Multiple Buffers

If you want to work on two different files at a time, each file needs its own buffer. Here are some of the commands used to work with buffers:

Command	Action
`<Ctrl-x>b daisy`	Create a new buffer called `daisy` or switch to the buffer `daisy`
`<Ctrl-x>k daisy`	Kill the buffer called `daisy`
`<Ctrl-x><Ctrl-f>lilac`	Find the file `lilac`, put it in a buffer, and switch to the new buffer
`<Ctrl-x><Ctrl-b>`	List all buffers in separate window

As you can see from these commands, it's possible to create several buffers, each with different contents. However, only one buffer appears onscreen unless you create a second window.

Working with Multiple Buffers and Multiple Windows

The most convenient way to get `emacs` to display two buffers, each in its own window, is to start `emacs` on a file, which creates the first buffer; then use the command `<Ctrl-x>4f` (*filename*) to display a second file in its own window. The command `<Ctrl-x>4` may be followed with **b**, **f**, or **.** as shown in the following examples:

Command	Action
`<Ctrl-x>4b [buffer name]`	Open buffer in new window
`<Ctrl-x>4f [filename]`	Open file in new window
`<Ctrl-x>4. [tag name]`	Open a tag file in new window

Note
In Berkeley UNIX, tags are used under a program called `ctags`. They are not discussed here.

The `<Ctrl-x>4b` command is equivalent to `<Ctrl-x>2<Ctrl-x>b`, and the `<Ctrl-x>4f` command is equivalent to `<Ctrl-x>2<Ctrl-x>f`.

Working with Files

Any information stored in UNIX is stored in files. When the `emacs` editor is started on an existing file, a copy of that file is brought into an `emacs` buffer. Any changes made to the buffer aren't permanent, unless they're written to a file.

The following examples show some of the most commonly used `emacs` commands for dealing with files.

- Start `emacs` on *filename*:

  `emacs [filename]`

- Save changes to file:

  `<Ctrl-x><Ctrl-s>`

- Other ways to save buffer contents:

  `<Esc>x write-file [filename]<Return>`   Usually used to change `filename`.

  `<Esc>x append-region-to-file [filename]`   The region must be marked

- Insert a file into the buffer at the cursor:

  `<Ctrl-x>i (filename)`

- Read a file only (no editing):

  `<Ctrl-x><Ctrl-r>filename`

- Visit and replace a file:

  `<Ctrl-x><Ctrl-v>filename`

Caution

If you are editing a file and visit another file, the new file replaces the original file in the buffer. The `emacs` editor will offer to save the old file, but only if you respond yes. Be careful not to type ahead after giving the Ctrl-x, Ctrl-v command because `emacs` may interpret your typing as new commands.

For Experienced Users: Customizing emacs

The `.emacs` file is used to create customized editing environments. When the `emacs` editor starts up, it looks at the `.emacs` file for instructions, which may be key bindings, mode setups, or variable settings. You can enter these instructions into the `.emacs` file just like any other file by using the `emacs` editor. Give the command

emacs .emacs

in your home directory. A typical `.emacs` file, with comments indicated by one or more initial semicolons, might look like the following:

```
;;;set the text mode as the default mode
(setq default-major-mode 'text-mode)

;;;turn on justification for the text mode
(setq text-mode-hook 'turn-on-auto-fill)

;;;set the right margin at 64
(setq fill-column 64)
```

```
;;;define a new key binding
(global-set-key "\<Ctrl-g>" 'enlarge-window)

;;;define a new key binding
(global-set-key "\<Ctrl-x> u" 'upcase-region)
```

Notice two things about these commands:

- The format is in the form used by the Lisp programming language because the editor itself is written largely in Lisp.

- You must precede a Ctrl key with a backslash (\).

These examples are just a few of the many possibilities available for personalizing your own editor. The best way to see what you might want to change is to get a copy of the written **emacs** manual and check the list of long commands and their key bindings.

emacs: Public-Domain Editor	
Entering and Exiting emacs	
emacs filename	Starts editor.
Ctrl-x, Ctrl-s	Saves text. *Caution*: May freeze display. Ctrl-q will unfreeze display.
Ctrl-x, Ctrl-c	Quits editor.
Adding or Inserting Text	
Just start typing.	
Moving the Cursor	
Ctrl-f	Moves forward a character.
Ctrl-b	Moves backward a character.
Ctrl-n	Moves to next line.
Ctrl-p	Moves to previous line.
Ctrl-a	Moves to beginning of line.
Ctrl-e	Moves to end of line.
Esc, f	Moves forward a word.
Esc, b	Moves backward a word.
Esc,]	Moves forward a paragraph.
Esc, [	Moves backward a paragraph.
Esc, <	Moves to beginning of buffer.
Esc, >	Moves to end of buffer.

Repeating a Command	
Esc, n, *[command]*	Repeats *command* n times.
Quitting a Command	
Ctrl-g	Aborts command.
Redrawing the Screen with Cursor on Middle Line	
Ctrl-l	Redraws screen with cursor in center.
Avoiding the Redrawing of the Screen	
Esc, n, Ctrl-o	Opens *n* blank lines for text.
Killing and Deleting Text	
Delete or Rub	Deletes the character just before the cursor.
Ctrl-d	Deletes the character at the cursor.
Esc, Delete or Esc, Rub	Kills the word before the cursor.
Esc, d	Kills the word after the cursor.
Ctrl-k	Kills from cursor position to end of line.
Esc, k	Kills to the end of the current sentence.
Ctrl-w	Kills region.
Restoring a Previous Kill	
Ctrl-y	Yanks back the text. Note: If you type Ctrl-k several times consecutively, one Ctrl-y will yank back all the lines.
Esc, y	Yanks back next previous kill from ring buffer. Can be used only after a Ctrl-y.
Undoing the Last Change	
Ctrl-x, u	Undoes last change.
Getting Help	
Ctrl-h, Ctrl-h	Gets help about the help program.
Ctrl-h, t	Starts the tutorial.
Ctrl-h, l	Lists the last 100 characters typed.
Ctrl-h, i	Runs `info`, a program for browsing that includes the emacs manual.
Ctrl-h, a *[descriptor]*	Lists commands containing *descriptor*.
Ctrl-h, b	Lists key bindings.
Ctrl-h, k *[key]*	Lists the command (key) runs.

Note

Many other options are available.

Searching and Replacing	
Ctrl-s *[string]*	Incremental search forward for `string`. Caution: May freeze display. Ctrl-q will unfreeze display.
Ctrl-r [string]	Incremental search backward for `string`.
Esc, % [string1] Return [string2] Return	Searches and replaces, depending on next key:

Key	Action
Spacebar	Makes the change and advances to next occurrence.
Del	Skips this change and advances to next occurrence.
Esc	Exits query-replace.
!	Replaces all remaining occurrences.
^	Backs up to previous occurrence.
Ctrl-h	Displays a help screen.

Defining a Region	
Ctrl-@	Sets mark at beginning of region.
(Cursor onscreen)	Sets point at end of region.
Ctrl-x, Ctrl-x	Interchanges mark and point.
Changing the Case of Text	
`upcase-region`	Capitalizes all text.
`downcase-region`	Lowercases all text.
Esc, l	Converts following word to lowercase.
Esc, u	Converts following word to uppercase.
File-Handling Commands: Input and Output	
Ctrl-x, Ctrl-s	Saves text.
Ctrl-x, Ctrl-c	Quits editor.

`append-region-to-file[filename]`	Appends region to a file.
`write-region [filename]`	Writes region to a file.
Ctrl-x, Ctrl-v *[filename]*	Visits *filename*, replacing old file.
Ctrl-x, Ctrl-r *[filename]*	Reads a file; no editing.
write-file *[filename]*	Allows changes to *filename*.
Ctrl-x, i *[filename]*	Inserts *filename* at the cursor.
Esc, ! *[UNIX_command]*	Captures *UNIX_command* in buffer.
`shell-command-on-region[UNIX_command]`	Filters region through UNIX.
Buffer Commands	
Ctrl-x, b *[file]*	Creates a new buffer called *file* or switches to the buffer *file*.
Ctrl-x, b	Switches to another buffer.
Ctrl-x, k *[file]*	Kills the buffer called *file*.
Ctrl-x, Ctrl-f *[file]*	Finds *file* and puts it in a buffer.
Ctrl-x, Ctrl-b	Lists all buffers.
Window Commands	
Ctrl-x, 2	Divides the current window vertically into two windows.
Ctrl-x, 5	Divides current window horizontally into two windows.
Ctrl-x, 1	Deletes all windows but the current one.
Ctrl-x, 0	Deletes current window.
Ctrl-x, o	Switches to other window.
Esc, Ctrl-v	Pages other window.
Ctrl-x, ^	Increases current window one line.
Ctrl-x, }	Makes current window wider.
Ctrl-x, 4b *[buffer_name]*	Opens buffer in new window.
Ctrl-x, 4f *[filename]*	Opens file in new window.
Ctrl-x, 4. *[tag_name]*	Opens a tag file in new window.

Formatting Text	
Esc, x, auto-fill-mode	Wraps word at right margin setting.
Esc, x, fill-region	Justifies region.
Esc, q	Justifies paragraph at right margin setting.
Esc, n, Ctrl-x, f	Sets right margin *n* characters.

Summary

In this chapter, you've seen how to use emacs, one of the most popular and powerful editors available for UNIX users. Many users prefer emacs over vi because it's more friendly and its commands are a little easier to remember. With an X version called xemacs (which works the same way), emacs is now available for GUIs, too.

Review Questions

1. How do you save buffer contents to a file?

2. What command will unfreeze a terminal display if Ctrl-s freezes it?

3. What command aborts an emacs command?

4. What command is used to kill a line of text?

5. What is the normal way to do "cut and paste" in emacs?

6. With what sequence do all the long forms of commands begin?

7. What does the command Ctrl-h, Ctrl-h do? Give an example of its use.

8. Give the command to search an entire buffer and replace county with County.

9. What is a *region*? How is it defined?

10. What command is used to justify text in a region?

11. How are margins set? Give an example.

Exercises

1. Create a practice file by writing a short letter to a friend or relative. Save the buffer contents without leaving the editor. Do each of the following:

• Make a global substitution. Find the word **the** and change it to **th##** by using the following command:

`<Esc>% the<Return>th##<Return>`

• Practice using the cursor-moving keys to move to each occurrence of **##** and change it back to **e**.

• Do some cutting and pasting. Move the second line to the end of the buffer.

• Leave the editor without saving your changes.

• Re-enter the editor and see if it contains your original letter to a friend.

• Repeat the global substitution. Change all **a**'s to **3**'s. Again, practice the cursor-moving commands.

2. Start the editor on a file and practice using the search commands and then the search-and-replace commands.

3. Start the editor on a file and practice using regions. Define a region and capitalize all text. Then try to set the right margin to 30 characters and justify the region. Leave the editor without saving any changes made.

4. Start the editor on a practice file and try using the help commands.

5. Try using the **emacs** tutorial by giving the command Ctrl-h, **t**.

6. Start the editor on a file. In the middle of the file, insert another UNIX file.

7. Start the editor on a file. Give the command Ctrl-x **2** to create two windows. Switch between windows and then try to cut and paste from one window to the other.

CHAPTER 7

MANIPULATING FILES AND DIRECTORIES: MV, CP, AND MKDIR

You will learn about the following in this chapter:

- How to rename (move) files by using the mv command
- How to copy files with cp

- How to use cp across directories
- How to make directories by using mkdir

N ow that you know the basic commands for reading files (see Chapter 4, "Files and Directories: ls, cat, more, and pr"), you can get into the real fun of directory and file manipulation. However, before doing that, look briefly at how UNIX names its files so that they don't get mixed up. We'll conclude this chapter by showing some typing shortcuts that you can use with *metacharacters* (abbreviations).

Filenames, Pathnames, Heads, and Tails

What happens if Bob, Lola, and Nerkie (each with his or her own UNIX account on the same system) all decide to create a file called whiz? Does UNIX become confused between the four whiz files? Does Lola find Bob's work in her file? Of course not! UNIX is much too clever for that. To understand what happens, first review the tree structure of the UNIX directory system. The full name of Lola's whiz file includes the name of the directory it is in. The full names of all three whiz files would be

```
/usr/bob/whiz
/usr/lola/whiz
/usr/nerkie/whiz
```

These are called the *pathnames* of the files because they give the path through the directory system to the file (see Figure 7.1). The last part of the pathname (the part after the last /) is called the *tail*, or *basename*, and the rest of the pathname is called the *head*. The path from the head to the tail is often called the *full pathname*.

FIGURE 7.1

A pathname, a head, and a tail.

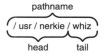

The head of the file in Figure 7.1 tells us that the `nerkie` directory branches off the `usr` directory and that the `usr` directory branches off the `/` directory (the root). For Bob, Lola, and Nerkie, all three pathnames have the same tail—that is, `whiz`. On the other hand, they all have different heads (`/usr/bob/`, `/usr/lola/`, and `/usr/nerkie/`), so UNIX has no problem distinguishing between them. Figure 7.2 shows a directory tree for the three `whiz` files.

FIGURE 7.2

Pathnames and the directory tree.

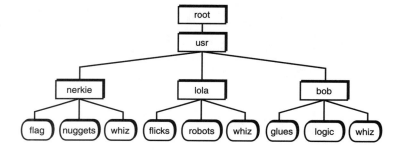

The slash (`/`) takes on two roles in a pathname. The slash at the very beginning stands for the root (or the top level of the file system). The other slashes serve to separate directory names or filenames from one another.

When a file is in your working directory, you can be casual and call it by its tail name. When the file is in a different directory, however, you need to tell UNIX which directory the file is in. It can certainly be quite frustrating to modify or delete a file, only to realize that it was the wrong file. One reliable method to prevent this is to use the full pathname. For example, if Nerkie wants to read Bob's `whiz` file, he can enter the command

`cat /usr/bob/whiz`

This will guarantee that only one file (Bob's `whiz` file) is read.

There are other ways to identify files—namely, by using the abbreviations and conventions discussed later in this chapter—but, if you are in doubt, use the pathname.

Look at one more example. Lola has created a directory called `Bigstuff`, and in it she has placed the file `walrus`. The full pathname of this file is

`/usr/lola/Bigstuff/walrus`

The tail name is

`walrus`

The head is

`/usr/lola/Bigstuff/`

If Lola is in the directory `/usr/lola/Bigstuff` and wants to read the files, she can simply call the file `walrus`. However, if she is in her home directory (`/usr/lola`), she can refer to the file as `/usr/lola/Bigstuff/walrus` or, more simply, as `Bigstuff/walrus`.

This illustrates an important special case, shown in Figure 7.3. If a file is in a subdirectory of the one you are in, the only part of the pathname you need to use is the subdirectory name and the tail. In other words, if the file is below you, relatively speaking, in the directory tree, full pathnames are not necessary. A partial pathname, such as `Bigstuff/walrus`, is called a *relative pathname* because it gives the path relative to your current directory. You can always use absolute or full path names, of course.

FIGURE 7.3
What to call a `walrus`.

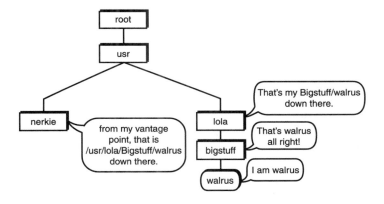

Caution

Many people use relative pathnames as a timesaver. Beware, however, of mixing up your current location and then modifying or deleting the wrong file. The handy **pwd** command gives you your current location.

Basic File and Directory Manipulation Commands

As a walrus in Lewis Carroll's *Through the Looking Glass and What Alice Found There* once said, "The time has come to talk of many things." We now will look at the commands `rm`, `cp`, `mv`, `ln`, `mkdir`, `rmdir`, `cd`, and `pwd`. These commands will let you manipulate your files and directories with ease and versatility. Their basic use is rather simple, but many of them can be used in more than one way. We will show you all you need to know soon enough, but first let's run through a sample session to highlight some of the most common uses.

Mimi has some files named `roses` and `daisies`. She wants to create a new directory called `Flowers` and move those files into it. So she types the following to make the new directory and move the files into that directory:

```
mkdir Flowers
mv roses daisies Flowers
```

Next, she wants to change to the **Flowers** directory so that she can do some work there. She types the following to change to the new directory:

```
cd Flowers
vi violets
```

The **violets** file joins the other files in that directory. When she finishes, she wants to return to her home directory, so she types a simple

```
cd
```

Her friend Rudolpho has written a poem for her in his directory, and she wants to have a copy. She types

```
cp /usr/Rudolpho/iris Flowers/iris
```

where the first pathname identifies the original file, and **iris** is the name of the copy in her directory.

As you can see, these are useful, simple commands. Now we will take a more detailed look at each. Again, we urge you to try the commands as you read along. Use one of the editors or the redirected **cat** command to create some files with which to work.

Tip

The following sections give you the rules governing several useful commands, but it's up to you to make good use of them. The first step is to practice with them, creating new directories, populating them with files, and then copying and moving files. Get comfortable with the procedures.

Directory Commands: mkdir, rmdir, cd, and pwd

Directories give you a place to keep your files. The first three commands (**mkdir**, **rmdir**, **cd**) let you create, remove, and move through directories. The last command (**pwd**) tells you where you are.

The Make Directory Command: mkdir

The **mkdir** command lets you build your own directory subsystem. If you are on a UNIX system, you should have a home directory; this is the directory you are placed in when you log in. We will assume that your directory is a subdirectory of **/usr**, so the full pathname of your directory is **/usr/**_yourname_ (that is, **/usr/james**, if your login name is **james**). The procedure is simple and quick. To create a subdirectory named, say, **FormLetters**, you enter

mkdir FormLetters

The general form of the **mkdir** command is

mkdir _name1 name2..._

where *name1, name2*, and so forth, are the names of the directories you want to create. You can make directories only within your own directory system (unless, of course, you have special privileges on the system). If *name1* is a tail and not a pathname, the new directory is attached to the directory you are in when making the command. For example, if Bob is in his home directory and issues the following command

```
mkdir Labs
```

the result is a new directory whose pathname is /usr/bob/Labs. After doing this, Bob could switch from his home directory to the **Labs** directory (see the **cd** command) and use the following command

```
mkdir Programs
```

to create the directory /usr/bob/Labs/Programs.

It's easy to make directories. The challenge is to design the directory system that's the most helpful to you. Failure to do so will result in a mess of directories and unorganized and unmanageable files. It's recommended that you use a naming convention for files and directories. One suggestion is that you begin subdirectory names with a capital letter, although users follow many conventions. Using this naming technique will help you distinguish files from subdirectories (see Figure 7.4, which has only a single directory, easily spotted by the capital letter).

FIGURE 7.4
The **mkdir** command:
before and after.

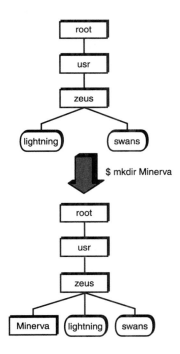

---

mkdir: Creates a New Directory

Name	Options	Arguments
mkdir	None	[*directoryname*...]

Description: The mkdir command creates a new subdirectory in the present directory.

Example: This command creates a new subdirectory called **Chapter4** that exists in the directory where you entered the command:

```
mkdir Chapter4
```

Notes: Don't use blank spaces in directory names; typing mkdir **Chapter 4** would create two directories. A handy convention is to name all directories starting with a capital letter or with all capitals.

Tip

Give thought to your own needs. Don't hesitate to create new directories. It's a good idea to use different directories to house different projects or different types of material. Give your directories and files names that tell you what the contents are. Use names like **Chapter3** and **UNIXbook** rather than **file1** and **directory2**. UNIX gives you the opportunity to make your directory system a model of clarity and convenience—take advantage of it!

The Change Directory Command: cd

After you create a new directory, you want to use it. The **cd** command lets you change from one directory to another. The following is the general form of the command:

```
cd directoryname
```

This command was once called **chdir**, but it is used so often that newer versions of UNIX have shortened the name to **cd**. After it is executed, the named directory becomes your *working directory*. For example, if you enter the commands

```
cd /usr/lola/Quarkdata
ls
```

the result will be a list of files in the directory /usr/lola/Quarkdata. Of course, there's a question of permissions. If Lola gave this command, she would have the power to alter the files in this directory. If Bob gave the command, normally he could look but not touch. (The standard setup allows you to look at someone else's files but not alter them. However, you can copy the file and alter the copy.) The **chmod** command, discussed in Chapter 9, "The UNIX Shell: Command Lines, Redirection, and Shell Scripts," lets you change the permissions governing your files.

The command

```
cd
```

with nothing following it will place you in your home directory.

<table>
| cd: Change Directory | | |
</table>

Name	Options	Arguments
cd	None	[*directoryname*]

Description: The `cd` command makes the named directory your current working directory. If no directory is given, the command takes you to your home directory.

Examples: This command would place you in the `/usr/reggie/Foods/Carbo` directory:

`cd /usr/reggie/Foods/Carbo`

To move up one directory level, use two periods, as follows (which will place you in the `/usr/reggie/Foods` directory):

`cd ..`

The Print Working Directory Command: pwd

When you have the power to change working directories, it's possible to forget which directory you are in. The command `pwd` causes UNIX to print the full pathname of your current working directory. If, when you try to copy or move a file, UNIX claims that the file doesn't exist and you know it does, try `pwd`. You may find that you are in a different directory than you thought and that you need to use a full pathname for a file. The use of `pwd` is simple. If you type

pwd

and if UNIX replies

`/usr/src/cmd`

you are currently in the `/usr/src/cmd` directory. This is a particularly good command to execute before you use other commands to manipulate files. For example, if you try to copy a file (in a different directory) to your current location, `pwd` will show you what your current location is.

pwd: Print Working Directory		
Name	Options	Arguments
pwd	None	None

Description: The `pwd` command prints the pathname of the current working directory.

The Remove Directory Command: rmdir

When you have no more use for a directory, the `rmdir` command lets you get rid of it. The standard form of the command is

`rmdir dir1...`

The `rmdir` command removes the one or more directories listed after the command. The command won't remove nonempty directories or, normally, directories belonging to others.

Tip
The **pwd** command is useful for making sure that you are where you think you are in the directory structure and you don't remove the wrong directory by accident.

rmdir: Removes Directories		
Name	Options	Arguments
rmdir	None	*directoryname(s)...*

Description: The `rmdir` command removes the named directories, providing they are empty.

Example: This command removes the directories **Lab1_Exercises** and **Lab2_Exercises**, if they don't contain any files:

`rmdir Lab1_Exercises Lab2_Exercises`

File Commands: rm, cp, mv, and ln

Handling old-fashioned files involved much paper shuffling. These four UNIX commands let you do the modern equivalent—electronic shuffling—with much greater ease.

Caution
Sometimes electronic shuffling is so easy that it's dangerous. The commands **rm**, **cp**, and **mv** are prime examples. When you remove (**rm**), copy (**cp**), or rename (**mv**) a file, it's possible—even easy—to wipe out, destroy, and permanently lose valuable files. ***Please be careful!*** (We wanted to alert you right now about these possibilities and will address them again in the following sections.) We will discuss ways to protect your files and yourself throughout this chapter and again in Chapter 9.

The Remove Command: rm

The `rm` command removes files. If you don't use it, your directories can become a jungle choked with unused and superceded files. Eventually your old files will take up so much disk space (fill up your quota, if you even have one) that you can't add new files. The `rm` command is simple to use. You just follow `rm` with a list of files you want to delete. Each filename should be separated by a space from the others. Thus,

```
rm dearjohn dearjoe dearfred dearigor
```

removes four files.

As you can see, it is very easy to remove files. In fact, it is so easy and so *irreversible* that you should stop and ask yourself the following questions:

- Am I sure I no longer want this file?

- Is this the file I think it is (not a file in a different directory with same name)?

- Am I really sure about my answers to the preceding questions?

Caution
Special caution is needed when using `rm` with the wildcard substitutions. We'll remind you again when you reach the section "Marvelous Metacharacters: Using Wildcards and Symbolic Substitutions." You may want to use the `-i` option described in the command summary.

Ordinarily, you should not remove directories with `rm`; use `rmdir` if that's what you want to do. The `-r` option in the command summary lets you remove directories, but you better be certain that you really do want to remove everything. The `rmdir` command is safer because it removes only empty directories.

Normally, you are not allowed to remove files from someone else's directory. To make things fair, someone else can't remove yours.

---

rm: Removes Files

Name	Options	Arguments
rm	-i, -r	`filename(s)...`

Description: The `rm` command removes each file in the argument list.

Options:

`-i` for	For each file on the list, whether or not to delete it; respond with y or n yes or no.
`-r`	Deletes a directory and every file or directory in it. (Be careful with this command option!)

Example: This will cause UNIX to query `rm: remove rodgers?` You reply with y or n:

```
rm -i rodgers
```

The Copy Command: cp

The **cp** command is used to create a copy of a file. You should have a copy command for several reasons:

- You can create backup copies (a *backup* is a second copy) of files. A file you are working on can be wiped out by a system problem or (believe it or not!) by mistakes on your part. Thus, backups are a good idea.

- You may want to develop a second, slightly different version of a file, and you can use a copy as a convenient starting point.

- Another reason stems from UNIX being a shared system. A colleague may write a program or collect some data you can use. A copy function gives you an easy way to place it in your own directory.

The simplest form of the copy command is

```
cp file1 file2
```

The command works from left to right; **file1** is the original and **file2** is the copy. The command works this way:

1. It creates a file called **file2**. If you already have a file by that name, it is eliminated and replaced by the new empty file.

2. The contents of **file1** are copied into **file2**.

You, of course, would use whatever names you want for the files; you aren't limited to **file1** and **file2**. For example, a user named **sam** might use the command

```
cp buypasta buytacos
```

to copy the contents of his **buypasta** file into a **buytacos** file.

> ### Caution
>
> Sam should be careful that he doesn't already have a valuable file called **buytacos** because it would be wiped out by the last instruction. This is one of the less friendly aspects of UNIX, but you can use **chmod** (Chapter 9) to protect your files. Also, you can use the **-i** option discussed in the command summary.

To copy a file from another directory into your own, you need to know the full directory name of the file. If you enter

```
cp bigthought idea
```

UNIX will search only your current directory for a file called **bigthought**. If the **bigthought** file is in, say, Bob's directory (assumed to be /usr/bob), the proper command is

```
cp /usr/bob/bigthought idea
```

Here, **/usr/bob/bigthought** is the pathname of the original file. (At the end of this chapter, we will show you some abbreviations that let you reduce the amount of typing you need to do when dealing with long pathnames.) Incidentally, Bob can use chmod (discussed in Chapter 9) to keep others from copying his files.

A second form of the copy command is

```
cp file1 file2... directory2
```

This copies the list of files given into the named directory, which must already exist. This instruction will become more useful to you once you begin establishing additional directories. The new files retain the tail name of the originals. For example, Sam has a **Backup** subdirectory in his home directory of **/usr/sam**. The next command

```
cp buypasta Backup
```

creates a file named **buypasta** in the **Backup** directory.

Note

Although both files are named **buypasta**, they exist in different directories and, thus, have different pathnames. For the preceding example, the pathname of the original file is **/usr/sam/buypasta** and the pathname of the copy is **/usr/sam/Backup/buypasta**. If the directory named **Backup** didn't exist, UNIX would assume that this command was in the first form we described. In other words, it would just copy the file **buypasta** into a file called **Backup**, all in the current directory (see Figure 7.5).

FIGURE 7.5
Copying files.

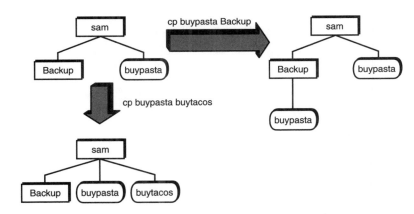

Sometimes, UNIX may give you messages such as cp: cannot create file2 or cp: cannot open file1. This is UNIX's way of confessing bafflement at your instructions. Check to make sure that you typed the names correctly, that you're not trying to place files in someone else's directory, or that you have used the correct pathname (you may need to use a full pathname). Using the full pathname is a safe way to make sure that you don't accidentally misplace a file.

cp: Makes Copies of Files

Name	Options	Arguments
cp	-i, -r	*file1 file2* or *file(s)* ... *directory*

Description: The command `cp` *file1 file2* creates a copy of the first file (*file1*) and gives it the name *file2*. If a file named *file2* already exists, it will be replaced by the new one. The second form of the command (`cp` *file(s)* ... *directory*) copies all the files listed and places them in the named directory.

Options:

-i	Protects you from overwriting an existing file by asking you for a yes or no before it copies a file with an existing name.
-r	Can be used to copy directories, subdirectories, and all their contents into a new directory. The structure of the new directory will have the same structure (subdirectories) and content (files) of the original directory.

Examples: This command copies the file **my_program** and calls the copy **my_program_backup**:

`cp my_program my_program_backup`

This command makes a copy of the file **guest_list** (from the **/usr/erik** directory) and places the copy in the **/usr/kalynn** directory:

`cp /usr/erik/guest_list /usr/kalynn`

The new pathname of the copy is **/usr/kalynn/guest_list**. Note that the original copy still exists in the **/usr/erik** directory. Either copy of the file can be changed *without* affecting the other copy.

The Move Command: mv

The `mv` command lets you change the name of a file and move a file from one directory to another. The simplest form of this command is

`mv` *file1 file2*

This command changes the name of *file1* to *file2*. The file contents are left unchanged. Suppose a person wants to change the name of a file from **a.out** to **findanswer**. This could be done with the following command:

`mv a.out findanswer`

Suppose, however, that the person already had a file called **findanswer**. The `mv` command is as ruthless as `cp`; it would wipe out the old file to make the name available for the contents of **a.out**.

You can use the `mv` command to change the name of a directory, too. The form is

`mv Oldname Newname`

and is the same as that for changing a filename. In other words, `mv` doesn't care whether `Oldname` is a file or a directory; it will just proceed and give it the new name. You can move entire directory paths in the same way, like this:

`mv /usr/bob/dir1 /usr/mary/bob_dir`

The final use of `mv` is to move files to an existing directory. The form is

`mv file1 file2... directory`

You can think of this command as moving one or more files to the specified directory. This is a very handy housekeeping command. For example, if Lola, an exotic physicist studying those exotic subatomic particles called quarks, has accumulated four files of quark data, she can create a directory called `Quarkdata` (using `mkdir`). Then she could type

`mv quark1 quark2 quark3 quark4 Quarkdata`

to put the four files in the new directory. This form of the command leaves the tail of the pathname unchanged. For example, the preceding command would change the pathname of `/usr/lola/quark1` to `/usr/lola/Quarkdata/quark1`. (At the end of the chapter, you will see a much quicker way to make the same move.) Of course, this use of `mv` won't work if the destination directory doesn't exist, or if you don't have permission to write in that directory (see Figure 7.6).

FIGURE 7.6
Two smooth moves.

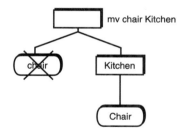

If you give a command like

`mv chair Kitchen`

how does UNIX know whether you want `Kitchen` to be a file or a directory? UNIX may be clever, but it isn't psychic; it doesn't know which you want. It *does* know, however, whether you already have a directory called `Kitchen`. If you have such a directory, UNIX puts the `chair` file there. If you don't have a directory called `Kitchen`, UNIX assumes that you want `Kitchen` to be a filename.

Note

This is possible even though it goes against our informal standard (convention) of naming files with all lowercase letters and directories beginning with capital letters. UNIX will do exactly what you ask it to do, whether or not it was what you **meant** to do. Therefore, always be careful about removing (`rm`), copying (`cp`), or moving (`mv`) any files. If you accidentally delete a *critical* file, don't despair (at least not immediately!). Speak to your systems administrator (SA) about what happened. In some cases he/she may be able to recover your file from a backup copy, but do not count on this. Convincing a busy SA (and they are always busy) to restore a file that was deleted through carelessness can be difficult, but not impossible. It is better to head off this problem by not creating it in the first place by being certain of what you are doing before you press Return.

`mv`: Move or Change a Filename

Name	Option	Arguments
`mv`	`-i`	`filename1 filename2 or filename(s)` `directoryname`

Description: The `mv` command allows you to change the name of a file. The first form of the command changes the name of *filename1* to *filename2*. However, because filenames can include the full pathname, it's possible to use the command to move a file to a new directory as shown in the second form of the command.

Option:

-i Protects you from overwriting an existing file by asking you for a yes or no before it copies a file with an existing name.

Examples: Assume that you are in the `/usr/flisk` directory and that `Hobo` is a subdirectory of that directory.

This changes the name of the file `mrak` to `mark`:

`mv mrak mark`

Note that there is no longer a file named `mrak`. Also, had a file named `mark` existed in that directory before the `mv`, it would have been overwritten (destroyed).

This command changes the name of the file `mark` (pathname `/usr/flisk/mark`) to `/usr/flisk/Hobo/mark`, thus moving the file to the `Hobo` directory:

`mv mark Hobo`

The following command changes the name of the file `mray` (pathname `/usr/flisk/mray`) to `/usr/flisk/Hobo/mary`, thus changing the directory and the tail of the pathname:

`mv mray Hobo/mary`

The Link Command: ln

With the ln command, you can assign multiple names to a single file. This allows you to refer to the same file by different pathnames (see Figure 7.7). This technique can be handy when you have many subdirectories because it lets you link one file to several different directories. (The names you assign are the links between the file and the directories.)

FIGURE 7.7

Setting up links.

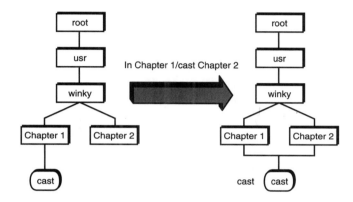

A general form of this command is

ln *file1 name2*

where *name2* can be either a new name you want to give to the file or an existing directory name. If it is a proposed filename, the result of executing this command is that *file1* will now have two names: *file1* and *name2*. If *name2* is the name of a directory, *file1* will also be known by the tail of its old name (*file1*) in the directory *name2*.

Let's clarify these two cases with two examples. Suppose that Tana is in her home directory (/usr/tana) and gives the following command:

ln lab3_program project_procedure3

UNIX checks to see whether the name project_procedure3 has been used yet. If it hasn't, UNIX gives the new name to the file, while still keeping the old one. (An ls command, for example, would show both, and an ls -1 command would show that each had two links.) Tana then could call up the file by either name. If there had already been a file named project_procedure3 in the current directory, ln, being more polite than cp or mv, would tell you and would not make the new link. If project_procedure3 already was a subdirectory, the situation would be like the next example.

Now suppose that Tana has a subdirectory called Project_code. The command

ln lab3_program Project_code

adds the lab3_program name to the Project_code directory, but it leaves the original name undisturbed. Thus, the same file is now in two directories and has two pathnames: /usr/tana/lab3_program and /usr/tana/Project_code/lab3_program. These are the same file, not copies. If you alter the file in one location, you would be able to see the changes in the other location. When Tana is in her home directory and wants to see the file, she can type

`cat lab3_program`

which is short for `cat /usr/tana/lab3_program`.

If she switches to the `Project_code` directory (see the discussion on `cd`), she can see the contents of the file by typing

`cat lab3_program`

which is short for `cat /usr/tana/Project_code/lab3_program`.

Without the `ln` command, she would have had to type

`cat /usr/tana/lab3_program`

to see the `lab3_program` file when in the `Project_code` directory.

Tip
Shortcuts like these are good to learn because they improve your efficiency. If you become more involved with the systems administration or computer programming aspects of UNIX, these types of shortcuts will become even more important.

Suppose that Tana, while in her home directory, issues the following command:

`rm lab3_program`

The file `lab3_program` disappears from her home directory. Does this mean that the file's contents disappear? No—the file still exists in the `Project_code` directory. Only when all the names or links to the file are removed will the file itself be erased.

Assume that you've established several subdirectories and that you want them to have access to the same mailing list. You could, of course, place a copy of the mailing list in each directory, but that would use too much disk space (see Figure 7.8). By using the `ln` command, you can link the file containing the list to a name in each directory. In effect, the same file will exist in each directory. Another advantage is that if you update the file from one directory, you've updated it for all directories.

FIGURE 7.8

A comparison of `rm`, `mv`, `cp`, and `ln`.

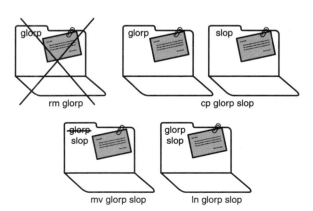

ln: Make File Links		
Name	Options	Arguments
ln	None	filename1 [filename2] or filename(s) directoryname

Description: The ln command lets you add one or more names to an existing file, thus providing a cross-reference system. Each name in your directory has equal priority for reading or writing to the file. However, if a file is linked to another user, generally only the originator of the file can write in it (see the chmod command in Chapter 9).

The form ln *filename1* creates a link between the current working directory and *filename1*. Since *filename1* can include a full pathname, it is linked to a file in another directory.

The form ln *filename1 filename2* is like the preceding action, except that the name of the new file is *filename2*.

The form ln *filename(s) directoryname* lets you put new filenames or links into other directories.

Examples: Assume that the current working directory is /usr/francie/Spring and that there is a file called homework1 in the /usr/francie directory.

The following command creates the filename homework1 in the current directory (usr/francie/Spring) and links that name to the file called homework1 in the francie directory:

ln /usr/francie/homework1

The full pathname of the new link is /usr/francie/Spring/homework1.

This command acts the same as the previous command, except that the newly created filename is test_review_1 instead of homework1:

ln /usr/francie/homework1 test_review_1

The full pathname of the new filename is /usr/francie/Spring/test_review_1.

The following command puts the filenames hist and eng from the current directory into the /usr/francie directory:

ln hist eng /usr/francie

Comparing cp, mv, and ln

The cp, mv, and ln commands form a family. All affect filenames, and they are used in a similar fashion. This similarity can occasionally confuse new users. If this occurs, files could be destroyed accidentally. A closer look at their workings can help prevent this, so let's take that look.

Suppose that you have a file named `jazz` in your home directory. To you, the file is named `jazz`, but, to the computer, the file is known by an identification number. Normally, you don't need to know this number. However, you can find it by using the `-i` option of `ls`. For example, the command

```
ls -i jazz
```

could yield the following output:

```
2312 jazz
```

where `2312` is the ID number. This ID number, termed the *i-node* number, is the true, permanent name for the file. If, for instance, you change the name by typing

mv jazz cool

the ID number remains the same. (Try it and see!)

In the UNIX way of things, the name you choose (`jazz`, `cool`, or whatever) acts as a link between the file and your directory system. These links tie the files to the directories. Using the idea of links, we can visualize the effects of the three file manipulation commands:

- The `ln` command establishes a new link between the file and a directory. All the old links (that is, names) continue to exist. No new files are created. Linking one file to different directories makes it appear as though several different files exist, but, in fact, there is just one file with multiple names. This is very useful when you want a particular file to be easily accessed from several directories without typing out pathnames.

- The `mv` command establishes a new link while removing an old link. If the link is to be a different directory, it makes it appear as though the file has been moved. However, only the link (or name) has been changed, and the file has the same ID number as before.

- The `cp` command actually creates a new file with a new ID number and with its own link (name) to a directory. The old file continues to exist.

In summary, the `cp` command creates new files that are copies of the originals. The `mv` command creates new names for existing files and dumps the old names. The `ln` command creates new names for existing files and simultaneously maintains the old names. Neither `mv` nor `ln` creates new files.

Searching Through Files: grep

The `grep` command possesses a beauty of function that far exceeds its beauty of name. It performs the invaluable service of searching your files for a key word or phrase and telling you what it finds. Suppose that you have several inventory files (`infile1`, `infile2`, `infile3`, and `infile4`) and want to find out which one contains the description of your widget. The following command will serve that high purpose:

```
grep widget infile1 infile2 infile3 infile4
```

The `grep` command will search the contents of each file in turn and will print those lines that contain the string of characters `widget`. The form of this command is

```
grep pattern file(s)
```

In Chapter 11, "Information Processing: `grep`, `find`, and `awk`," we explore `grep`'s abilities much more fully. For the moment, we will point out just two more aspects:

- If the pattern has a space in it, enclose the pattern in single quotes so that `grep` will know that the second word is part of the pattern and not a file to be searched. For example, if you were interested only in a glaxon widget, you could type

  `grep 'glaxon widget' infile1 infile2 infile3 infile4`

  and you would receive every line containing the string `glaxon widget` in any of those four files.

- The wildcard substitutions (described later in the section "Marvelous Metacharacters: Using Wildcards and Symbolic Substitutions") can make it easier to specify filenames. For instance, as you will soon learn, the first example could have been typed

  `grep widget infile?`

The `grep` command is one of the most heavily used UNIX commands. It is used by both novices and experts to improve productivity. Experts often combine `grep` with other commands (such as `ps` to see processes) to provide a wealth of system information. As you become more involved with the system, you will find `grep` growing on you. Don't worry if it does; it's just a sign of a healthy relationship.

One pleasure of UNIX is the freedom it gives you in creating files and directories and manipulating them. Whether you are a collector keeping an inventory, a business person dealing with accounts, a researcher working with experimental data and computer programs, or a homeowner monitoring the household budget, easy file handling is a key to happy computing.

What Can You Do with a UNIX File?

Files are the heart and soul of the UNIX operating system. They store everything from letters to programs to UNIX itself. Thus, it is not surprising to discover how many commands UNIX has for handling files. Table 7.1 lists the most commonly used file-handling commands.

TABLE 7.1   What You Can Do with a UNIX File

Task	Command Format
Read it	`cat filename` or `more filename`
Change or edit it	`vi filename`
Print it	`lpr filename`
Simple formatting	`pr filename`
Make a copy	`cp filename newname`
Mail it	`mail loginname < filename`
Remove it	`rm filename`
Move it to a subdirectory	`mv filename directoryname`
Rename it	`mv filename newname`
Link a file	`ln filename newname`
Count it (see Chapter 9)	`wc filename`
Sort it (see Chapter 9)	`sort filename`
Search for keyword	`grep 'keywords' filename`
Check the spelling (see Chapter 10, "More Text Processing: join, sed, and nroff")	`spell filename`
Complex formatting (see Chapter 10)	`nroff filename`
Redirect output from some commands to another file	`sort filename > newfile`
Combine files	`cat file1 file2 > file3`
Append files	`cat file1 >> file2`

Caution

The **mv** and **cp** commands are dangerous. If a file exists with the same name as the new filename, the old file is wiped out.

Marvelous Metacharacters: Using Wildcards and Symbolic Substitutions

You can get tired and bored punching in file and directory names, especially when you have to use full pathnames. Although specifying full pathnames reduces the risk of overwriting files in some situations, it can become tedious. UNIX provides some tricky ways to save time. We'll look here at some alternative ways to identify filenames.

One clever ability of UNIX is pattern searching. That is, UNIX can find filenames that match a pattern you supply. For example, you can have UNIX list all your files that start with chubby or remove all your files that end with old. Or you can have UNIX concatenate (cat) all your files having names with exactly four characters. The secret lies in the use of special characters (and some experience) called *wildcards*, which can stand for one or more characters in a filename. The wildcards are ? and *. The rules for using them are

- A ? matches any one character.

- An * matches any grouping of zero or more characters.

Some examples should make these rules clear. First, suppose that your directory contains the following files:

```
co.5      coward      hog      huge      part2.2      thug
cow       coy         hug      part2.1   start2.3
```

The command ls used by itself will list all these files, whereas the command ls cow will list only the cow file. The command

```
ls co?
```

however, will list cow and coy, but not co.5 or coward. We can describe the process this way: You provide the pattern co?, which means a co followed by exactly one character (any character). UNIX searches for filenames that match this pattern, and it finds cow and coy. It doesn't list co.5 or coward because they both have more than one character after the co.

Here are other examples of using ls and ? with the previous sample directory:

Command	Response
ls hu?	hug
ls hu??	huge
ls ???	cow coy hog hug
ls ?o?	cow coy hog

The process of finding out which files match the pattern you give is called *filename expansion*. For instance, in the last example, we could say that the pattern ?o? was expanded to match cow, coy, and hog. Note that you use two ?s to represent two characters, and so forth.

The * character is more general yet. As promised, it represents any number of characters. The following are some sample commands and the responses:

Command	Response
ls h*	hog hug huge
ls *g	hog hug thug
ls hug*	hug huge
ls *hug	hug thug
ls *.*	co.5 part2.1 part2.2 start2.3

Let's take a closer look at how these examples work. The first example lists all files beginning with h. The second command lists all files ending in g. The third command lists all files starting with hug. Note that, in this case, the * even matches the *null character* (that is, no character at all). As you can see, the pattern hug? matches huge but not hug because hug? has exactly four characters. However, hug* matches both hug and huge.

The fourth command matches all names ending with hug. Again, the null character is matched. The final example matches all names containing a period in them, except for files whose name begins with a period. (Recall that ls doesn't show such files unless you use the -a option.)

The * and ? characters, as well as the > character, belong to a group of characters having special meanings and uses in UNIX. These characters are called *metacharacters*, an imposing term that hints at their latent power. Besides metacharacters, UNIX also possesses *metasequences*. An example is the pattern-matching sequence [ ]. Like ?, this sequence matches one character, but more restrictively. The trick is to place a list of characters to be matched between the brackets. The following are some examples:

Command	Response
ls co[xyz]	coy
ls [cdegh]o[gtw]	cow hog

The first example matches all three-character names beginning with co and ending in x, y, or z. The second example would also have matched cog and how, among others, if they had been in your directory.

Note

The [ ] sequence matches one character and *only* one character. For example, [nice] matches an n, an i, a c, or an e; it doesn't match ice or nice.

You also can specify a range of characters by using the [ ] notation. For example, [2-8] represents the digits 2, 3, 4, 5, 6, 7, and 8, whereas [A-Z] represents all the capital letters. Thus,

`ls [A-Z]`

would match all filenames consisting of a single capital letter, and

`ls [A-Z]*`

would match all filenames starting with a capital letter and ending in anything. The last example points out that you can combine the different pattern-matching operations into one command. This is a quite useful option.

Very interesting, you say, but of what use is this? In part, the usefulness depends on what sort of names you give your files. Consider the earlier example that we gave of the mv command:

`mv quark1 quark2 quark3 quark4 Quarkdata`

Lola could have accomplished the same result with

`mv quark? Quarkdata`

or

`mv quark[1-4] Quarkdata`

Of course, the first instruction would also move any other files matching that pattern, such as `quarky` or `quarkQ`.

Here's another example. Suppose that you created a directory called **Backup** and wanted to place in there copies of all files in your home directory. The following entry would do the job:

`cp * Backup`

Caution

In general, be cautious about using a solo *. Consider, for example, what the next command does:

`rm *`

Because * matches anything, the command removes all the files in your current working directory. Well, you're hardly likely to give that command unless you mean it, but it can crop up accidentally. Suppose that Lothario wishes to get rid of 20 files called `hortense1`, `hortense2`, and so forth. He could type

`rm hortense*`

and all would be well. But, if he accidentally pressed the Spacebar and typed

`rm hortense *`

UNIX would first look for a file called `hortense`, remove it if found, and then proceed to carry out the * and remove all files. This serious mistake happens frequently (until you've done it yourself), so *be careful*!

wing is another example. You want to `cat` the file `fourtney.Bell`. If you have no
s starting with `f`, you can type

If you have other files starting with `f`, perhaps

`cat fo*`

or

`cat f*l`

will work, depending on the names of the other files.

Like many rules, these have exceptions. In particular, these metacharacters do not match an initial period, a slash, or a period immediately following a slash. There are good reasons for protecting an initial period. First, setup files, such as `.profile`, often have names beginning with a period. This is to make the files unobtrusive, because `ls` doesn't list such files unless you use the `-a` option. If the metacharacters did match an initial period, you might accidentally remove a file that didn't show up with the normal `ls` command. A second reason, which we discuss soon, is that the shell recognizes `.` and `..` as representing the current and parent directories. The slash is protected so that filename matching is confined to the current working directory. The slash, if you recall, serves to separate names in a pathname.

Wildcards are great time savers. The more you work and play with UNIX, the more often—and the more naturally—you will use their help. Just be sure to use them with caution; an accidental `rm *` could be disastrous to your files.

Directory Abbreviations: . and .. and ~

UNIX offers you some useful abbreviations for directory names. We'll unveil them here.

If Nerkie wants to copy two files, `tillie` and `max`, from Bob's subdirectory `gossip` into his own subdirectory `Lowdown`, he could type

`cp /usr/bob/gossip/tillie /usr/bob/gossip/max /usr/nerkie/Lowdown`

What a job with lots of typing! UNIX offers some shortcuts to those of you who desire less typing (and inevitable typos). They are abbreviations for particular directories as follows:

Directory	Command Shortcut
Your current working directory	. (a simple period)
The parent directory from which your current working directory branches	.. (two periods)
A home directory	~ (a tilde)

The following are some examples and what they stand for, assuming that Nerkie uses them while in the `usr/nerkie` directory:

Abbreviated Command	Meaning for Our Example
~	/usr/nerkie
~bob	/usr/bob
~Lowdown	/usr/Lowdown
~bob/gossip	/usr/bob/gossip

Notice the difference between ~`Lowdown` and ~`/Lowdown`. The first one would cause UNIX to took for the home directory of a user named `Lowdown`, whereas the second would lead UNIX to look through Nerkie's home directory for a subdirectory called `Lowdown`.

The following are some more examples showing how Nerkie could reduce his typing. Suppose that he wants to copy the same two files as before (`tillie` and `max`) from Bob's `gossip` subdirectory into his subdirectory `Lowdown`:

`cp ~bob/gossip/tillie ~bob/gossip/max Lowdown`

(Because Nerkie is in his home directory, UNIX will recognize `Lowdown` as a subdirectory.)

An easier way to do the same thing would be to move into Bob's directory before giving the copy command:

`cd ~bob/gossip`
`cp tillie max ~/Lowdown`

Yet another possibility would be to switch into his subdirectory and then give the copy command:

`cd Lowdown`
`cp ~bob/gossip/tillie ~bob/gossip/max`

These directory abbreviations can be combined with the wildcard substitutions. For instance, Nerkie can copy the entire file contents of Bob's `gossip` directory into his own `Lowdown` subdirectory with

`cp ~bob/gossip/* Lowdown`

If Nerkie is already in the `Lowdown` directory, he could have simplified this even more with

`cp ~bob/gossip/*`

Next are some more examples and what they stand for, assuming that Nerkie uses them while in the `/usr/nerkie` directory.

.	/usr/nerkie
..	/usr
./Lowdown	/usr/nerkie/Lowdown

If Nerkie uses `cd` to switch to the `/usr/nerkie/Lowdown` directory, the meanings of the last two become

.	/usr/nerkie/Lowdown
..	/usr/nerkie

The directory abbreviations often come in handy when you decide to make wholesale revisions in your directory system. They give you a convenient way to shift large blocks of files about. Suppose that Nerkie is working in his `/usr/nerkie/Programs/Fortnerkie` directory and wants to copy several files, all of which have names ending in `.f`, from `/usr/nerkie/Programs` to his current directory. If he didn't know about these directory abbreviations, he could use

`cp /usr/nerkie/Programs/*.f /usr/nerkie/Programs/Fortnerkie.`

But now that he knows better, he can just type

`cp ../*.f .`

That is, copy everything from the directory above that ends in `.f` into the current directory. Not only is this quicker to type, but it also offers fewer opportunities to make typing errors. Ah, how lucky Nerkie is to have a UNIX system at his service!

Summary

The hierarchical structure of the filing system is one of the major features of the UNIX operating system. You can manipulate files and directories with the commands you've seen in this chapter. The `mv` and `cp` commands are often used, and you've seen how to create new subdirectories to copy files into.

Review Questions

Matching Commands to Functions

Match the functions shown on the left to the commands shown on the right.

1. `cd`	a.	Makes a new subdirectory named `D2`
2. `pwd`	b.	Lists contents of the working directory
3. `mv dearsue dearann`	c.	Changes the name of `dearsue` to `dearann`
4. `mail sue`	d.	Initiates sending mail to `sue`
5. `cat part.? > final`	e.	Prints all lines containing the word `sue` in the file `dearann`
6. `ls`	f.	Copies the file `stats` in `hoppy`'s home directory into a file called `stats` in the current working directory
7. `mkdir D2`		
8. `grep sue dearann`	g.	Gives you your current working directory
9. `rm fig*`	h.	Concatenates all files whose names consist of `part.` followed by one character, and places the result in the file `final`
10. `cp /usr/hoppy/stats`		
	i.	Moves your working directory up one level
	j.	Removes all files whose names start with `fig`

Creating Commands

Use the hypothetical file structure in Figure 7.9 to create the commands that will accomplish the following actions (in some cases, there is more than one way). Assume that you are in the directory called `home`.

FIGURE 7.9
Your hypothetical work-
ing directory.

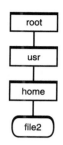

1. List all files and directories in your account.

2. Read the file `file2`.

3. Make a copy of `file2` and call it `file5`.

4. Make a subdirectory named `D2`.

5. Put yourself in subdirectory `D2`.

6. Move `file2` into `D2`.

7. While in subdirectory `D2`, list all files in directory `home`.

8. Assuming you are in the subdirectory `D2`, create a subdirectory `D3` at the same level as `D2`—that is, not a subdirectory of `D2`. (*Hint:* One method is a two-step sequence.)

9. Assume that you are in the `home` directory. Place today's date in a file in `D3`, calling it `f8`.

10. Remove subdirectory `D3`.

Exercises

1. Find your full pathname.

2. List the contents of your home directory.

3. Some UNIX systems have games on them. Try to find the directory in which they are stored and list them.

4. Create a new subdirectory named `D7`. Put yourself in `D7` and try to copy any two files into the `D7` directory. You should use full pathnames for the experience.

5. Create a backup copy of your `D7` files into a new subdirectory named `D8` by using metacharacters.

6. Try creating a new filename using `ln`.

7. Use `grep` on your mailbox file (`mbox`) to find the occurrence of a word such as `dear` or `hello`.

8. Clean up your filing system by removing the files from `D8` and then removing `D8` itself.

CHAPTER 8

THE UNIX SHELL: COMMAND LINES, REDIRECTION, AND SHELL SCRIPTS

You will learn about the following in this chapter:

- The shells available to most users
- How to use options and arguments on the command line
- How to use redirection to alter input and output
- The basics of writing a shell script
- How to use foreground and background processes

M uch of UNIX's awesome strength comes from its shell, the program that handles your interaction with the computer system. The UNIX shell plays two roles:

- It acts as a command interpreter.

- It's a programming language.

Sounds good, but what do these terms mean? Calling the shell a *command interpreter* means that it interprets your commands. If, for example, you type the **date** command, the shell tracks down where the **date** program is kept and then runs it. Calling the shell a *programming language* means that you can string together a series of basic commands to perform some larger task. The pipelines and the shell scripts discussed in this chapter are examples of that ability.

As a UNIX user, you have several shells from which to choose. One is the **sh** program. This program is the standard Bourne shell, common to all modern UNIX versions. The second is the C shell (**csh**) program, which comes with BSD UNIX. A third option is the Korn (**ksh**) shell. When you log on to a UNIX system, UNIX starts up one of these programs to act as your shell. Normally, BSD UNIX patrons use the **csh** shell. Although you have the option of using **sh** or **ksh** instead, either temporarily or as your everyday shell, we'll assume that you're using **csh**. Actually, much of what we'll say applies equally to all three shells. We'll let you know which discussions pertain just to one shell.

Clearly, if you want to know UNIX, you should get to know your shell. We hope to help you do that in this chapter. First, we will discuss the usual form for commands to the shell. Then we will discuss redirection again and introduce pipes. Next we will talk about special `csh` capabilities: history, filename completion, aliasing, and job control. Even the more casual UNIX user will want to pick up on these topics. If you want to get deeper into the shell, read on and be introduced to shell scripts, shell variables, shell metacharacters, and your `.login`, `.cshrc`, and `.profile` files.

Okay, let's begin by looking at the command line.

The Shell Command Line

When you sit down to a UNIX system, you have hundreds of UNIX commands at your call. Many will become indispensable to you, some you will use occasionally, and some you may never see. There are some basic commands that almost every user needs to know, and frequent use will burn them into your brain. The more you use the system, the more commands you'll know by heart, but with so many commands available, remembering the details can be a problem. Fortunately, most UNIX commands are used similarly. Unfortunately, there are many exceptions, but we can view this as a sign of the UNIX system's vibrant vitality.

You've seen the main elements of a command in Chapter 3, "Electronic Mail and Online Help: `mail`, `talk`, and `man`," but you probably would enjoy seeing them again. The elements are the command name, the options, and the arguments. (Technically, anything following the command name is an argument, but we will use the term *argument* to mean the file, the directory, or whatever it is that the command acts on. We will use the term *option* to indicate a modification of the command.) When put together on one line, these elements constitute the *command line*. An example of a command line is

```
ls -l /usr
```

Here the command name is `ls`, the option is `-l` (that is, the *long* form), and the argument is the directory name, `/usr` (see Figure 8.1).

FIGURE 8.1
Command-line structure.

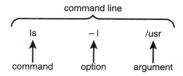

Computers, being the simple-minded machines they are, require that you follow rules when typing in a command line. Here are some of them:

- Each element should be separated from the others by at least one space. UNIX uses the spaces to tell when one element ends and another begins, so if you type

  ```
  ls-l /usr
  ```

UNIX will think you're looking for a command called `ls- l`, and if you type

```
ls -l/usr
```

UNIX will think you're looking for an option called `-l/usr`. In either case, you will leave UNIX dumbfounded. Why can't UNIX figure out what you really meant? After all, there aren't any other command names beginning with `ls`, so UNIX should have known that you intended `ls-l` to be `ls -l`. Ah, but UNIX is so flexible that you could have *created* a new command called `ls-l`. Thus, UNIX takes the safe route and doesn't try to second-guess what you meant. Because many users forget to put a space between a command name and the option flag, we remind you once again: *put a space after the command name*. On the other hand, *don't* put spaces within an element:

Right	Wrong
`ls -l /usr`	`ls - l /usr`
`ls -s /bin`	`ls-s /bin`

- The proper order of elements is *command name*, *options*, and *arguments*. Often, you don't need any options and, sometimes, you don't need an argument; just omit the elements you don't need. Here are some examples of right and wrong command-line orders.

Right	Wrong
`cat -n hobo`	`cat hobo -n`
`cat hobo`	`hobo cat`
`ls -a`	`-a ls`

- Options usually are indicated with the flag notation, where one or more characters follow a hyphen. Typical examples are the `-n`, `-a`, and `-l` flags that you just saw. More than one option can be used at a time (unless they contradict each other), and the order usually isn't important. Multiple option flags may be separated from each other by spaces or, if they require no further input, may be strung together on the same hyphen. (In some instances, only one of these two approaches may work, depending on the particular command.) For example, if you want to get a long listing (`-l`) of all files (`-a`) in reverse order (`-r`), you could type any of the following RIGHT examples:

Right	Wrong
`ls -l -a -r`	`ls -l-a-r`
`ls -lar`	`ls -l a r`
`ls -r -al`	
`ls -r -la`	

What do we mean by "require no further input"? We mean an option that's called up just by giving a letter or symbol alone. For example, the `-l` and the `-a` options of `ls` need no further input. On the other hand, the `-o` option of `cc` must have a filename supplied with it.

- Some commands take, or can take, more than one argument. These should be separated from each other by spaces:

Right	Wrong
`cat cabbage king walrus`	`cat cabbagekingwalrus`
	`cat cabbage, king, walrus`

- You can combine several commands on one line by separating them with semicolons. For example, if you wanted to compile the C program in the file **lulu.c** and run the resulting **a.out** program, you could type

```
gcc lulu.c;  a.out
```

- You can spread a command over more than one line by typing a backslash (\) just before you press Return. When you type a Return without a backslash, the **csh** shell executes the command. Here we **cat** the file **dolphins**, splitting the command line:

```
% cat \
dolphins

Dolphins can use their sonar to observe the heart and
lungs of a human swimmer. Thus, to a dolphin, a human
looks more like a dolphin (albeit a sickly one) than
does a fish.
%
```

The Bourne and Korn shells work much the same, except that they supply a > prompt for the continued lines to let you know that it thinks the command isn't finished.

A command can be your own creation. For example, you saw in the last chapter that you can run a computer program simply by typing the name of the file in which the executable program is stored. Later in this chapter, you will see how to use shell scripts to produce your own commands. First, though, take a fuller look at redirection.

Redirection

Redirection is one feature that makes UNIX pleasant to use. You've already seen one type of redirection in Chapter 4, "Files and Directories: `l s`, `cat`, `more`, and `pr`," when we discussed the > operator. Now we will trot out a full stable of redirection operators for your appreciation: >, >>, <, and ¦. For good measure, we will throw in the **tee** command.

Redirecting Output to a File: >

You've seen the > operator before. It allows you to redirect the output of a command or program to a file. An example is

```
cat listl list2 > list3
```

In this case, the output of `cat` is the joined contents of the files `list` and `list2`. The file `list3`
is created, and this file is then filled with the joined contents of `list1` and `list2`. For instance,
if the contents of `file1` are

```
milk 2 qt
bread 1 loaf
hamburger 2 lb
```

and if `file2` contains

```
lettuce 1 hd
spaghetti 1 lb
garlic
basil
butter
```

the newly created `file3` will contain

```
milk 2 qt
bread 1 loaf
hamburger 2 lb
lettuce 1 hd
spaghetti 1 lb
garlic
basil
butter
```

The general format for using the > operator is

```
command > filename
```

The *command* (which can include options and arguments and can be your own executable program) should be one that produces some sort of output normally routed to the screen. It could
be something like `ls`, but not something like `rm list1`, which performs an action but doesn't
produce screen output.

Perhaps the most important point to remember is that the right side of the command should
be a file. (However, UNIX treats I/O devices as files, so the right side of the command could
represent a printer or another terminal. See the upcoming sidebar, "I/O Devices and Files.")

Suppose that you redirect data to a file that already exists:

```
% cat flipper zippy > dolphins
```

With the `sh` shell, this command would wipe out the prior contents of `dolphins`. With the `csh`
shell, however, you get your choice of two behavior patterns. The first is the same as for the `sh`
shell—any prior contents of the file are lost. The second is that the shell refuses to execute the
command. Instead, it warns you:

```
dolphins: File exists
```

The shell has protected your file. To get this file protection, use the following **csh** command:

```
set noclobber
```

To turn off file protection, use this command:

```
unset noclobber
```

Typically, you would place the set **noclobber** command in your **.cshrc** file so that it's executed automatically when you log in. We'll discuss this in more detail later.

I/O Devices and Files

UNIX's marvelous redirection operators are available because UNIX treats I/O (input/output) devices as files. This means that each device is given a filename. These files usually are kept in the directory **/dev**, which contains a separate file for each terminal, printer, phone hookup, tape drive, floppy disk, and so forth. For example, this text is being typed on a terminal named **/dev/tty06**. (How can you tell what your terminal's filename is? Type the command **tty** and UNIX will tell you the device name.) If you **ls** the contents of **/dev**, you'll get to see all device filenames.

How can you use these names? Normally, you don't have to. For instance, remember how you got the **cat** command to use the terminal for input? You typed

cat

and UNIX interpreted the lack of a filename to mean that it would use the terminal as an input. However, you could also have used

ls /dev/tty06

if you were using **tty06**. This would be using the filename directly, but omitting a filename is simpler in this case.

When you give a command such as **ls**, it's really the same as

ls > /dev/tty06

if you're using **tty06**. Thus, when you use a command such as

ls > save

you are just replacing one file with another as far as UNIX is concerned. This equivalence is what makes it simple to include the redirection feature.

When you use the redirection operators, you don't need to use device filenames. UNIX itself takes care of the bookkeeping, but it's the file system that makes redirection convenient.

Overriding File Protection: >!

Suppose that you've selected the **noclobber** option but want to override the file protection it offers. You can use a special **csh** version of the redirection operator: >!. For example, the command

`% ` **cat revision1 revision2 >! report**

replaces the contents of report with the combined contents of **revision1** and **revision2**. The **!** tells the **csh** shell that resistance is useless; it must obey your command.

Redirecting and Appending Output to a File: >>

Suppose that you want to add information to an existing file. The >> operator was designed to do just that. To add the contents of the file `newcustomers` to the file `customers`, just type

```
cat newcustomers >> customers
```

The new material is appended to the end of the `customers` file. Suppose that there was no `customers` file. Then the file named `customers` would be created to receive the contents of `newcustomers`.

The general format for using >> is

```
command >> filename
```

where *command* is a command or sequence of commands that produce an output, and *file-name* is the name of a file.

Redirecting Input from a File: <

The last two operators send data to files; the < operator gets data out of files. You can use it with commands or programs that normally take input from the terminal. For example, you could use an editor to write a letter and store it in a file called `letter`. You could then mail it to another user (assume a login name of `cbiscuits`) with the following command:

```
mail cbiscuits < letter
```

The < operator tells `mail` to take input from the file `letter` instead of from the terminal.

The general form for using this command is

```
command < filename
```

The *command* should be one that normally takes input from the keyboard.

Combined Redirects

Suppose that the program `analyze` produces some output that you want to save in a file called `results`. At the same time, you want `analyze` to get its input from the `datafile` file (see Figure 8.2). You can do that with the command sequence

```
analyze < datafile > results
```

This command causes `analyze` to look for input in `datafile` and place its output into `results`. The redirection instructions can be in either order. The next example would work also:

```
analyze > results < datafile
```

Don't use two or more inputs (or outputs) in the same command. The following example is incorrect:

```
analyze < data1 < data2
```

FIGURE 8.2

Combined redirects using the hypothetical command `analyze`.

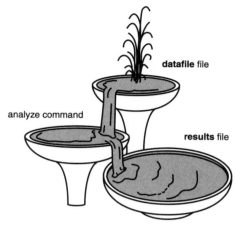

datafile file

analyze command

results file

analyze <datalife>results

The Pipeline: ¦

Chuck Biscuits has lots of files in his directory. He wants to know how many but feels (rightly so) that the computer, not he, should do the counting. The `ls` command, he knows, lists the names of his files, and the `wc` command (see Chapter 9, "File-Management Commands and Others: `wc`, `sort`, `lpr`, and `chmod`,") counts words. Can he use the > and < operators to some-how link these commands together? Not really, for these operators always link a command to a file, never a command to a command. He could create a temporary file and do it this way:

`% ls > temp`	List files, store in temp)
`% wc -w temp`	Count words in temp)
`% rm temp`	Remove temp)

However, this is a little awkward, and there's a real need for an operator that links a command to a command.

If there's a need, UNIX tries to fill it. For this particular need, UNIX provides the *pipeline* oper-ator, represented by the ¦ character. (On some keyboards, this is a solid vertical line; on oth-ers, it's a vertical line with a small gap in the middle.) This operator *pipes* the output of one command into a second command. For example, Chuck can solve his problem with this com-bined command:

`ls ¦ wc -w`

In this case, the *output* of `ls` (that is, a list of filenames) is accepted as the *input* of `wc -w`, which then counts the number of words. Because the list of filenames is shunted to `wc`, the list doesn't appear onscreen. All Chuck will see is the final output of `wc`. Thus, this simple com-mand that uses a pipe replaces three commands and counts the number of files you have in your directory.

The general format for using the pipe is

```
command ¦ command
```

The output of the first command becomes the input of the second command. You can string together as many pipes as you need; you also can use > and <. Suppose that you've written a program called `bigword` that selects words longer than eight letters from its input and prints them. What will the following compound command do?

```
bigword < MyLife ¦ wc -w
```

This command causes `bigword` to search the file `MyLife` for words longer than eight letters. These words are then counted by `wc -w`, and the end result is the number of big words that you have in the file `MyLife`.

Here's an example with two pipes. Suppose that you have a program, `randomword`, that chooses 100 words at random from its input. (Perhaps you are an author who needs a few extra words to sprinkle through your work.) You want to sort these words alphabetically and process the list with a program of your own called `caps`. Here's how to do it:

```
randomword < MyLife ¦ sort ¦ caps
```

In this example, `randomword`'s output is sent to `sort` (see Chapter 9), and `sort`'s output is then sent to `caps`. Only the output of `caps` is sent to the terminal, so the rest of the process is invisible to the user.

Split Output: `tee`

Suppose that you're running a program and want to see the output as it's produced as well as save the output in a file. One way is to run the program twice: once without using > and once using it. This is a bit wasteful and, thanks to `tee`, is unnecessary. Actually, `tee` isn't an operator like > or ¦ but is a command. It takes its input and routes it to two places: the terminal and the file of your choice. You can think of it as a tee fitting to the pipeline. It's used this way:

```
ls ¦ tee save_ls
```

The pipe relays the output of `ls` to `tee`; `tee` then sends the output to the terminal and to `save_ls`, the file that you chose for saving the output.

The output to the terminal can be piped further without affecting the file's contents. For example, you can try this command:

```
ls ¦ tee save_ls ¦ sort -r
```

The file `save_ls` will contain a list of your files in alphabetical order (because that's what `ls` produces), but your terminal screen will show your files in reverse alphabetical order, for the other output of tee has been routed to `sort -r`, which sorts in reverse order (see Figure 8.3).

The general format for using the `tee` command is

```
command ¦ tee filename
```

FIGURE 8.3

Using the `tee` command.

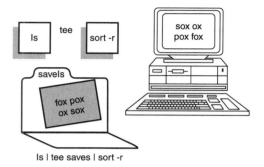

ls | tee savels | sort -r

Here, the output of *command* is piped to `tee`, which routes copies of *command*'s output to the terminal and to the file *filename*. Actually, `tee` has two options, as described in the upcoming summary.

As you've seen, the redirection operators give you some very flexible means for routing data through the system. They are an important component of the design of UNIX, so make yourself familiar with them. Again we see how UNIX provides you a powerful tool set of commands, if you are creative enough to use them.

UNIX redirection offers one form of controlling how your tasks are performed. The UNIX job control system offers another way with different possibilities. We will look at it next.

---

tee: Splits Output

Name	Options	Arguments
tee	[-i, -a]	*filename(s)*

Description: The `tee` command routes its input to the terminal as well as to the named file or files.

Options:

-i   Ignores interrupts

-a   Causes the output to be added to the end of the named file

---

Example: This command produces the long listing of the contents of the /usr directory:

```
ls -l /usr | tee -a clutter
```

This listing is sent to the terminal screen and is added to the end of the **clutter** file.

Job Control

A *job* is a task that you have the computer do for you. Editing a file is a job, compiling a program is a job, creating a directory is a job, and listing your files is a job. Job control gives you the option of suspending a job and resuming it later and of switching a job between foreground and background. When you master job control, you will find yourself using it more than you probably imagined.

Stopping and Restarting a Job: Ctrl-z and `fg`

You are in the midst of editing a large file or of running an interactive program when you receive mail that you want to reply to immediately. You can stop your current job by pressing Ctrl-z and can then attend to your mail. When you want to restart the job, type

fg

(for foreground) to resume your job where you left off. If you were editing a file in `vi`, for example, you would be returned to the line you were working on.

Simple? Simple! Press Ctrl-z to stop the job and `fg` to resume it. What if you stop a job and forget about it? If you do, you will be given a warning when you try to log off. The `csh` shell will say

```
Stopped jobs
```

and not let you log out. However, if you persistently try to log out, `csh` will eventually let you and will kill your stopped jobs. A better idea is to bring the job to foreground and terminate it properly.

Note

With some keyboards, many people accidentally press Ctrl-z rather than type **ZZ** when attempting to leave `vi`. This leads to some mysterious `Stopped .jobs` messages. Of course, after such people read this section, they won't find the messages so mysterious.

Background Jobs

To run a program in background, follow the command with an ampersand. For example, to get a listing of your files in background, you could type

```
ls -la > listing &
```

UNIX will place the job in background and give you a message like

```
[1] 1492
```

The first number is a personal job control number that you see how to use in the next section. The second is the process identification (PID) number, which is a system number assigned uniquely to your job. Meanwhile, you could do another job while the background task is being executed. Eventually, UNIX would notify you that the task was done, and you would find that the file listing had been added to your directory. Remember, though, that if a job normally sends output to the screen, it will do so even if running in background (see Figure 8.4).

FIGURE 8.4
Job types.

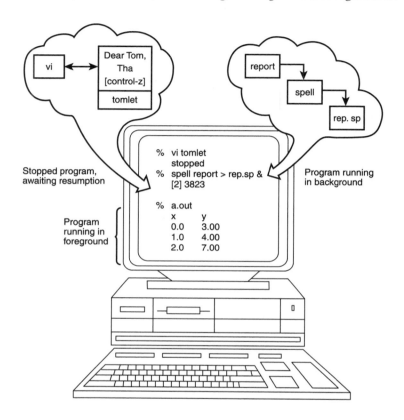

If you want to return the background job to the foreground—that is, on your terminal—just type

fg

> **Note**
>
> sh, csh, and ksh support the & background commands, but fg and Ctrl-z are csh and ksh features only.

Multiple Jobs: jobs and bg

You are a blur of activity. You've stopped a job, started two jobs in background, started and stopped another job, and then started yet another job. But, what was the first job you started? And, what job will come into the foreground the next time you type **fg**? You need some way to check on what you've done and identify the various tasks you have under way. Perhaps you also need a vacation. Well, UNIX may not help with the vacation, but it can deal with the other problems.

The simplest, quickest way to review what you're doing is to type

jobs

This command will then list and label the jobs that you've initiated at your terminal. (If you're using two terminals simultaneously, each will have its own job list.) Here is a sample response:

```
[2]    Stopped    vi whatamess
[3]    Stopped    vi *7
[4]  - Stopped    gcc ~wiseone/bigprogramms/begin.c
[5]  + Stopped    vi fing
[6]    Running    ls -R / ¦ sort -o jnk
```

The first column identifies the job with a number in brackets; we will call this the *job number*. The + in the fourth line indicates the *current* job, and the - in the third line marks the next most current job. (The **jobs** command has an interesting conception of "current." All stopped jobs are more current than running jobs. The most recently stopped job is the most current. Of running jobs, the job initiated the longest ago is the most current.) Jobs labeled **Stopped** are, indeed, stopped. A job labeled **Running** is running in background. The final column gives the job's name.

How do you use this information? Suppose that you want to resume work on job **[2]**. One way is to type

fg %2

The **%** character is used to introduce a job number, so this instruction means to bring job **[2]** into foreground. More simply, you can omit the **fg** and just type

%2

	Tip

If you type **fg** with no further information, the job labeled with the + sign is brought into foreground.

You can also take a stopped job and restart it in the background, and you can stop a job already running in the background. You actually have two choices for putting a stopped job in the background. The first uses the **&** operator. For example, to start job **[4]** in background, you can type

%4 &

Or, you can use the **bg** (for background) command:

bg %4

The result is the same in either case. The job is placed in background and you receive a message such as

```
[4]    gcc ~wiseone/bigprograms/begin.c &
```

telling you the name of job [4] and that it's now running in the background.

To stop, say, job [6] running in the background, just type

stop %6

Job Numbers and PID Numbers

Earlier, we mentioned that each job you stop or put into background is given a job number (in brackets) and a PID number. Why two numbers? And what are their uses?

First, the job numbers assigned by job are personal to you and your terminal. The first job you stop or put in background after logging in on a given terminal is called [1], the next one [2], and so on; the sequence is fairly predictable. They are small, easily typed integers, and they are the labels recognized by the **csh** job-control system. However, these numbers aren't unique; your neighbor could very well also have a job [1] and a job [2]. To keep things straight, the computing system needs a method to assign each job a unique identification; that's the purpose of the PID number. Another difference is that only jobs that you stop or place in the background are given job numbers, but every job you run is assigned an ID number. In short, a job number is a local, useful-to-you label, and the PID number is a system-wide, useful-to-UNIX label (see Figure 8.5).

FIGURE 8.5
Job numbers and PIDs.

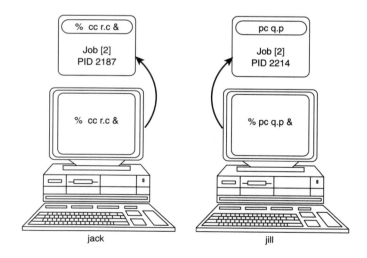

You can get both labels displayed by using the **-l** option on **jobs**; see the following **jobs** summary.

---

jobs: List and Identify Stopped and Background Jobs

Name	Options	Arguments
jobs	[-1] None	

Description: The jobs command lists stopped jobs and jobs running in the background. The format is as follows:

```
[1]  + Stopped    vi whatamess
[2]  - Stopped    vi fing
[3]    Running    ls -R / ¦ sort -o jnk
```

The first column is the assigned job number enclosed in brackets. The second column contains a + for the current job and a - for the next most current job. The third column states whether the job is stopped or running in background. The final column gives the name of the job.

The jobs command ranks by *currency*. From most current to least current, the order is as follows: most recently stopped job to least recently stopped job followed by the first initiated background job to the most recently initiated background job. In the example, the user went back to [1] after stopping [2] and then stopped [3] again.

The job numbers are assigned for a given terminal; if you use two terminals simultaneously, each will have its own list of job numbers.

Option:

-1   This option gives a long listing that also includes the process identification (PID) number, a unique system-wide number. Different users can have jobs with the same job number, but no two jobs have the same process ID number.

Process Status: ps

The ps command also reports on the processes currently going on in the computer. This command works with all three main shells (csh, sh, and ksh), so it's more general than jobs. It also supplies more information, particularly if you use some options too technical to discuss here. Let's see what a plain usage gives us:

```
% ps
    PID  TT  STAT  TIME  COMMAND
    326  A5  R     0:00  ps
%
```

We get five items of information. The PID is the process ID number, the same one that jobs reports. The TT column identifies the terminal on which the process is running. The STAT column is the status; R means running. The TIME column is the time taken so far by the job, and the COMMAND column gives us the name of the command. So, in this case, the ps command reports on itself.

Now let's put a process in the background and repeat the command:

```
% sort bigfile > nicefile &
[1] 680

% ps
    PID  TT  STAT  TIME  COMMAND
    680  A5  R     0:03  sort bigfile
    680  A5  R     0:00  ps
%
```

Here we've used a file big enough that the sorting is still going on when we invoke **ps**. Now we get the PID for the sorting process as well as for the **ps** process itself. Note that the **ps** command has a different PID from last time because calling it again starts a new process.

Let's look at a couple of options. The -**x** option is interesting because it also lists processes that you didn't start from your terminal. That may sound cryptic, so let's look at an example:

```
% ps -x
    PID  TT  STAT  TIME  COMMAND
    147  A5  R     0:06  -csh (csh)
    762  A5  R     0:00  ps
%
```

Now you see the **csh** command listed. (Don't worry about the peculiar format.) When we logged on to the system, the system started up a **csh** process to handle our interaction with UNIX. This reminds us that **csh** is just another program. It runs as long as we remain logged in. When we log off, our shell quits, too.

The -**a** option (for all) is interesting, too. It lists additional processes for others on the system. This feature is quite useful if you're using several shells. Let's try the -**ax** combination. Here's an abbreviated version of what you might get:

```
% ps -ax
    PID  TT  STAT  TIME  COMMAND
    157  A3  R     0:31  -csh (csh)
    213  A3  R     0:16  vi poultrylife
    456  A4  R     0:06  -csh (csh)
    801  A4  R     0:00  ls -l
    147  A5  R     0:10  -csh (csh)
    803  A5  R     0:00  ps
    102  A9  R     1:34  -csh (csh)
    666  A9  R     0:12  vi eggreport
%
```

Not only does this show us what others are up to, it also reveals that each user has his or her own version of the **csh** shell handling that user's needs. If we just did the -**a** option, **ps** wouldn't report the shells.

ps: Process Status Report		
Name	Options	Arguments
ps	[-a, -x]	None

Description: The **ps** command prints information about processes—that is, jobs now in the system. The output consists of the process identification number (**PID**), the terminal (**TT**), CPU time used (**TIME**), the state of the process (**STAT**), and the command (**COMMAND**). The PID is a number uniquely assigned to the process. The state is described by a four-letter sequence. The first letter can be **R** (for running); **T** (for stopped); **P**, **D**, or **S** (for various states of temporary inactivity); or **I** (for idle). The other three letters relate to more technical matters; refer to the online manual if you're interested in more information about them.

Options:

-a	This option displays ps information for all terminals, not just the user's.
-x	This option causes ps to report processes, such as the login shell, that weren't started at the terminal.

Terminating Unruly Jobs: `kill`

Into every computer user's life comes the program that just won't quit. The computer insists on taking some trivial error seriously and expends considerable time doing useless things with great speed and accuracy. If a program is doing this in the background, you can't stop it with a simple interrupt (using Ctrl-c or Break). You need a special tool: `kill`. To use `kill`, you need to know either the job number or the PID number. Suppose that these numbers are [3] and 3456, respectively. Then either of the following commands will terminate the troublesome job:

```
kill %3
```

or

```
kill 3456
```

Occasionally, a complex process won't succumb to this command. In this case, try the potent `-9` option, as in

```
kill -9 %3
```

---

kill: Terminate Jobs

Name	Options	Arguments
kill	[-9]	Job number or process ID

Description: The kill command terminates the specified job. You can specify the job either by the job number assigned by jobs or with the process identification number (PID) given by ps or jobs -1. The format when using job number *n* is

kill %*n*

The format when using the PID number is

kill *number*

Option:

-9   This is a "sure kill" that can be used if the ordinary kill fails. This actually is a special case of a more general option.

Example: The job spell Essay > err & has job number 3 and a PID of 3492. You can terminate the job with

kill %3

or

kill 3492

Job-Control Summary

Table 8.1 lists the job-control operations that we've discussed.

TABLE 8.1   Job-Control Commands

Command	Definition
Ctrl-z	Stops the job you're working on.
command &	Makes `command` run in the background.
jobs	Lists stopped and background jobs, assigning them job numbers. The job numbers are given in brackets, as [1]. The current job is identified with a + and the next most current with a -. Because you can go back and forth between jobs, the current job may not be the last one on the list.
fg	Brings the + marked job from the jobs list into the foreground, starting it if stopped.
fg %*n*	Brings job *n* from the jobs list into foreground, starting it if stopped.
%*n*	Short for fg %*n*.
%*n*&	Restarts job *n*, placing it in background.
bg	Puts the + marked job from the jobs list into background, starting it if stopped.
bg %*n*	Puts job *n* from the jobs list into background, starting it if stopped.
stop %*n*	Stops the specified background job.
kill %*n*	Kills job *n*—that is, terminates the job rather than merely suspend it.

Job Control in the Bourne and Korn Shells

Of the operations discussed in the preceding sections, the only one available in the Bourne shell is putting a job in background with the **&** operator. If you need to terminate a job there, use the **ps** command to find the process ID number, and use **kill** with that PID number as just described. This is also a handy way to kill process if you're using the Korn shell (**ksh**).

System V UNIX from Bell Labs has a command called shl that provides job control capabilities similar to those of the C shell.

History: A System That Remembers

The **csh** shell has the remarkable ability to keep a history of the commands you've used. The number of commands that it remembers is usually around 20, but you can change that number if you like. The **history** function makes it easy to repeat earlier commands and possible to modify them before repeating them.

Initiating Your History Service

Your system administrator may not have enabled the history feature for you. If the forthcoming examples don't seem to work, you may have to activate the history service yourself. You can use the following command to start the history service:

```
set history=20
```

Here, 20 represents the number of command lines that will be recalled. You can use another value for this number, but 20 is the standard. Version 4.3 of BSD UNIX lets you use spaces on either side of the equal sign, but some earlier versions don't allow them.

If you type **history** at the UNIX prompt, the command will stay in effect until you log out. To have history turned on automatically each time you log in, place this command in your .cshrc file, as described later.

Repeating an Earlier Command: Event Identifiers

We will look at an example to see how the history function lets you easily repeat commands. Hilary Dale, after doing a few things on the system, types the following command:

```
history
```

UNIX responds with the following list:

```
1 mail
2 cd energy
3 vi wlls.c
4 gcc walls.c floors.o windows.o roof.o temp.o
5 a.out
6 vi checkfile
7 vi walls.c
8 history
```

This, obviously, is a list of the commands she has executed. (UNIX refers to each command line as an *event*.)

Apparently (starting at command 3), she modified part of a C program, compiled it along with the unchanged portions, ran the new version, checked it, found something wrong, and then fixed up the **walls.c** program. Her next step will be to repeat command 4. She can, of course, retype the entire command, or she can use some nifty history features. She can type any of the following entries to return that command:

Command	Description
!4	Identification by command number. This form means, "Run the fourth command from the history list."
!g	Identification by command name. This particular command means, "Run the most recent command from the history list beginning with the character g."
!-5	Identification by relative position. This form means, "Look back five commands and run that command."
!?cc?	Identification by pattern. This form means, "Find the most recent command line with the pattern cc in it, and run that command." The question marks on either side identify the pattern.

Each command (which we will call *event identifiers*) will repeat command 4 by first printing what the command was. The ! character alerts UNIX that the command uses the history list. The two commands that use patterns, !c and !?pat?, have the advantage that you probably won't have to look up the history list numbers to use them.

The !c event identifier doesn't need to be limited to one character after the !. Suppose that a history list had a mkdir command followed by a more command. Because it was most recently executed, !m would rerun the more command, and !mk would run the mkdir command. You can use as many letters as you need to identify your chosen command unambiguously.

The !?pat? form can use a pattern from anywhere in the line; the commands !?oof? or !?wind? would have worked just as well. The command ?wall?, however, would have rerun command 7 instead of command 4 because it was the most recent command line containing that pattern.

A special case of a history repeat command is

!!

Not only does this command look very assertive, but it also repeats the previous command. Thus, it's the same as !-1, but it's faster to type.

Note

Because the ! symbol has a special meaning to the C shell, you have to use the combination \! if all you want is an ordinary, non-**history** exclamation mark. The backslash tells the C shell to interpret the following character as an ordinary character instead of as a special character. For example, the Usenet system for transferring mail between UNIX sites uses the exclamation mark to separate site names in a mail address. If, for instance, you want to send mail to **well!unicom!don**, you would use this command from the C shell:

```
mail well\!unicom\!don
```

Adding to a History Command

History substitutions (the official term for translating event identifiers into ordinary commands) do a lot more for you than just repeat earlier commands. For one thing, they can be incorporated into longer commands. Suppose that you've just run the following command:

```
sort namelist1 namelist2 namelist3 namelist4
```

As the output begins pouring down the screen, you realize that you forgot to redirect the output. You can press Ctrl-c or whatever key generates an interrupt signal for your system. This doesn't count as a command and doesn't go on the history list. Then, you can type

!! > finallist

UNIX translates this as

```
sort namelist1 namelist2 namelist3 namelist4 > finallist
```

and you are in business! Similarly, the command

```
!5 ¦ more
```

would rerun your fifth command and pipe its output through **more**.

The history reference doesn't need to be the first part of your command line. For example, if you wanted to time a command that you had just run, you can give the command

time !!

You can also make ! ! part of a single command string. For example, if your last command was

```
ls -F /usr/doc
```

and you next want to see what was in the directory **/usr/doc/csh**, you could type

!!/csh

and the history facility will interpret this as

```
ls -F /usr/doc/csh
```

Whenever UNIX sees the special character ! in a command line (with some exceptions, as in > >!), it checks the history list and makes the appropriate substitution, putting spaces where you put them and omitting spaces where you omitted them.

Simple Command-Line Editing

You're putting a C program together and have just typed

```
cv peter.c piper.c picked.c a.c peck.c of.c pickled.c
```

You press Return, and UNIX replies

```
cv: not found
```

Oops—you typed **cv** instead of **cc**. Cheer up, you don't have to retype the whole line. This next command line will patch it up:

```
^cv^cc
```

The caret (^) at the beginning of a command line tells UNIX that you want to make a correction in the preceding command. (On some terminals, the ^ character is represented by a vertical arrow.) The characters between the first and second ^ are then replaced by the characters following the second ^. UNIX will print the corrected line,

```
cc peter.c piper.c picked.c a.c peck.c of.c pickled.c
```

and then execute it.

Substitution occurs at the first instance of the pattern, so make your pattern unambiguous. Suppose that you enter

```
cc that.c old.c black.l magic.c
```

You want to correct `black.l` to `black.c`. The command

```
^l^c
```

is no good because it will change the first `l` to a `c`—in other words, the "corrected" version will read:

```
cc that.c ocd.c black.l magic.c
```

The correct solution is to type

```
^.l^.c
```

or

```
^k.l^k.c
```

which identifies the `l` as being the one at the end of `black.l`.

Command-Line Editing in the Korn Shell

In the Korn (`ksh`) shell, you may be able to press Esc, k to repeat your last command. It will take you through your history of commands (starting at the most recent) and place you in editor mode (`vi`, if you have it set up). For example, if you have a long file containing phone numbers and want look someone up, you could type

```
$ cat phone_numbers.txt
```

UNIX will display

```
m wess     555-5343
e hunt     555-2311
j jones    555-2669
.
.
m hogan    555-7465
```

"Stop!" you say as the long list scrolls off the screen before you can press the interrupt key. You now realize that you really wanted to use `more` instead of `cat`. Do you have to retype that whole long filename prefixed with `more` instead of `cat`? No, just press Esc, k once (assuming that you want to go back to your most recent command) and you will appear on the command line in `vi` editor mode:

$ `<Esc-k>`	Retrieves previous commands from history
$ `cat phone_numbers.txt`	Previous command is retrieved; you're placed in vi editor mode
$ `more phone_numbers.txt`	Type **xxx** to delete `cat`, **i** (insert mode), type **more**, press Esc, and then press Return to execute the command

UNIX will display your file one screen at a time using `more`:

```
m wess    555-5343
e hunt    555-2311
j jones   555-2669
```

This allows you to edit your command line by using familiar `vi` editor commands (which can be a real time-saver). Also, if you wanted to repeat a command executed earlier in your history, simply press Esc, k repeatedly until it appears. After it appears on the command line, you can edit it (using `vi` commands) or simply press Return to execute it.

Selecting Parts of a Command Line: Word Identifiers

Sometimes you may want to use just part of an earlier command. For instance, you may want to `vi` a file that you `cat`ted earlier (how's that for UNIX lingo?). The history system has a way for you to specify not only the command line but also individual words from the line. The words are numbered from left to right, and the first word (the command name) is number 0. To avoid confusion with command-line numbers, the word numbers are preceded by a colon (:). There also are some special symbols used: ^ is word number one, $ is the last word, and * stands for all words after word 0. The : can be omitted with these last three symbols. A *word identifier*, then, is a construction such as `:2` or `$`. A word identifier isn't used alone but is appended to an event identifier so that UNIX will know which command to look at (see Figures 8.6 and 8.7).

FIGURE 8.6
History representation of works of an event.

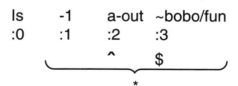

FIGURE 8.7
Structure of a complete word specification.

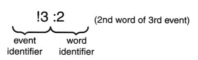

Suppose that your fourth command was

```
cat that.c doormat.c hat.c pat.c
```

Here's how different history references would be translated:

Reference	Meaning
!4	cat that.c doormat.c hat.c pat.c
!4:0	cat (0th word of 4th command)
!4:1	that.c
!4^	that.c
vi !4:2	vi doormat.c
edit !4$	edit pat.c
more !4:2-4	more doormat.c hat.c pat.c
lpr !4*	lpr that.c doormat.c hat.c pat.c

Tip

You can use the hyphen (-) to give a range of words.

The special symbol * means much the same as ^-$. The difference is that ^-$ can represent one or more arguments, while * can represent 0 or more arguments. Let's clarify that. Suppose that this is part of your history list:

```
cat dwarf giant
cd dungeon
ls
```

Then these are some history substitutions:

Reference	Meaning
more !1:^-$	more dwarf giant
more !1*	more dwarf giant
cat !3*	cat (with no argument)
cat !3^-$	error (looks for at least one argument for ls and finds none)

One other convention can simplify life a bit. If you're referring to the immediately preceding command, you can omit the line identifier. For example, if the last command were number 5, the following would be equivalent:

```
cat !5:2
cat !!:2
cat !:2
```

However, a solitary ! without following characters means nothing.

The UNIX history service may not tell you when Hannibal crossed the Alps or the essential features of feudalism, but it can reduce the amount of typing you do and thus reduce the number of keyboard errors. It also can be used in UNIX programming and, as discussed in the next section, can enhance the alias system.

---

history: Prints a List of Last Commands Given

Name	Options	Arguments
history	None	None

Description: The history command lists the last *n* commands or events run by the C shell. To set *n* in the .cshrc, add the line

```
set history=n
```

The history list can also be used to substitute for commands using the ! symbol:

- Identifying commands or events:

!*n*	Command number *n* from the history list
!-*n*	The *n*th command before the present one
!*c*	The most recent command beginning with character *c*
!?*pat*?	The most recent command containing the pattern *pat*

- Identifying words within an event (the first word is number 0):

:*n*	The *n*th word in an event
:^ or ^	Same as :1
:$ or $	The last word in an event
:*n*1-*n*2	Words *n*1 through *n*2
^-$	Words 1 through the last word
*	Words 1 through the last, or no word at all if there is no word 1

- Special notations:

!!	The preceding command line
!	The preceding command line (must be followed by a word identifier)
!*	The options and arguments, if any, of the preceding command

Examples: This command repeats the previous command:

`!!`

This command causes event 5 on the history list to run:

`!5`

The previous command is run, substituting `ls -l` for `ls`:

`^ls^ls-l`

The command more is run on history event 5, from word 3 to the end of event 5:

`more !5:3-$`

Note: You can add several modifiers to history substitutions. They consist of letters or symbols preceded by a colon. We'll leave it to you to investigate the online manual for details; see the sections on `csh` and `newcsh`. Most modifiers are more useful as components of UNIX programming than as casual aids.

Customizing UNIX: The Alias

The C shell offers you a marvelous opportunity to rename, redefine, and rearrange commands in a way that suits your needs. The method is easy and is called making *aliases*. We will get you started with a few examples, and you can take it from there.

Establishing a Simple Alias

Perhaps you have a combination of command and options that you use often. For example, when you list files, you may like using the combination

`ls -Fla`

You use this combination to mark your directories (`-F`), to see your permissions (`-l`), and to make sure that you list dot files (`-a`). The `alias` facility lets you create your own abbreviations for such commands. To make, say, `l` an abbreviation for `ls -Fla`, you can evoke the aliasing ability by typing

`alias l ls -Fla`

Henceforth, until you log out, whenever you type `l`, UNIX will interpret it to mean `ls -Fla` (see Figure 8.8).

FIGURE 8.8

A command with an alias.

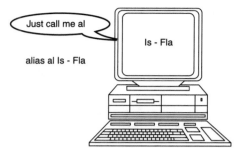

The alias name can be a standard UNIX name. For example, if you type

alias cp cp -i

UNIX will use your definition of **cp** rather than its own.

The usual form for an **alias** command is

alias *abbreviation command*

You can use aliases for commands and executable files but not for directory or nonexecutable filenames. (The **ln** command provides a similar service for these files.)

To get rid of an alias, use the **unalias** command:

unalias *abbreviation*

This removes the named abbreviation from your current alias list. To see what your alias list is, just type

alias

and UNIX will show the aliases now in effect in your account. Some may have been created by the people who set up your account, such as the system administrator.

Permanent Aliases

After you develop an alias that you like, you can let UNIX remember it for you and you can establish it automatically every time you log in. The trick is to store the alias(es) in the **.cshrc** or **.profile** file (depending on the shell you're using). Use an editor to enter that file and add a new line consisting of the alias. Type the line just as you would if you were giving UNIX an **alias** command directly.

Aliases with Arguments

Suppose that you want to use the **l** alias (for **ls -Fla** shown earlier) on the **/dev** directory. Just type

l /dev

UNIX will recognize your alias whether it's the only command on a line or whether it's part of a larger command. Therefore, UNIX will interpret your command to be

ls -Fla /dev

Aliases for Compound Commands

An alias can stand for more than one command. Suppose that you have a subdirectory, **neat-stuff**, to which you often switch and to which you normally perform an **ls** when you are there. Thus, your normal sequence of commands is

```
cd neatstuff
ls
```

You can make the following alias do the same thing:

```
alias ns 'cd neatstuff; ls'
```

(The single quote marks ensure that the whole list of commands is included in the alias.) Then you need type only

ns

instead of the other stuff. The single quotation marks were used so that UNIX would know that the whole phrase, consisting of two commands separated by a semicolon, was part of the alias.

Making Aliases for Complex Commands: \!*

Of course, the **l** alias may be troublesome if you have a long list of files. Perhaps you want to pipe the listing through the **more** command so that you can see the output a page at a time. You could try this:

```
alias L 'ls -Fla ¦ more'
```

This alias works fine as long as you use it in your working directory, but it messes up if you try to apply it to another directory. If, for instance, you type

L /dev

the command is interpreted as

```
ls -Fla ¦ more /dev
```

which is meaningless. What you need is an alias that will translate to

```
ls -Fla /dev ¦ more
```

The problem is that you have to get the **/dev** argument into the middle of the command instead of at the end. The answer to this problem is to combine the powers of the history service with the alias procedure. We will show you the answer and then explain it. The answer is

```
alias L 'ls -Fla \!* ¦ more'
```

Here you see a new construction: \!*. The !* symbolism—straight from the history feature—stands for the arguments, if any, of the preceding command. The \ (backslash) is an *escape*. In this case, it inactivates the history symbol (!) while you type in the alias. Otherwise, UNIX would look at the command that you made just before defining the alias and would insert its arguments in the definition. Here is an example of what we mean. Suppose that you typed the following two lines (leaving out the backslash):

```
cc pat.c wat.c
alias Ls 'ls -Fla !* ¦ more'
```

Then, UNIX would set up this alias for you:

```
alias Ls 'ls -Fla pat.c wat.c ¦ more'
```

This isn't too useful because `Ls` will list only those two named files. With the backslash, you escape this problem. History substitution will take place when the alias is used, not when it's defined. Thus, the command

```
L /dev
```

causes UNIX to execute the following command:

```
ls -Fla /dev ¦ more
```

First, UNIX reads the line `L /dev`. Next, it substitutes for `L`; this makes the `L /dev` command the one that precedes the use of the alias, so `!*` is interpreted as `/dev`.

This was just one specific example, but you can use the `\!*` construction whenever you create an alias that needs to place arguments within the defining expression. Here is one more example:

```
alias cd 'cd \!*; ls'
```

This alias will cause UNIX to list the new directory whenever you change directories. That is, the command

```
cd ~lola
```

will be translated to

```
cd ~lola; ls
```

Aliases in Aliases

Yes, you read right. After you define an alias, you can use it as part of a definition of a new alias. In this manner, you can build up a little empire of aliases. Aliases don't need to be confined to UNIX procedures, either. They can be defined in terms of programs or procedures that you've written. By using aliases, you can program in UNIX without really knowing how to program. No wonder thousands of UNIX users never go anywhere without their aliases.

Note

The `sh` shell doesn't have aliasing. However, you can accomplish many of the same things by using shell scripts (described briefly soon). Compared to the alias, the shell script is a little more awkward to use but it's more versatile.

alias: List Aliases or Make Aliases

Name	Options	Arguments
alias	None	
alias		*abbreviation command*
unalias		*abbreviation*

Description: The `alias` command prints a list of aliases. To make new aliases, use the second form given above. Permanent aliases can be kept in the `.cshrc` or `.profile` file. To remove aliases, use the third form.

Examples: This command teaches UNIX a new name for the `ls` command:

```
alias list ls
```

Giving the command `pp` is the same as causing the typing of `cat /usr/poopsie/phone`:

```
alias pp cat /usr/poopsie/phone
```

For more details on using `alias`, see the text examples or the online manual discussion under `csh`. (This section of the manual is about 20 pages long, with less than one page of text discussing `alias`.)

The Filename Completion Service

Suppose that you've created a nice, descriptive filename such as `garlic.division.report`. You may find yourself not wanting to type the entire name when you go to edit the file. If the `csh` filename completion service is active, you can type a few initial letters, press Esc, and `csh` will complete the rest of the name for you:

`% vi gar<Esc>`	You type this
`% vi garlic.division.report`	The shell completes the name

Of course, there are some restrictions. The shell isn't psychic, so you must type enough characters to distinguish the name from others. If `garlic.division.report` is the only file beginning with a **g**, you can use only one character. But if you also have a file called `garfish.division.report`, you have to type **garl** and press Esc.

Suppose that you have a file called `garlic.division.debts`. Filename completion still can help. If two files match the pattern you type, the shell will extend the name for as many characters as the names have in common and then beep. You can type the rest of the name, or enough of it to choose between the two:

`vi garl<Esc>`	You type this
`vi garlic.division.`	Shell extends name
`vi garlic.division.r<Esc>`	You add the **r**
`vi garlic.division.report`	Shell completes name

If the system administrator hasn't turned on this feature for you, you can use this command:

```
set filec
```

As with similar examples we've discussed, you can place this command in your `.cshrc` file to activate file completion automatically.

Shell Scripts

UNIX lets you use standard UNIX commands as building blocks to construct new commands of your own devising. The shell makes this possible. Normally, the shell takes its input from the terminal. (Its normal input consists of the commands you type.) But, like other UNIX programs, it also can take input from a file. A file containing UNIX commands is called a *shell script*. For example, you can use an editor to create a file with the following command line:

```
ls -l
```

Suppose that you name this file **ll** (for long list). Then you can have the shell run this command by typing

```
csh ll
```

and the command in the `ll` file is executed. The `csh` command invokes the shell, and the shell runs the instructions found in the `ll` file. (Actually, using `csh` creates a new shell which then takes over control. When it finishes running the shell script, the new shell "dies," returning control to your original shell. See the upcoming sidebar, "Multiple Shells.")

Now suppose that you type

`ll`

You are informed

`ll: cannot execute`

but you don't need to accept this. Just type

`chmod u+x ll`

and try typing `ll` again. Now the command runs just by typing the filename! Chapter 9 discusses the `chmod` (change mode) command, but what it does here is rather simple: It changes the mode of the `ll` file so that you (u) add (+) executable (x) status to the file. You now have a convenient abbreviation (`ll`) for a lengthier command (`ls -l`).

Multiple Shells

There's just one `csh` shell program in BSD UNIX, but there are many instances of the shell. As the examples with **ps** show, each time you log in, the system starts up a shell process for you. (A process is a program being run.) Each user has his or her own shell process. Of course, only one program runs at any moment, but UNIX switches from running your shell to running Laura's shell to running Pete's shell, and so on, attending to each of your needs in turn. Your shell process knows about your commands, but not Pete's, and vice versa. Thus, the separate shell processes keep your work from getting muddled up with the work of others.

More remarkable, perhaps, is that you yourself can have more than one shell process going for you. For example, executing a shell script creates a new shell that runs the script and expires when it finishes. You can use **ps** to test this claim. First, create a file called, say, **do.ps** and containing this command:

```
ps -x
```

Next, run this script, doing a **ps** -x before and after:

```
% ps -x
   PID TT STAT    TIME COMMAND
   147 A5 S       0:18 -csh(csh)
   834 A5 R       0:00 ps -x
% csh do.ps
   PID TT STAT    TIME COMMAND
   147 A5 S       0:18 -csh(csh)
   837 A5 S       0:00 csh do.ps
   843 A5 R       0:00 ps -x
% ps -x
   PID TT STAT    TIME COMMAND
   147 A5 S       0:18 -csh(csh)
   851 A5 R       0:00 ps -x
%
```

The shell you were granted at login has a PID of 147. The temporary shell that ran the shell script had a PID of 837. Similarly, each invocation of **ps** has its own PID. If you make the script executable and type its name, that, too, creates a temporary shell. Try it and see.

You don't have to run a shell script to create a new shell. Just type **csh** and press Return. The screen may look the same, but you're using a new shell. Again, you can confirm this using **ps -x**:

```
% ps -x
  PID TT STAT   TIME COMMAND
  147 A5 S      0:18 -csh(csh)
  866 A5 S      0:18 -sh(csh)
  868 A5 R      0:00 ps -x
%
```

Again, don't worry about the odd format for reporting the **csh** shell. The main point is that you now have two of them. You can continue typing **csh**'s, creating a shell with a shell within a shell…. To reverse the process, press Ctrl-d. Each Ctrl-d kills off the most recently created shell. Try it.

Why would you start up a new shell? Normally, you wouldn't. But some actions you take may result in starting a new shell. For instance, some programs, such as the **vi** editor and **mail**, let you issue UNIX commands while still in the program. When that happens, UNIX starts up a new shell just to run that command.

Interestingly enough, you also can start an **sh** shell by typing the **sh** command. In that case, your prompt will change to a **$** symbol. Again, press Ctrl-d to return to the parent shell.

You may find that the executable version works faster than typing **csh 11**, particularly if your .cshrc file is full. (Be patient, we'll get to that file yet!) This is because BSD UNIX uses **sh** instead of **csh** to run shell scripts. The **sh** program is smaller and less powerful than **csh**, but in compensation it's quicker. If you don't make a shell script file executable, you still can use **sh** to run it:

sh 11

Let's summarize the main points before we move on to more interesting examples:

- A shell script consists of a file containing UNIX commands.

- A shell script can be run by typing **csh** *filename* or **sh** *filename*.

- If you use the **chmod** command (Chapter 9) to make the file executable, you can type just the filename to make it work.

Shell scripts are quite versatile and flexible. First, you can include more than one command in a script. Second, you can have your command use command-line arguments, just like the built-in commands do. Third, you can create loops and other programming features in a script. We'll look at the first two features now and leave the other features for more advanced references.

Multiple Commands

You aren't limited to one command per script. For example, when you've spent too many hours at the terminal, you might need a script like the following:

```
who am i
pwd
date
```

Just put one command per line, as though you were typing instructions from the terminal. Or you can put several commands on the same line by using the semicolon as a separator:

```
who am i; pwd; date
```

Place either version in a file called huh, and typing huh will produce an output such as

```
% csh huh
fleezo   ttyA5   Oct  11 10:55
/usr/fleezo/stocks
Mon Oct 11 10:55:21 PDT 1999
%
```

It would be nice if the script could print descriptive messages. UNIX doesn't let you down here, for the echo command gives you the means. In its simplest form (which is all we need here), echo sends a copy of its arguments to the screen—for example,

```
% echo 34
34
% echo We will meet at Toms.
We will meet at Toms.
%
```

Now you can upgrade huh to the following:

```
echo You are
who am i
echo The directory you are in is
pwd
echo The date is
date
```

Running the new huh produces this sort of output:

```
% csh huh
You are
jjones  tty14   Oct  11 12:08
The directory you are in is
/usr/jjones/cs_180/labs
The date is
Mon Oct 09 12:08:23 PDT 2000
%
```

(The output would be neater if we had a command that just gave the user's name without the other information. We'll show one possibility later in this chapter.)

What if you want one of your scripts to use an argument? Suppose that you are in the directory /usr/me and want a long listing of the /usr/me/profits directory. Can you type

ll profits

to get that listing? You can type it, of course, but the shell will ignore the **profits** and just list your current directory. That is, your command will be interpreted as

ls -l

and not as

ls -l profits

But there's a scheme that won't ignore your profits; it's our next topic.

---

echo: Echo Arguments

Name	Options	Arguments
echo	None	_[any_string_of_characters]_

Description: The echo command writes its arguments to the standard output screen. Without arguments, it produces an empty line.

Example:

```
% echo say New York unique 10 times fast
say New York unique 10 times fast
%
```

Command-Line Arguments for Shell Scripts

When you use a shell script, the shell keeps track of any arguments you type after the script name. Your script can use these arguments by referring to them by the following scheme: **$1** is the first argument, **$2** is the second argument, and so on. In addition, **$*** is short for all arguments, and **$0** is short for the name of the shell script itself. **$1** and its companions are called _positional parameters_, for the number indicates the position of the original argument. Figure 8.9 illustrates how the scheme works. First, here is the script itself, stored in the file i.remember:

```
echo This is the $0 command
echo My first argument is $1
echo My third argument is $3
echo Here are all my arguments: $*
```

Next, here is a sample invocation:

```
% csh i.remember three cats each wearing hats
This is the i.remember command
My first argument is three
```

```
My third argument is each
Here are all my arguments: three cats each wearing hats
```

Thus, $1 is three, and so on. Incidentally, the explicit numbering scheme extends only to $9, but the $* will encompass however many arguments you give.

FIGURE 8.9

Scripts and arguments.

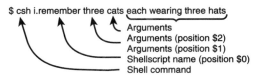

Now you can modify **ll** to make it more useful. One version would be

```
ls -l $1
```

Another possibility is

```
ls -l $*
```

How do they vary? The first version will list just one directory (the first one fed to it), whereas the second will list all the directories given to it.

Here's another example. Suppose that you create a shell script containing the following command:

```
mv $1 $1.$0
```

Call the script **pig**. Then, assuming that you have a file called **porky**, what will the following command do?

```
csh pig porky
```

Well, **$1** is the first argument (**porky**), and **$0** is the name of the script (**pig**), so this command is interpreted as

```
mv porky porky.pig
```

You now have a command that will add **.pig** to the name of any file! This could be quite useful to swinologists and to users of the PIGSCRIPT programming language (**OGAY OTAY**...).

Another important feature of shell scripts is that they can use redirection and pipes. Suppose that you have the following shell script in an executable file called **printandsave** (the **lpr** command sends stuff to be printed on a line printer):

```
cat $* ¦ lpr
date >> prfile
echo $* >> prfile
echo >> prfile
```

And suppose that you give this command:

```
printandsave file1 file2 file3
```

What happens? The best way to check what this does is to run it on your system. But if you can't wait for that, here is what happens. The first line concatenates all the files (`file1`, `file2`, and `file3`) that you feed to the shell script as arguments. (Recall that `$*` stands for all the arguments to the shell script.) This combined file then is piped to the printer and printed. The next line adds the current time and date to the end of a file called `prfile`. (If no such file exists, it's created.) The next line adds the names of the files you printed to the end of `prfile`. The final line adds a blank line to `prfile`. Thus, the net effect of this shell script is to print some files and to keep a record of which files you printed and when.

> ### Note
>
> The script uses a `prfile` in your current directory. If you want to use this command in various directories, be more specific about the name. For instance, Ben could establish an **Accounting** directory and use `/usr/ben/Accounting/prfile` as the storage file.

Shell Variables

As the shell carries on its activities on your behalf, it has to keep track of a number of things, including the name of your home directory, which prompt you use, and where to look for commands. To do this, the shell uses *shell variables*. You can think of variables as names that can have values assigned to them. The shell has built-in variables that keep track of your home directory, and so on. It uses other shell variables to control features such as history and file-name completion. And it also lets you define variables of your own. First, let's look at some of the built-in variables, and then see how you can create and use your own variables.

Built-In Variables

The `csh` shell maintains two kinds of shell variables: the ordinary shell variable and the *environment* shell variable. The difference is that an ordinary variable is known just to the shell in which it's created. If you start up a new shell, it doesn't know (aside from special exceptions) the shell variables of the original shell. Environment shell variables, on the other hand, are known to the shell in which they are defined and all descendant shells.

To find out which ordinary shell variables your shell knows, use the `set` command:

```
% set
filec
history 20
home     /usr/msmith
mail     /usr/spool/mail/msmith
noclobber
path     (. /bin /usr/bin)
shell    bin/csh
user     msmith
%
```

The shell prints the variables it knows. The list you get might very well be longer than this. The name on the left is the name of a variable, and any stuff to the right is the variable's value. Thus, the variable user has the value msmith.

You should recognize some of these variables. The history shell variable, if you'll recall, turns the history service on and specifies the number of command lines to remember. The noclobber and filec variables turn on file protection and filename completion. So our example shows that all three services are active.

Note

Some shell variables, like **noclobber**, have no value. In that case, we say the variable is set.

Next, to see the list of environment variables, use the setenv command:

```
% setenv
HOME=/usr/msmith
SHELL=/bin/csh
TERM=adm5
USER=msmith
PATH=.:/bin:/usr/bin
%
```

Using uppercase names for environment variables and lowercase for regular shell variables is a BSD UNIX tradition. Also, note that the setenv command list puts an equal sign between the variable name and its value.

You probably noticed that there seems to be a sort of overlap. One list has home, and the other has HOME, and so on. Each time you create a new shell, BSD UNIX automatically creates shell variable copies of certain important environment variables. So home is a copy of HOME, user is a copy of USER, and so on. What are these certain important environment variables? Here are some of them:

- HOME is set to the pathname of your home directory.

- USER is set to your login name.

- PATH names the directories that the shell will search to find commands. A colon separates the directory names; there are no spaces. The directories are searched in the order given. For example, if you give the command cat, the shell first searches your current directory (.) for an executable file by that name. If it doesn't find one there, it looks in /bin. If it still hasn't found cat, it looks in /usr/bin. And if it still hasn't found a cat program, the shell reports back that it can't find that command. Notice that this particular sequence of directories in PATH means that if you have an executable file called cat, it's executed rather than the standard system cat, which would be in a subsequent directory.

- **TERM** identifies the kind of terminal you habitually use. Knowing this, the shell knows what to interpret as a Backspace key, and so on.
- **SHELL** identifies which shell program you use.

To use these variables, you need a convenient way to obtain the value of a particular variable and to change that value.

Obtaining the Value of a Variable

The shell uses the metacharacter **$** to specify the value of a shell variable or of an environment variable. (What could be more American than denoting value with **$**?) Compare these two commands and responses:

```
% echo TERM
TERM
% echo $TERM
adm5
%
```

Using **TERM** prints the word literally, but using **$TERM** causes the *value* of **TERM** to be echoed. By using echo and **$**, you can print the value of any particular variable.

You also can use the **$** construction as part of other expressions. Suppose that Zeke is working in a distant directory and wants to copy a file into his home directory. He could type

```
cp rainstats /usr/zeke
```

but he also could type

```
cp rainstats $HOME
```

The shell would see **$HOME** and know that Zeke wanted the value of the **HOME** environment variable, which is /usr/zeke. Then it would make that substitution. Alternatively, he could use $home to access the value of the home shell variable (recall that home and HOME happen to be set to the same value).

This may not seem like much of a savings, but consider the possibilities for shell scripts. If Zeke wrote a shell script with the line

```
cp $1 /usr/zeke
```

only he could use it. But if he used

```
cp $1 $HOME
```

then anyone could use this script, and the copy would go to the user's home directory.

Here's another example. Remember that in discussing the huh script earlier, we hankered for a command that yielded just the user's name. We can construct such a command very simply with user. Just create an executable file called myname containing the line

```
echo $user
```

We will assume that you have a myname function available from now on.

Setting Shell Variables

Calling something a *variable* implies that you can change its value. To create regular shell variables and to give them values, use the **set** command:

```
set age = 65
set name = Scrooge
set bebop
```

The format is

```
set name = value
```

where *name* is the name of the variable and *value* is the value of the variable. The value can be a number or a word, or it can be omitted entirely. For instance, the last example creates, or sets, the variable **bebop**, but doesn't give it a value.

The shell variables we created are added to the list. We can check this by using **set** to get the full list of shell variables:

```
% set
age      65
bebop
history 20
home     /usr/escrooge
mail     /usr/spool/mail/escrooge
name     Scrooge
noclobber
path     (/bin /usr/bin)
shell    bin/csh
user     escrooge
%
```

Normally there should be no blanks in a value-giving command, but you can use quotation marks (single or double, but not mixed) to assign a phrase to a variable:

```
set lunch = "hot and sour soup"
set dinner = 'rack of Lamb'
```

To get rid of a variable, use the **unset** command. For instance, the following command turns off overwrite protection for redirection:

```
unset noclobber
```

The environment variables work similarly, but not identically. First, you use **setenv** instead of **set**. Second, you don't use an equal sign:

```
setenv COLORS 8
setenv EXINIT "set noai wm=15"
```

This creates an environment variable called **COLORS** and gives it the value **8**. It also creates an environment variable called **EXINIT**, which is used to modify how the **vi** editor behaves. Use **unsetenv** to delete an environment variable.

We've mentioned how shell variables modify some UNIX features, such as history and redirection. If you have some settings you prefer, you probably don't want to have to type them each time you log on. Fortunately, UNIX lets you have your favorite variables set automatically.

Customizing Your Environment: Your `.login` and `.cshrc` Files

When you log in, UNIX creates a shell for you. Some shell variables and environment variables (such as **home** and **PATH**) are given to it at this time. Then the shell looks in your home directory for a file called `.cshrc` and follows the instructions it finds there. Next it looks for a file called `.login` and follows the instructions in it. (The system treats `.cshrc` and `.login` as shell scripts.) The difference between the two files is that `.cshrc` is executed each time you start up a new **csh** shell, whereas `.login` is executed only when you log in. Usually the system administrator provides you with standard versions of these files. (Remember, filenames beginning with a period aren't listed by a simple **ls**. You need to use **ls** **-a** to see them.) The contents of these files will vary from system to system, but here are typical examples:

```
% cat .cshrc
set history=20
set noclobber
set filec
set mail=/usr/spool/mail/$user
alias cp cp -i
alias mv mv -i
alias rm rm -i
alias copy /bin/cp -i
% cat .login
set noglob
set term=(tset -S -n -m 'dialup:?tvi920')
setenv TERM $term[1]
setenv TERMCAP "$term[2]"
unset term
unset noglob
mesg y
set path=(/bin /usr/bin .)
setenv EXINIT 'se noai wm=15 terse nowarn sm'
set ignroeeof time=15
%
```

Without going into all the technical details, let's note some high points:

- Both files are used to set shell variables. In general, environment variables are defined in `.login`. Because they carry over to subsequent shells, they need to be defined only once.

- You can use these files to set up your favorite aliases when you log in. Aliases generally go into `.cshrc` so that they will be available to each shell you start up.

- Because these are ordinary text files, you can edit them and add to them. This customization is quite common among computer professionals, but anyone can do it. For instance, if your setup doesn't have the history feature turned on, just add the line

```
history=20
```

   to your `.cshrc` file. Or, you can change `20` to `40` if you want the system to recall more command lines.

Let's look at some commands you can add to these files. Suppose that you want to be greeted when you log on. Then you can put an echo command in the `.login` file:

```
echo Welcome back, $user!
```

To control various `csh` services, you can modify your `.cshrc` file by adding or deleting lines to set `noclobber`, `history`, and `filec`, for example:

```
set noclobber
```

You could put them in `.login`, but then they would affect only your login shell and not any subsequent shells you might create. (Remember, some actions, such as certain commands from the `vi` editor, create a new shell without you having asked for one.)

If you want to keep your own record of when you log in, insert a line like this:

```
date >> loginlog
```

Then each time you log in, the `date` command is run, and its output is diverted to the `loginlog` file, giving you a record of the date and time of your logins.

If you have a supply of shell scripts or other programs that you use often, here is a useful practice:

1. Establish a subdirectory to hold these executable files.
2. Add that subdirectory to your path search list.

Then, no matter what directory you are in, you can run those programs just by typing the name. For example, Bess could establish a `bin` subdirectory and add this line to her `.login`:

```
path=(/bin:/usr/bin:/usr/bess/bin:.)
```

Tired of the `%` prompt? The `csh` recognizes a shell variable called `prompt`. If you set it to some value, the shell will use that value for your prompt. For example, you can place the following in the `.cshrc` file:

```
set prompt= "Yes, O wise one? "
```

This change won't take place until the file contents are executed, which happens automatically the next time you log in. Or you can use the `source` command to put it into effect immediately:

```
source .cshrc
```

The phrase `Yes, O wise one?` is called a *prompt string*. Notice the space at the end of the string. That's to separate the prompt string from your typed commands.

If you use ! as part of the prompt string, it's replaced by the command number used in the history list. This results in numbering your command lines onscreen.

Shell Metacharacters

In this chapter, we have used several special characters, including $ and !. At this point it may be useful to summarize the special characters encountered so far and to add a few more to the list.

The shell recognizes several characters (*metacharacters*) as having special meaning, such as * and !. The shell also has ways to remove these special meanings. We'll summarize the more common metacharacters now and then show how to neutralize them.

Function	Metacharacter
Wildcard substitution	* ? [ ] (see Chapter 6)
Redirection	> >> < ¦
Background process	&
Command separator	;
Continue command on next line	\
Value of a variable	$
History prefix	!

To this list add the backquote character (`) Don't confuse this with the regular quote/apostrophe. A pair of backquotes does for commands what the $ does for shell variables. That is, a command name in backquotes is replaced by the output (or value, so to speak) of the command. Compare these two command-response pairs:

```
% echo date
date
% echo `date`
Mon Oct 11 11:22:04 PDT 1999
%
```

The backquotes are useful in shell scripts; see the "Review Questions" section for examples.

Neutralizing Metacharacters

Now suppose that you want to use some of these symbols literally, perhaps in a command like

```
echo Type a * if you are happy
```

Try it. You'll find that the * is replaced by a list of all your files! After all, that's what * means to the shell. To get around this difficulty, UNIX offers metacharacters that neutralize metacharacters. For this purpose, it uses the backslash (\), single quotes ('), and double quotes (").

The backslash negates the special qualities of whatever character immediately follows it. Nonspecial characters are left that way. Here is an example:

```
% echo \* \I \ \\ \[
* I \ [
%
```

Note that it even negates itself, so \\ is rendered \. The single \ is read as *blank* and is printed as a blank, just as \I is printed as I.

Now suppose that you want to print the sequence *?*. You could use

```
echo \*\?\*
```

or you could type

```
echo '*?*'
```

The single quotes turn off the special meaning of every character between them:

```
% echo 'Send $100 to who?'
Send $100 to who?
%
```

The double quotes are slightly less restrictive. They turn off all the metacharacters *except* $, `, and \. Thus,

```
% echo `myname`
mariella
% echo '`myname` is nice & sweet'
`myname` is nice & sweet
% echo "`myname` is nice & sweet"
mariella is nice & sweet
%
```

The single quotes cause the backquotes and the & to be printed literally. The double quotes also cause the & to be printed literally, but the `myname` is replaced by its output, mariella. (Recall that myname is one of our shell script examples and consists of the command echo $user.)

Another use for quotes is to combine several words into one argument. Suppose that addition is a shell script. If we give the command

```
addition five fleet fools
```

$1 is five, $2 is fleet, and so on, as usual. But if we say

```
addition 'five fleet fools'
```

$1 is the whole phrase five fleet fools.

Summary

This ends our discussion of the shell for a while. You've encountered many shell features in this chapter: command lines, redirection, job control, shell scripts, shell variables, the `.cshrc` and `.login` files, and shell metacharacters. Using them can greatly enhance your UNIX powers and pleasures. We will use them in subsequent chapters, and we suggest that you play with these features until they become familiar. Using them will do much more for your understanding than just reading about them.

But now it's time to return to the nitty-gritty of learning some of the multitudinous commands known to the shell. We will resume that task in the next chapter.

Review Questions

1. Of the following commands, some are correct and some have errors in them. Identify the incorrect commands and then fix them.

   a. `ls-l blackweb`

   b. `ls rupart -s`

   c. `ls -s-l`

   d. `ps -a`

   e. `cat duskhaven > lp`

   f. `jolly >cat`

   g. `pal = ginny mae`

   h. `setenv NETWORTH = 45`

2. The file `exc` contains the line `chmod u+x $1`. What will the following commands do?

   ```
   csh exc fopman
   csh exc exc
   ```

3. Our `huh` shell script had output such as

   ```
   you are
   godzilla tty92 Feb 21 23:24
   ```

   Modify the script so that the output is

   ```
   You are godzilla
   ```

4. Suppose that you often `cd` to the `/usr/lisa/progs/pasc/proj` directory. What could you put into your `.cshrc` to make this easier to do?

5. Here is the result of a `history` command:

```
1 cd English
2 head My.Summer Faulkner Tragedy
3 cd /usr/nerkie/project.c
4 ls
5 history
```

Translate each of the following history references, assuming each is typed as the sixth command.

a. `!l`

b. `!c`

c. `!?erk?`

d. `!2 ¦more`

e. `vi !he:2`

f. `wc !2*`

g. `more !3 ^/ guesses`

6. Suppose that all the following aliases are in effect:

```
alias rm rm -i
alias c 'cd; ls'
alias cr 'cd \!*; rm *'
```

How, then, would the following commands be interpreted?

a. `rm junkfile`

b. `c`

c. `c junkdirectory`

d. `cr junkdirectory`

7. Here is the result of a `jobs` command:

```
[1]  +Stopped     edit lice
[2]   Running     spell sports > error.sp
[3]  -Stopped     spell chess > error.ck
```

What would each of the following commands accomplish?

a. `%3`

b. `fg`

c. `stop %2`

d. `bg %3`

e. `kill %1`

Exercises

1. Try some pipes. To provide suitable tools, you can use the commands wc, which counts the words in its input, and **sort**, which sorts its input alphabetically. Create a file of text called **mystuff** and try these commands, and then devise your own.

```
wc mystuff > savecount
cat mystuff ¦ sort
sort mystuff ¦ tee sorted ¦ wc
```

2. Put a **ps** command in your .login and .cshrc files and find out the process number of the shell that reads that file. Is it the same shell that later interprets your commands?

3. Devise a shell script that **cat**s a file and copies it into your home directory. Make the copy have a name that adds .cpy to the original name.

4. Implement the personal command directory approach we outlined in the section on .login.

CHAPTER 9

FILE-MANAGEMENT COMMANDS AND OTHERS: WC, SORT, LPR, AND CHMOD

You will learn about the following in this chapter:

- Some handy UNIX commands such as wc, sort, and uniq

- How to handle printing with lp and lpq

- How to change file permissions with chmod

- How to use the mesg command as well as how to block it

- How to use the tty and stty commands

F iles are the heart of UNIX's storage system, so it's no surprise that UNIX has many commands for managing and manipulating files. This chapter will look at commands for counting the number of words in a file, looking at the beginning or end of a file, sorting a file, comparing files, printing files, and modifying file permissions. It also will mix in a few miscellaneous commands. As you read through the descriptions, remember to sit down and try out the commands. All these commands allow you to use metacharacters such as the wildcard matches. Many of the commands expect a filename as an argument. If you don't provide a filename, the keyboard is expected to provide input.

File-Management Commands

With UNIX's file-management commands, you can obtain detailed information about your files. The next several sections explain the word-counting command wc, the file-checking commands tail and head, and the file-sorting command sort.

Word Counting: wc

The wc command tells you how many lines, words, and characters you have in a file. If you have a file named gourd, you can find this information by typing

wc gourd

UNIX responds with, say,

```
79  378  2936  gourd
```

This response tells you that there are 79 lines, 378 words, and 2936 characters in the file gourd. You can have more than one file as an argument. For example, the command

```
wc gourd mango
```

would produce a result like the following:

```
 79  378  2936  gourd
132  310  2357  mango
211  688  5293  total
```

Not only does wc count the lines, words, and characters in each file, it also finds the totals for you!

The most commonly used options for wc are -l, -w, and -c. The first one counts lines only, the second counts words only, and the last option counts characters only. Of course, you can combine them:

```
wc -lw darkeyes
```

This command would count the number of lines and words in darkeyes but not the number of characters.

---

wc: Word Count

Name	Options	Arguments
wc	-lwc	[*filename(s)*]

Description: The wc command is actually a counting program. By default, it works with the -lwc options, counting the lines, words, and characters in the named files. If more than one file is given, wc gives the counts for each file plus the combined totals for all files. If no file is given, wc uses the standard input—the terminal. In this case, you should terminate the input with a Ctrl-d. Multiple options should be strung together on the same hyphen.

Options:

-l	Counts lines
-w	Counts words
-c	Counts characters

Example: This command counts the number of words in the file **essay**:

```
wc -w essay
```

File Checking: `tail` and `head`

The **head** and **tail** commands give you a quick way to check the contents of a file (see Figure 9.1). By default, the **tail** command shows you the last 10 lines of a file. For example, to see the last 10 lines of the file **feathers**, type

tail feathers

The summary for the **tail** command shows how to select more or fewer lines.

FIGURE 9.1

head and tail look at a file.

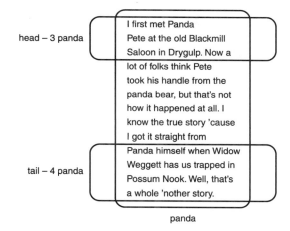

Both System V and Berkeley Standard Distribution (BSD) UNIX have the **tail** command, but the **head** command is an enhancement that may not be available on all systems. As you might expect, the command

head overheels

shows you the first 10 lines of the **overheels** file. Or, by typing

head -15 overheels

you can see the first 15 lines.

tail: Give the Last Part of a File		
Name	Options	Arguments
tail	[+/-number][lbc]	filename(s)

Description: The **tail** command shows the tail end of a file. By default, it displays the last 10 lines.

continued on next page

Options:

+ *number*	Starts *number* from the beginning.
- *number*	Starts *number* from the end.
1bc	Indicates whether *number* is to be counted in lines (1), blocks (b), or characters . Option 1 is assumed if no letter is given.

Examples: This prints the last 20 lines of the file **gate**:

```
tail -20 gate
```

This command prints the file **gate** starting with the 30th character until the EOF (end of file) character is reached:

```
tail +30 gate
```

Comments: Constructions of the form **tail -15 -c gate** aren't allowed. All the options have to be strung after one + or -.

---

head: Looks at the Head of a File (BSD)

Name	Options	Arguments
head	[-*number*]	*filename(s)*

Description: The **head** command shows the first 10 lines of the named files, unless the number option specifies a different number of lines.

Option:

-*number*	For *number*, substitute the number of lines you want to have printed.

Example: This command prints onscreen the first 15 lines of the file **hunter**:

```
head -15 hunter
```

Sorting: sort

One of UNIX's great labor-saving commands is **sort**, which can sort files numerically or alphabetically. The sorting function can be used simply or with some fancy options. We will just take a basic look this time and will save the fancy stuff for Chapter 11, "Information Processing: **grep**, **find**, and **awk**."

The **sort** command, when used without options, sorts files alphabetically by line. Actually, the idea of "alphabetical" order has to be extended, since a file can contain nonalphabetic characters. The basic order used is called the *machine-collating sequence*, and it may be different on different machines. For UNIX, the following points are generally true:

- Uppercase letters (capitals) are sorted separately from lowercase letters. Within each case, the standard alphabetical order is used.

- Numbers are sorted by the first digit. The sorting order is 0, 1, 2, 3, 4, 5, 6, 7, 8, 9.

- The remaining symbols—such as), %, +, and !—aren't grouped. Some may come between the numbers and the alphabet, and others before or after all numbers and letters.

Let's look at how a particular example might work. Suppose that the contents of **grabbag** are

```
Here is a small
file with some
words in it
and also
some numbers
like
1
23
and
102.

 The first line is blank; this one begins with a blank.
```

This is how the command **sort grabbag** would arrange the contents on a typical UNIX system:

```
 The first line is blank; this one begins with a blank.
1
102.
23
Here is a small
and
and also
file with some
some numbers like
words in it
```

Notice that the line beginning **The first...** wasn't placed with the other alphabetical lines, because the first character of that line isn't the letter **T** but a blank. Thus, the line was placed according to where blanks go. Also note that **102** is listed before **23**! This is because **sort** treats numbers as words and sorts them by their first digit. (The **-n** option treats numbers as numbers and sorts them arithmetically; it would place the numbers in **file1** in the order **1**, **23**, **102**.) Finally, notice that **sort** lists capital letters before it lists lowercase letters.

If you feed more than one file to **sort**, it will merge the files and then sort the results. This is great for combining, say, inventory lists.

Normally, `sort` sends its output to the terminal screen. To save the results, you can use redirection. For example, to sort and merge the files `redsox` and `whitesox` and then store the results in a file called `pinksox`, type

sort redsox whitesox > pinksox

Or, you can use the `-o` option described in the sort summary.

sort: Sorts and Merges Files		
Name	Options	Arguments
sort	[-d, -f, -n, -o, -r]	*filename(s)*

Description: The `sort` command sorts and merges the lines from the named files and sends the result to the screen (see Figure 9.2). By default, lines are sorted in machine-collating sequence, which is an extended alphabetical order that encompasses letters, digits, and other symbols. Capital letters are sorted separately from small letters.

Options:

-b	Ignore leading tabs and spaces.
-d	"Dictionary" order, using only letters, digits, and blanks to determine order.
-f	Ignore the distinction between capital and lowercase letters.
-n	Sort numbers by arithmetic value instead of by first digit.
-o *filename*	Place the output in a file called *filename* instead of onscreen. The name can be the same as one of the input names.
-r	Sort in reverse order.
-u	Identical lines appear only once in the result.

Example: This command would sort the lines of the file **grabbag** and put the results in the file **sortbag**:

`sort -f -r -o sortbag grabbag`

Capitalization will be ignored by the sorting process, and the lines will be in reverse alphabetical order.

FIGURE 9.2

sort versus sort -f.

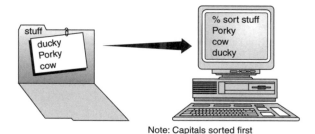

Note: Capitals sorted first

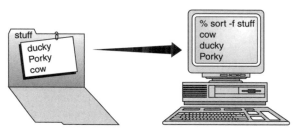

Note: -f option ignores case

Redundancy Elimination: uniq

Suppose that you have two mailing lists that you've sorted and merged. You notice that some addresses are duplicated, and you want to get rid of the repeated versions. You can do this with **uniq**. It will read a file, compare adjacent lines, reject repetitions, and print the remaining lines on the terminal or into a file that you choose. Think of it as a filter to eliminate duplicate lines.

Assume that the merged file **foodlist** has the following contents:

```
apples
artichokes
bananas
bananas
grapes
```

The command **uniq foodlist** will produce the following output:

```
apples
artichokes
bananas
grapes
```

As you can see, **uniq** eliminated one copy of the word **bananas** from the file. If you want to direct the output to a file, just provide that file's name after the name of the file to be processed. Thus, the command

```
uniq foodlist newfoodlist
```

would produce the same output but would route it to the file **newfoodlist** instead of to the screen.

There is one thing to be aware of when using `uniq`. Because `uniq` works by comparing adjacent lines, duplicate lines must be next to the originals or else `uniq` won't spot them. For example, if you used `uniq` with input of the form

```
apples
grapes
artichokes
bananas
grapes
```

your output would contain duplicate grapes lines because the **grapes** lines aren't adjacent to each other. You would receive the following output, which probably isn't what you want:

```
apples
grapes
artichokes
bananas
grapes
```

Fortunately, there are several ways to eliminate duplicate lines from a file regardless of what order they appear. You can sort the file first with the **sort** command, and then use the **uniq** command. An even better method would be to use **sort -u** *filename* to sort the file and eliminate duplicates all in one command.

`uniq`: Removes Duplicate Lines from a File

Name	Options	Arguments
uniq	[-u, -d, -c]	*inputfile* [*outputfile*]

Description: The `uniq` command reads the input file, compares *adjacent* lines, and, without any options specified, prints all unique lines and a single copy of any duplicated lines. If a second filename is given, the output is placed in that file instead of onscreen.

Options:

-u	Prints only those lines with no duplicates—that is, a line that appears two or more times *consecutively* in the original file isn't printed at all.
-d	Prints just the duplicated lines—that is, unique lines aren't printed.
-c	Prints the number of times each line appears in the file followed by the line itself.

Example: The following command would scan the file **ioulist** for lines that appear more than once consecutively. One copy of each such line would be placed in the file **urgent**.

```
uniq -d ioulist urgent
```

Making a Printed Copy

Graphical user interface (GUI) terminals are fun, but for some purposes (conducting inventories, debugging program code, and so on), you really need printed paper output. You can use the commands in this section to give you a printed output.

lpr, lpq, and lprm

The `lpr` (for *line printer*) command sends one or more files to a line printer (see Figure 9.3). To have the file `fall_report` printed, type

lpr fall_report

FIGURE 9.3
Using a line printer.

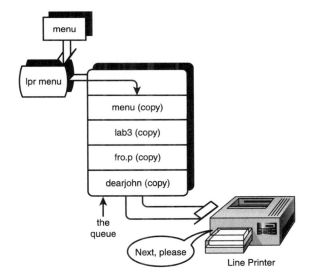

Chaos would result, however, if this command sent your file directly to the printer because other `lpr` commands might arrive in the middle of your print job and interrupt it. Instead, this command sends a copy of your file to a *printer queue*, where it waits its turn to be printed. Think of a queue as a waiting area for files to be printed. Because a printer can't physically print a file as fast as it is received, sometimes there is a waiting line for the printer.

The `lpq` command lets you check the contents of the line printer queue. For each file, it will print (onscreen, not on paper) the user name, an identification number, the file size, and the filename. Some systems also print how long the file has been in the queue. The following is an example of output from one system:

```
% lpq
Owner    Id    Chars    Filename
jowls   00217  31472    /usr/spool/lpd/cfa00217
```

Note

The filename is that of the copy in the queue, not of the original file.

Have you ever sent a 5,000-word file to the printer and then realized that it was the wrong file? The `lprm` command lets you remove a file (if it's yours) from the queue. Use the owner name (your login name), the identification number, or the filename as reported by `lpq` for the queue. Any of the following commands would remove the sample file just described:

```
lprm jowls
lprm 00217
lprm /usr/spool/lpd/cfa00217
```

To print several files, list them all after the command:

```
lpr Winter_report Spring_report Summer_report Fall_report
```

Each file will be separated from its neighbors by a banner page proclaiming your identity and by a blank page. If you want the files printed as one unit, combine all the files (temporarily) and send them to the printer as one unit:

```
cat Winter_report Spring_report Summer_report Fall_report ¦ lpr
```

Choosing a Printer

Many systems have more than one printer available. In general, a system will have a *default* printer to which print jobs normally are sent. You may, however, be able to choose a specific printer by using the -P option. You have to know the name used to identify the printer, and that will be a local matter. If, for example, `hplj` identified a particular laser printer on which you want to print the `resign` file, you would give the following command:

```
lpr -P hplj resign
```

You also would similarly use the -P option with the `lpq` and `lprm` commands.

If you use a particular nondefault most of the time, you may want to make it your default printer. You can do that by setting the environment variable **PRINTER** to the name of the desired printer. As discussed in Chapter 8, "The UNIX Shell: Command Lines, Redirection, and Shell Scripts," you do that with the following command in **csh** (the C shell):

```
setenv PRINTER hplj
```

You can place this command in your `.login` (or `.profile` in some cases) file so that it's executed automatically when you log in.

---

lpr, lpq, and lprm: Using the Line Printer

Name	Options	Arguments
lpr	See *Options* below	[*filenames*]
lpq		
lprm		*file identification*

Description: The **lpr** command sends the named files to the line printer queue from whence they are printed in an orderly fashion. If you omit a filename, **lpr** accepts input directly from your terminal; terminate the input with Ctrl-d.

The **lpq** command reports on the files in the line printer queue, assigning each file an owner name, an identification number, a file size, and a filename. The filename is that of the temporary queue file, not the original filename.

The **lprm** command removes files from the queue. It should be followed by one of the following identifications:

ownername	Removes all queued files having *ownername* as the owner
identification-number	Obtained from the **lpq** command
filename	Obtained from the **lpq** command

Options: These vary wildly from system to system, so check your online manual or local guru. For example, on some systems, there is an **-r** option (for reply) that informs you when printing is finished. On other systems, there is an **-r** option (for remove) that removes the file from your directory once it's printed. On some systems, the -r option deletes the original file after the file is spooled.

Examples: This prints the contents of the files **some** and **stuff**; the files will be separated by a banner bearing your name:

```
lpr some stuff
```

This command removes from the queue the print job identified by **lpq** as number **03847**:

```
lprm 03847
```

Permissions: chmod

The **chmod** (for change mode) command gives you the final say on who can read and use your files and who can't. This command considers the UNIX users' world to be divided into three classes:

- You, the user (**u**)

- Your group (**g**)

- Others (**o**)

What's this bit about a group? UNIX was developed at Bell Labs for use there in research. So, originally, a group would correspond to a particular research group. What constitutes a group for you will depend on your system. Perhaps it might be students in the same class, workers in the same department, or it might be arbitrary. Whatever the system, users in the same group are assigned the same group number, and this number is stored in the **/etc/passwd** file, which also contains your login name, your home directory assignment, and your encrypted password. So UNIX knows which group you are in and who else is in it (even if you don't).

In addition to three classes, **chmod** considers three kinds of permissions:

- *Read permission* (**r**) includes permission to **cat**, **more**, **lp**, and **cp** a file.

- *Write permission* (**w**) is permission to change a file, which includes editing a file and appending to a file.

- *Execute permission* (**x**) is permission to run an executable file, such as a program.

You can check to see what permissions are in effect by using the **-l** option for **ls** on the pertinent files. For example, the command

```
ls -l a.out expgrow.c
```

could produce the following output:

```
-rwxr-xr-x 1  doeman    25957 Jan 27 15:44  a.out
-rw-r--r-- 1  doeman      671 Jan 27 15:17  expgrow.c
```

The symbols on the left (`-rwxr-xr-x`) contain the information about permissions. There are 10 columns. The first can contain a **d** for directories and other letters for special kinds of files. Don't worry about that column for now. The first column has nothing to do with file or directory permissions but instead indicates what the name refers to: directory is a **d**, character mode device driver is a **c**, block mode device driver is a **b**, and other special symbols are used by specific versions of UNIX.

The next nine columns are actually three groups of three columns each. The first trio reports on user permissions, the second on group permissions, and the final on permissions for others. We can spread out the three groupings for **a.out** like this:

User	Group	Other Users
rwx	r-x	r-x

Within each grouping, the first column shows an r for read permission, the second column a w for write permission, and the third column an x for execute permission. A hyphen in any of these columns means no permission.

Thus, for the preceding a.out file, the user has read, write, and execute permissions (rwx). Members of the same group have read and execute permissions (r-x) but no write permission. Other users also have read and execute permissions (r-x) but no write permission. Permissions for the earlier expgrow.c account are similar, except that no one has execution permission.

This all means that anyone on the system can read or copy these two files. Only the person who owns the file, however, can alter these two files in this directory. (However, if you copy this file into your directory, you then can write as well as read and execute. You need to have read permission to be able to copy the file.) Finally, anyone who wants to can run the program a.out by typing the name of the file. (If the other user is in a different directory, he must use the full pathname of the file.) In most systems, these particular permissions are established by default; chmod lets you change them.

The chmod command is used a bit differently from most other UNIX commands. The simplest way to use it is to type chmod and then type a space. Then comes an *instruction segment* with three parts and no spaces. The first part of the segment consists of one or more letters identifying the classes to be affected. The next part is a + or - sign for adding or subtracting permissions. The final part is one or more letters identifying the permissions to be affected (see Figure 9.4). After the instruction segment is another space and the name(s) of the file (s) to be affected by the changes. This may sound a little confusing, but it is simple once you look at the following:

```
chmod g+w growexp.c
chmod go-rx a.out
```

FIGURE 9.4
Parts of a *chmod*
command.

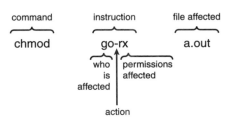

You can read Figure 9.4 as "change mode for groups and others to remove read and write permissions from file a.out."

The first example grants other members of your group (g) the right to write (w) in the file growexp.c. The second example takes away both read (r) and execute (x) privileges from members of your group (g) and from others (o). If you repeated the ls -l command now, the result would be

```
-rwx------  1  doeman    25957 Jan 27 15:44  a.out
-rw-------  1  doeman      671 Jan 27 15:17  expgrow.c
```

You can include more than one permission instruction by separating the permissions with commas. For instance, the command

```
chmod g+w,o-r project.big
```

would let other group members write in the `project.big` file and would deny other users permission to read that file. There must not be any spaces within the instruction segment.

You can use `chmod` on your directories. Just use the directory name instead of the filename. What are the effects of these permissions on directories? *Read permission* for a directory lets you read (using `ls`, for example) the names of the files in the directory. *Write permission* lets you create new files in the directory and remove files from the directory. Finally, *execute permission* for a directory lets you `cd` to that directory.

Perhaps you wonder what the point is in changing permissions for yourself (`u`). First, you can create a shell script file of UNIX commands. If you give that file *execute* status, typing that filename will cause the commands in the file to be executed. This is discussed in Chapter 8. Second, by removing write permission, you can protect yourself from accidentally changing a valuable file.

chmod: Change Modes or Permissions on Files

Instruction Name	Components	Arguments
chmod	ugo, +-, rwx	*filename(s)* or *directory name(s)*

Description: The `chmod` command grants or removes read, write, and execute permissions for three classes of users: user (you), group (your group), and others. A `chmod` command has three parts: the command name (`chmod`, of course), the instruction string, and the name of the file to be affected. The instruction string also has three parts: letter(s) indicating who is affected, a + or - symbol indicating the action to be taken, and letter(s) indicating which permissions are affected.

The code is as follows:

Who	
u	The user
g	The user's group
o	Others (everyone other than u or g)

Action	
+	Add permission
-	Remove permission

Permission	
r	Read
w	Write
x Execute	

Example: Suppose that you (login name **sam**) gave the command `ls -l` and found the following permissions for your payroll file:

```
rwxrwxrwx 1 sam 1776 Jan 4 9:33 payroll
```

If you want to remove the write and execute permissions for your group and other users, type

```
chmod go-wx payroll
```

The **g** refers to group, the **o** to others. The **-** means remove permissions **w** and **x**.

Messages: mesg

Normally, accounts are set up so that if someone tries to write to you while you are on a terminal, you will get a message to that effect. This makes UNIX a friendly and neighborly environment. Sometimes, however, you may not want to be interrupted. For those times, UNIX gives you ways to turn off the messages. The **mesg** command controls attempts to talk to you.

To prevent people from reaching you with **talk**, type

mesg n

When you feel more open to the world, you can re-establish your communication links with

mesg y

If you forget your state, just type

mesg

and UNIX will let you know your current state. The command will endure until you log out.

The command **mesg y** can be included in the standard `.cshrc` file (or `.profile`, depending on your system). You can change that if you like, so that you can log in with **mesg n** (see Figure 9.5).

FIGURE 9.5

mesg at work.

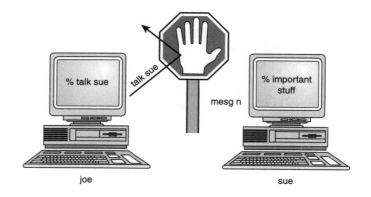

mesg: **Permit or Deny Messages from** talk		
Name	**Options**	**Arguments**
mesg	None	[y, n]

Description: Typing **mesg y** allows other users to communicate with you using talk. Typing **mesg n** forbids other users from communicating with you using talk. Typing simply **mesg** will display your current mesg status—**is y** or **is n**, as the case may be.

Commands for Your Terminal: tty and stty

The tty command tells you the pathname of your terminal. For example,

```
tty
```

might elicit the response

```
/dev/tty08
```

or

```
/dev/pts/08
```

This means that you are using terminal number 8, and the terminal is treated as a file in the /dev (for device) directory. The tty in the response means that your terminal is physically connected to the machine, whereas pts means that you are connected via a network connection (commonly called a *psuedo terminal*). While substituting your terminal identifier, try executing

```
ps -ef ¦ grep /dev/tty##
```

on your system. You'll see all the executing programs/processes tied to your terminal.

The `stty` command sets terminal options, such as the baud rate (transmission speed), parity, and echo, and sets which key is the erase key. Much of `stty` concerns the interface between the terminal and the computer, but we will just look at some of the less technical aspects. Normally, the system takes care of these matters for you, but you might want to change some of the choices.

The first step is to determine the current situation. Type

stty

and UNIX will report back the baud rate and option settings that vary from the default (standard) values. You can get more information by typing

stty all

for Berkeley UNIX or

stty -a

for SVR4 variants. Either command inspires UNIX to report on *all* normally used options. Finally, typing the command

stty everything

tempts only Berkeley UNIX to print *everything* that `stty` knows. For our modest purpose, `stty all` suffices. The following is an example of a response to that command:

```
new tty, speed 9600 baud, 24 rows, 80 columns; tabs
crt tostop
decctlq
erase   kill   werase   rprnt   flush   lnext   susp    intr   quit   stop    eof
#       ^U     ^W       ^R      ^O      ^V      ^Z/^Y   ^C     ^\     ^S/^Q   ^D
```

Much of this probably is best ignored, but here is what the output means. The first line states that the system is using the `tty` driver program for handling terminals. The communication rate is set to 9600 baud, the terminal display has 24 rows and 80 columns, and tabs are treated as tabs, rather than replaced by spaces.

The second line sets some options to values appropriate for a CRT (cathode ray tube) display. The **tostop** option causes background jobs to stop if they attempt to write to the terminal. Believe it or not, quite a few sites still haven't made the leap into the GUI world. They may prefer, for example, to run an older version of Oracle Forms in character mode to conduct their business.

The **decctlq** entry means that if you stop terminal output by using the stop character, you must restart output by using the start character (see Ctrl-s and Ctrl-q in the following list).

The final two lines identify which keys perform which tasks. For the setting list here, we have the following key assignments:

Key	Description
#	Erases the last character typed
Ctrl-u	Erases the current line just typed
Ctrl-w	Erases the word just typed
Ctrl-r	Reprints the line just typed
Ctrl-o	Flushes output
Ctrl-v	Causes the next character to be interpreted literally instead of as a special character
Ctrl-z	Suspends jobs
Ctrl-y	Restarts suspended jobs
Ctrl-c	Interrupts jobs
Ctrl-\	Causes jobs to quit
Ctrl-s	Suspends screen output
Ctrl-q	Restarts screen output
Ctrl-d	Generates an end-of-file signal.

Your system may show a different list. Most of the time, these settings will be preset for you, and you will be encouraged not to experiment with them, but there are exceptions. For instance, you may want to change some settings, such as the erase character. That's easy enough. To set the erase character to, say, Ctrl-h, type the following command:

stty erase ^h

For the ^h characters, you can either press Ctrl-h or type the caret character (^) and then the **h**. To make the change permanent, place it in your **.login** file.

Using the UNIX Clock: time and calendar

Never let it be said that UNIX won't give you the time of the day. It gladly informs you whenever you give the **date** command. UNIX can support the **date** command because it keeps track of the time internally. This ability helps it to perform such diverse tasks as timing commands (**time**) and providing you with a reminder service (**calendar**).

time

The **time** command tells you how long a simple command takes. Its general form is

time *command*

After you give this instruction, the *command* (which can be any UNIX command or program execution) is run, and when it is finished, you are given a breakdown of how much time was used. The output of `time` looks like the following:

```
7.9u 1.2s 0:35 25% 13+18k 74+0io 1pf+0w
```

The first item is user time to the nearest tenth of a second. This is time spent actually executing your command. The second time is system time, also to the nearest tenth of a second. It is time used by the system in supporting your command. Next comes the total time from start to finish, in whole seconds. Because the system may be time-sharing between your task and others, this number may be greater than the sum of the first two times. The percent figure reports on how much of that total time was spent on your job. The final figures relate to memory. These time commands are very important when you are renting CPU time, which can be quite expensive. These values also provide an indication of the resource usage of a particular command.

`time`: Time a Command

Name	Options	Argument
time	None	*command*

Description: The `time` command, when followed by a command name, runs the named command and gives you a breakdown of the time used. Three times are given:

User time	The CPU time used solely for the execution of your command.
System time	The additional CPU time spent in the system in the course of setting up and servicing the command.
Real or elapsed time	The actual time that passes from the moment you initiate the command until the command is finished. If UNIX is switching back and forth between your demands and those of other users, all that time is included, too.

Then the command lists the percentage of system time that your command used while running. After that comes some memory details. Much of the information returned will be of more interest to the systems administrator (SA) than to a normal user.

Example: This command will cause the command `cc woo.c` to run:

```
time cc woo.c
```

continued on next page

> *continued from previous page*
>
> When execution of the command is finished, UNIX will print the time summary for `cc woo.c`:
>
> ```
> 1.9u 0.6s 0:08 29% 15+13k 21+1io 5pf+0w
> ```
>
> A total of 1.9 seconds were used to support the command, and the system spent another 0.2 second supporting the command. The total elapsed time was 8 seconds (rounded to the nearest second), and your command got 29 percent of the time during that period.

calendar

The `calendar` command provides a built-in reminder service. (Don't confuse it with the `cal` command, which generates monthly and yearly calendars.) Actually, you don't even execute the `calendar` command. Your responsibility is to create a `calendar` file in your login directory. In this file, you place dated reminders such as

```
September 22      Dentist at 2:30
9/24      dinner at Antoine's, 8pm
PAY AUTO INSURANCE         Sept 28
```

Early each morning, UNIX looks through all the login directories for files named `calendar`. Whenever it finds one, it reads the file and looks for lines containing the date for today or tomorrow. It will mail the lines that it finds to the directory's owner. Thus, you receive a reminder via mail the day before the date and then on the day itself.

The date can be anywhere on the line, and you can use recognizable abbreviations. However, `calendar` doesn't recognize dates in which the day precedes the month. Thus, you won't be reminded of lines containing dates such as **25 December** or **25/12**.

> ### calendar: A Reminder Service
>
> **Description:** To use this service, create in your login directory a file called `calendar`. Put notes to yourself in this file. Every line in this file containing a recognizable date is mailed by UNIX to you twice: on the day before the date listed and on the date itself. The date can be anywhere on the line. It should include the month and the day, in that order, and you can use reasonable abbreviations.
>
> **Examples:** The calendar file can contain entries such as
>
> ```
> Buy goose March 19
> call gus mar. 20 at 3 pm
> 3/23 Report due
> ```

Summary

This chapter examined quite a few UNIX commands, which should give you an idea of the power and variety of the UNIX system. Again we urge you to try them and experiment. You may even want to look through the manual, because, in many cases, we have given only the more common options.

Review Questions

1. Explain what each of the following commands is used for:

   a. `chmod`

   b. `mesg`

   c. `time`

   d. `calendar`

   e. `sort`

   f. `tty`

   g. `lpr`

2. Some commands in the following list are correct; some have errors in them. Identify the incorrect commands and then correct them. Describe what the command does, too.

   a. `wc -w blackweb`

   b. `tail blackweb`

   c. `sort -f- n iou.list`

   d. `tail blackweb -15`

   e. `cat Rupart > lpr`

   f. `blackweb> wc`

Exercises

1. While in your home directory, do the following:

   a. List the contents of your home directory.

   b. Count the number of files you have by using the command sequence shown earlier in the chapter (with pipes).

   c. Find your longest file.

   d. Read the beginning of three files by using **head** and pipe the results through more.

2. Create two new files using an editor as follows:

   a. File **AA** contains

```
3
4
```

and file **BB** contains

```
a
b
c
```

   b. Now try the following commands:

```
head -2 AA BB
tail AA BB
cmp AA BB
comm AA BB
diff AA BB
cat AA >> BB
sort AA
sort BB
wc -l B*
```

3. Try a few commands like the following:

```
who | sort | more
who | sort | tee CC
head CC
```

CHAPTER 10

MORE TEXT PROCESSING: join, sed, AND nroff

> **You will learn about the following in this chapter:**
>
> - How to use the join command to merge files
>
> - How to use sed, a powerful editing tool
>
> - How to use the nroff text-formatting tool
>
> - Some ways to use the shell for scripting
>
> - Macro languages and preprocessors

Today, much computing effort goes into the creation and alteration of text. Therefore, it's not surprising that UNIX has many facilities dealing with text processing. There are several aspects to this subject. First, there's the basic process of creating text files. You've seen how to use editors such as vi to do this. Second, there's the process of modifying a file, perhaps to correct the spelling of a word you've persistently misspelled or to change a name in a form letter. Or you may want to rearrange text. A third aspect is formatting the file—that is, setting margins, lining up the right side of the text, controlling line spacing, and so on. These tasks can be accomplished by using the standard editors, but often they can be done more conveniently and efficiently by using the UNIX commands join for rearranging, spell for detecting spelling errors, sed for editing, and nroff for formatting. All four of these tools are designed to work as "filters," so let's discuss this unifying feature before we move to the individual commands.

UNIX Filters

Many UNIX utilities, including pr, wc, sort, and those discussed in this chapter, are designed to be *filters*. Typically, a filter takes input from the standard input (usually your PC or laptop keyboard), processes it somehow, and sends the output to the standard output (usually your screen). By using UNIX redirection and pipes, a filter can just as easily take its input from a file or another command instead of from the terminal. (Also, most filters can take input from files used as arguments.) Similarly, you can use UNIX redirection and pipes to route the output of a filter to a file or to another command. This agility makes for a flexible, powerful system. You don't need one command for keyboard input and a separate command to handle files. You don't need a carload of complex programs when you can achieve the same results by linking the right combination of filters with pipes. Designing programs to act as filters is an important part of the UNIX philosophy.

Understand that a filter adds nothing superfluous to its output; **sort** doesn't preface its output with a merry

```
All right, sweetheart, here's your output!
```

This may make UNIX utilities seem a little cold and impersonal, but you wouldn't want a message like that piped along to **wc** or **lp** with the rest of the output.

Note

If you don't use pipes but want the personal touch, you can make shell scripts like this:

```
echo There! It\'s all sorted.
sort $*
```

A backslash is used before the single quote metacharacter because we want it to be a simple apostrophe.

Now let's get on to particulars by looking at **join**.

Combining Files: join

The **cat** command lets you combine files vertically—that is, it allows you to append one file to another. The **join** command lets you combine files horizontally, with the lines of one file being tagged to the end of the corresponding lines of another file. The **join** command is more demanding, however:

- The lines in a file must be in sorted order. More specifically, they should be in ascending ASCII sequence, such as the **sort** command produces.

- For two lines to be combined, they must have the same *join field*. Normally, join uses blanks and tabs to divide a line into fields, and the first field is taken to be the join field. The **join** command then prints the join field, the rest of the fields from the first file, and the rest of the fields from the second file.

Let's try it. First, suppose that we begin with the files shown by the following **cat** commands:

```
% cat rbi.and.ba
Abe Booth       88          .332
Billie Hays     82          .345
Tank Derron     73          .302
% cat pos.and.fld
Abe Booth       RF          .978
Billie Hays     CF          .989
Tank Derron     LF          .982
%
```

Although you can't tell from the appearance, this file uses tab characters to align the fields.

The Tab and Space Characters

Many keyboards have a Tab key. Pressing Tab causes the cursor to move to the right, typically eight spaces at a time. A tab produces *absolute* moves—that is, it moves to predefined locations onscreen. Thus, whether the cursor is in column one or six, a tab moves the cursor to column nine. (A *relative* move would move the cursor, say, eight spaces from the current cursor position.)

A tab is part of the ASCII character set; it's character 9. The space also is a character—character 32. Each takes up the same amount of storage space as, for instance, B or any other alphabetic character. One consequence of this is that text containing tabs may look like text containing spaces but nonetheless be different. Suppose, for example, that the tabs are spaced by eight and that you type

sam<Tab>**adams**

It would appear like this onscreen:

sam   adams

Typing

sam<Spacebar><Spacebar><Spacebar><Spacebar><Spacebar>**adams**

also produces that appearance:

sam   adams

But the first takes up just 9 memory slots (8 letters, 1 tab), whereas the second uses 13 memory slots (8 letters, 5 spaces).

The unexpected presence of tabs may produce surprises when you do editing. In **vi**, for instance, you may try to remove one space and find that eight disappear, for you really were removing a tab.

The chief values of tabs are saving storage space and producing nicely aligned columns of data. This second point means that tabs often occur in the sort of text used with **join**.

Now let's use the **join** command:

```
% join rbi.and.ba pos.and.fld
Abe Booth 88 .332 Booth RF .978
Billie Hays 82 .345 Hays CF .989
Tank Derron 73 .302 Derron LF .982
```

In this case, the join field was the column of first names. That's why the last names appear twice; they belong to a different field.

Also notice that the **join** command uses a space character to separate the fields on output. You can modify that behavior by using the -**t** option. If you use, say, -**t***c* in the command line, where *c* is some character, **join** will use the *c* character to identify fields during input and to separate fields during output. For this example, let's use the tab character. That way, the first and last names would be in one field, and the output would line up better. To use a tab with the -**t** option, however, you have to enclose it in single quotation marks. Otherwise, the shell will think that you are just spacing out the command line.

Let's try it. We'll use **<Tab>** to indicate where you type the Tab key. Notice that you still have to type a space after the tab to separate it from the filenames.

```
% join -t'\t'  rbi.and.ba pos.and.fld
Abe Booth      88           .332  RF              .978
Billie Hays    82           .345  CF              .989
Tank Derron    73           .302  LF              .982
```

join: Joins Lines from Two Files

Name	Options	Arguments
join	[-t, -j]	*file1 file2*

Description: The join command combines matching lines from *file1* with lines from *file2*. The lines should be sorted in ascending ASCII order. Each line is divided into fields by a separator character. By default, blanks and tabs are separators. Each line has a join field (the first field by default). Lines match if the join fields match. In that case, the join field is printed, and then the remaining fields from *file1*, and then the remaining fields from *file2*. Lines without matching join fields aren't permitted. Advanced users may want to check a manual for additional options.

Options:

-t*c*	Use the character *c* as the separator character.
-j*n m*	Use field *m* of file *n* as the join field.

Examples: This joins lines using the default behavior:

join spring fallThis uses the colon for the field separator and the third field of parts1 as the join field:

join -t: -j 1 3 parts1 parts2

Checking Your Spelling: spell

You've just completed an important letter but are worried about your spelling. You could sit down and check each word with a dictionary, or you can let UNIX do that for you. Suppose that your letter is in the file **sendcash**. You can give the command

spell sendcash

and UNIX will compare each word in your file with words in a spelling list it maintains. If one of your words isn't on the list or can't be derived from some standard rules (adding an *s* or an *ing*, for example), that word is printed on the terminal. (If you make lots of spelling errors, you may need to use redirection to save all your errors in a file.)

Suppose that **sendcash** looks like this:

```
Dear Ruggles,

I'm at a real nice place. It's the sub-basement of Mildew
Hall at Forkney College, have you ever been their? If you
have, you will knoe that I need mony bad! Please, please
send some soon! The autchthons here are spooky. I'm
looking forward to recieving your next letter.

                              Love,
                              Buffy
```

The output of the **spell** command would look like this:

```
autchthons
Buffy
Forkney
knoe
recieving
Ruggles
```

This example points out some of the pitfalls of **spell**:

- It may not recognize some proper names.

- The **spell** command can check to see whether a word is on its list but can't tell whether you used it correctly. It caught the words **knoe**, **mony**, and **recieving** but didn't catch that **their** should have been spelled **there**. In other words, **spell** doesn't replace good old-fashioned proofreading.

- **spell** doesn't tell you the correct spelling.

- You may know some words, such as **autchthons** (meaning inhabitants) and certain four-letter words, that aren't on **spell**'s list.

Nonetheless, **spell** is a big help, especially with long files. Now let's see about editing files.

The sed Stream Editor

The **sed** command does wholesale editing work. It has many of the capabilities of **ed** or **ex**, but it's used differently. Rather than let you interactively modify a file, it just takes a file as input, reads and modifies it one line at a time, and sends its output to the screen. You can think of the contents of the input file as streaming through the editor, modified as it flows through—hence the name *stream editor* (see Figure 10.1). This design makes **sed** efficient for large files. Perhaps more important, it allows **sed** to be used with pipes and redirection, thus making **sed** into a handy tool for many tasks. In particular, it often is used in shell scripts.

FIGURE 10.1

sed is a stream editor.

sed's/TROWT/TROUT/g'

Note

The **sed** editor was developed from **ed**, not **ex**, which is why it's not the **sex** editor. However, **ex** duplicates many **ed** commands.

sed Basics

Give **sed** an input file and minimal instructions, and it will print the contents of the file line by line:

```
% sed '' tale.start
     Once upon a time a delightful princess named Delita lived in
the Kingdom of Homania. One day, as Princess Delita walked
amidst the fragrant flowers and artful bowers of the West Garden,
she spotted a glistening stone. Picking it up, Delita discovered
that the stone looked wet but was dry to the touch. Suddenly the
%
```

Note

sed's first argument consists of its instructions, and it usually is enclosed in single quotes. For our example, we used single quotes containing nothing.

Here, **sed** reveals the contents of the file `tale.start` just as the `cat` command would. The difference, of course, is that **sed** will accept further instructions. For instance, look at this:

```
% sed   's/Delita/Melari/g'   tale.start
    Once upon a time a delightful princess named Melari lived in
the Kingdom of Homania. One day, as Princess Melari walked
amidst the fragrant flowers and artful bowers of the West Garden,
she spotted a glistening stone. Picking it up, Melari discovered
that the stone looked wet but was dry to the touch. Suddenly the
%
```

Here we have added an **ed** substitution command to the command line. The command pattern is

```
sed 'ed-command' filename
```

The **sed** command looks at each line in turn, applies the command (if applicable), and prints the result. In our example, the first, second, and fourth lines contained the name **Delita**, so those lines were printed with the substitution of **Melari** for **Delita**. The other lines were printed unchanged.

Note that the original file, `tale.start`, is left unchanged by **sed**. If you want to save your changes, you have to use redirection. For example, we could have typed

```
sed 's/Delita/Melari/' tale.start > tale.1
```

This command would have placed **sed**'s output in the file `tale.1` instead of onscreen.

Understand, too, that **sed** is best used for wholesale changes to the whole file. It's great if you want to replace every **Delita** with **Melari**. If you want to change just one or two occurrences of a word and leave other occurrences of that word unaltered, you are better off using one of the regular editors.

You've just seen that **sed** can be used to make substitutions. What other abilities does it have at its disposal? Let's take a look.

sed Editing Instructions

A typical instruction has two parts: an *address specification* telling which lines are affected, and a *command* telling what to do to the affected lines. If there's no address given, all lines are affected. The address can be specified numerically or by pattern matching, much as in **ed**. The commands, too, largely stem from **ed** and, hence, **ex**.

Table 10.1 lists the most common commands. They work much as they do in **ed**, and we'll bring out details in the examples to come.

TABLE 10.1   Common sed Commands

Command	Action
a\	Appends following line(s) to affected lines
c\	Changes affected lines to following line(s)
d	Deletes affected lines
g	Makes substitutions affect every matching pattern on a line instead of just the first
i\	Inserts following line(s) above affected lines
p	Prints line, even under the -n option
q	Quits when specified line is reached
r *filename*	Reads *filename*; appends contents to output
s/old/new/	Substitutes new for old
w *filename*	Copies line to *filename*
=	Prints line number
! *command*	Applies *command* if line is *not* selected

The **sed** command's normal method, as we have said, is to print the modified line if a change has taken place and to print the original line if no change was made. This norm is overridden by the -n option, which causes only those lines affected by a **p** command to be printed. We'll give an example soon, but first let's see how to specify an address.

Specifying Lines

The **sed** command uses two methods. The first is to specify an address with a number. You can use a single number to indicate a particular line. For instance, to delete the third line of our sample file, try

```
% sed '3d' tale.start
     Once upon a time a delightful princess named Delita lived in
the Kingdom of Homania. One day, as Princess Delita walked
she spotted a glistening stone. Picking it up, Delita discovered
that the stone looked wet but was dry to the touch. Suddenly the
%
```

Or you can use two numbers separated by a comma to indicate a range of lines:

```
% sed '2,4 s/e/#/' tale.start
     Once upon a time a delightful princess named Delita lived in
the Kingdom of Homania. On# day, as Princess Delita walked
amidst the fragrant flowers and artful bow#rs of the West Garden,
she spotted a glistening stone. Picking it up, Delita discov#red
that the stone looked wet but was dry to the touch. Suddenly the
%
```

Here, the substitution command affected only the second through fourth lines. (Recall that a simple substitution command affects only the first occurrence of a pattern on a line. Thus, only the first e on each affected line is replaced by a #.)

The second approach to identifying lines is to specify a pattern; the pattern is contained between slashes. The next example prints only those lines containing Kingdom. It uses the -n option, which suppresses printing of those lines not affected by a p command.

```
% sed -n '/Kingdom/p' tale.start
the Kingdom of Homania. One day, as Princess Delita walked
%
```

If you omitted the -n, the Kingdom line would be printed twice, and the rest once.

The patterns can be literal, as in the last example, or they can involve certain metacharacters. This next example deletes lines containing princess or Princess:

```
% sed '/[Pp]rincess/d' tale.start
amidst the fragrant flowers and artful bowers of the West Garden,
she spotted a glistening stone. Picking it up, Delita discovered
that the stone looked wet but was dry to the touch. Suddenly the
%
```

We'll take up sed's pattern-matching scheme after we finish with more basic matters.

One of the more basic matters is that these two modes (numerical, pattern) of specifying lines can be combined. For instance, to delete all lines from line 1 through the first line containing fragrant, do this:

```
% sed '1,/fragrant/d' tale.start
she spotted a glistening stone. Picking it up, Delita discovered
that the stone looked wet but was dry to the touch. Suddenly the
%
```

Now let's look a bit further at some of the commands.

sed Command Highlights

The last few examples show how to use the d and p commands. These work much as in ed, but ed's a, c, and i commands have become a\, c\, and i\. We'll use the append command (a\) to show the proper form for using these three commands:

```
% sed 'a\\
Once upon a time a delightful princess named Delita lived in the Kingdom of
Hey la la\! Doo de dah\!
Homania. One day, as Princess Delita walked amidst the fragrant flowers and artful
Hey la la\! Doo de dah\!
bowers of the West Garden, she spotted a glistening stone. Picking it up, Delita
Hey la la\! Doo de dah\!
discovered that the stone looked wet but was dry to the touch. Suddenly the
Hey la la\! Doo de dah\!
Hey la la! Doo de dah!
%
```

Because we didn't give any sort of line identification, our addition was added after every line of the original. (Adding a blank line instead of our choice would have double-spaced the original.) Notice, too, how the append command is used. First comes the **a**; then two backslashes (\\) are used. The first backslash tells **sed** to take input from the next line. The second backslash tells the **csh** shell that the command is to be extended to the next line; you should press Return immediately after the second backslash.

Note

The **sh** shell doesn't require the second backslash—indeed, **sh** and **ksh** will balk at it.

This next line contains the text to be added, and the closing quote mark indicates the end of the command. You could add more than one line by using more paired backslashes:

```
% sed 'a\\
doobie doobie\\
do' dumbsong
```

The insert command (**i**) works much the same, except it places the new line(s) before each original line. The change-line command (**c**) has the same form, too:

```
% sed 'c\\
Oh marvelous delight! Sing to me!' tale.start
Oh marvelous delight! Sing to me!
Oh marvelous delight! Sing to me!
Oh marvelous delight! Sing to me!
Oh marvelous delight! Sing to me!
Oh marvelous delight! Sing to me!
%
```

Each of the original five lines was changed to the new text. Of course, you usually would attach some sort of address specifier to a change command so that it would affect just some lines.

The **q** command causes the editor to quit after it reaches the specified line:

```
% sed '2q' tale.start
     Once upon a time a delightful princess named Delita lived in
the Kingdom of Homania. One day, as Princess Delita walked
amidst the fragrant flowers and artful
%
```

You can use this form instead of **head** for looking at the beginnings of files. Unlike **head**, **sed** is available on non-BSD UNIX.

The next command we want to highlight is the substitution command. You've already seen that the form of this command is

s/*oldpattern*/*newpattern*/

where *newpattern* replaces *oldpattern*. In this form, the command affects only the first occurrence of *oldpattern* in a line. Adding the **g** command (for global) to the end of the instruction causes every occurrence in the line to be affected. Compare these two examples:

```
% sed -n '1s/e/#/p' tale.start
    Onc# upon a time a delightful princess named Delita lived in

% sed -n '1s/e/#/gp' tale.start
    Onc# upon a tim# a d#lightful princ#ss nam#d D#lita liv#d in
```

One very important feature of the **s** command is that it can use **sed**'s pattern-matching abilities for *oldpattern*. Let's see how that works.

Pattern Matching in sed

The **sed** command uses patterns to specify lines in its substitution command. These patterns can be literal, or they can use metacharacters to specify more general patterns. The scheme is similar to the shell's filename expansion scheme (*, ?, and all that) but isn't quite the same. Table 10.2 shows the metacharacters used by **sed**. (You can use these same metacharacters in **vi**.)

TABLE 10.2   Common sed Metacharacters for Pattern Matching

Metacharacter	Action
\	Turns off the special meaning of the character that follows
^	Matches the beginning of a line
$	Matches the end of a line
.	Matches any single character
[ ]	Matches any one of the enclosed characters; characters can be listed ([aqg4]) or be given as a range ([c-h])
[^...]	Matches any character not in the ... list
*pat**	Matches zero or more occurrences of *pat*, where *pat* is a single character or a [ ] pattern
&	Used in the *newpattern* part of an s command to represent reproducing the *oldpattern* part

Table 10.3 shows some brief examples illustrating the use of the metacharacters in Table 10.2.

TABLE 10.3   Quick Examples of the Metacharacters in Action

Command	Result
/Second/	Matches any line containing **Second**
/^Second/	Matches any line beginning with **Second**
/^$/	Matches an empty line—that is, one with nothing between the beginning and end of the line. (This doesn't match a line of blank spaces because a space itself is a character.)
/c.t/	Matches lines containing **cat**, **cot**, and so on. This pattern can be part of a word—for instance, **apricot** and **acute** would be matched.
/./	Matches lines containing at least one character.
/\./	Matches lines containing a period. The backslash negates the special meaning of the period.
/s[oa]p/	Matches **sop** or **sap** but not **sip**, **sup**, or **soap**; only one letter is permitted between the **s** and the **p**
/s[^oa]p/	Matches **sip** or **sup** but not **sop** or **sap**
s/cow/s&s/	Replaces cow with scows
/co*t/	Matches **ct**, **cot**, **coot**, **cooot**, and so on. That is, it matches a **c** and a **t** that are separated by any number (including zero) of o's. Note that use of the * is different from the shell's use.

Now let's see how these metcharacters can be used and combined in the context of **sed** commands.

Simple sed Solutions

Let's try some examples that are typical of the problems **sed** can solve. Suppose that you want to remove all the blank lines from a file called **rawtext**. You could do this:

```
sed '/^$/d' rawtext
```

However, as pointed out previously, this locates empty lines only. The text might contain lines that aren't empty but have only blanks. The next command gets those lines, too:

```
sed '/^ *$/d' rawtext
```

Notice that the * follows a blank, so the search pattern says to find lines that contain only zero or more blanks between the beginning and the end of the line (see Figure 10.2).

FIGURE 10.2

The **sed** command can match patterns.

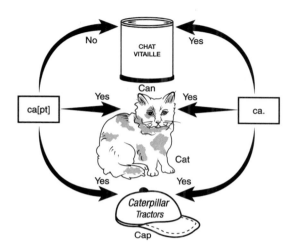

Suppose that you want to add a blank line to each line. One solution was suggested earlier:

```
% sed 'a\\
' rawtext
```

Here we have appended a line consisting of one blank space to each line. Another approach is

```
% sed 's/$/\\
/' rawtext
```

This time we substituted a carriage return for the end of the line. The carriage return is an invisible character, and we made the substitution by typing a backslash and then pressing Return.

Next, suppose that you want to print all lines containing the word *hopefully*:

```
sed -n '/[Hh]opefully/p' rawtext
```

The -n option suppresses the printing of other lines, and [Hh] catches both capitalized and uncapitalized occurrences.

Now suppose that you want to remove all the comments from an old FORTRAN program you have to maintain. FORTRAN comments have a C in the first column, so this would work:

```
sed '/^C /d' prog.f
```

If your system allows both lowercase and uppercase, use

```
sed '/^[cC]/d' prog.f
```

Keep in mind that the ^ indicates that the C (or c) must be at the beginning of a line.

Assume that you want to print a letter and want to shift the left margin five spaces to the right:

```
sed 's/^/     /' letter
```

Just substitute five spaces for the beginning of each line.

Now suppose that you have a file in which you want to change the name *Bob* to *Robert* and *Pat* to *Patricia*. Oops! How do you enter more than one command? Read on.

Multiple Commands

Sometimes you may need more than one editing command. Just add in each command, one command to a line. (Be sure to enclose the entire command list in single quotes.)

```
% sed 's/Bob/Robert/g\
        s/Pat/Patricia/g' actii
```

The backslash following the g tells the `csh` shell to continue the command to the next line; omit the backslash if you use the `sh` shell. Each time a new input line is accepted, it's subjected to each command in the order given. For example

```
% sed 's/cat/dog/g\
        s/dog/pigs/g' petreport
```

would first convert all `cat`s to `dog`s and then all `dog`s (including former `cat`s) to `pig`s.

There's one problem with our first example. A line like

```
Patience is needed, Pat.
```

will become

```
Patriciaience is needed, Patricia.
```

because a `sed` search doesn't distinguish between patterns that are complete words and those that are just part of a word. The pattern /Pat / (with a space) will pass up `Patience`, but it also would miss `Pat` followed by a period. You have to anticipate ways in which `Pat` might not be followed by a space:

```
% sed 's/Bob/Robert/g\
        s/Pat[ \.,;:\!?\'\"\]]/Patricia/g' actii
```

Have we thought of all the possibilities? Perhaps not. And did we put backslashes in the right place? Maybe we should try another approach:

```
% sed 's/Bob/Robert/g\
        s/Pat[^a-z]/Patricia/g' actii
```

Rather than think of all the possible ways Pat might be used, we simply eliminate the possibility we don't want, namely, that Pat is the beginning of a word. (Recall that [^a-z] means any character other than those from *a* through *z*.)

Tags

However, our pattern still has a fault. When something like `Pat!` is found, the whole string, including the !, is replaced by `Patricia`, and the ! is lost. We need a way to replace the `Pat` while keeping the !. We can do this with *tags*. To "tag" part of a pattern, enclose it with a \(to the left and a \) to the right. Then, in the *newpattern* part of the command, you can refer to the first such enclosed pattern as \1, the second as \2, and so on. Using this method gives this command:

```
sed 's/\(Pat\)\([^a-z]\)/\1ricia\2/g' actii
```

Here, the \1 stands for `Pat`, and the \2 stands for `[^a-z]`. We simply squeeze `ricia` in between these two patterns. Just as **&** gives you a means to refer to an entire expression, the \(...\) and \1 notation lets you refer to a part of an expression.

Shell Scripts and sed

If you find yourself using a particular **sed** concoction often, you may want to put it into a shell script. For instance, our double-space example could be rendered

```
sed 'a\
' $*
```

and placed in the file **twospace**. Notice that we used just one backslash instead of two. We're assuming that you'll use **sh** and not **csh** to execute the shell script. That's the default, for instance, when you make the script an executable file. However, if you do use **csh** to execute the script, you need to use two backslashes. After that file is made executable, you can type

twospace jane.letter ¦ pr ¦ lpr

to format the letter and print it. Or you could make the printing part of the script:

```
sed 'a\
' $* ¦ pr ¦ lpr
```

This last example points out how **sed** lends itself to UNIX programming and to shell scripts. Because it produces an output rather than modify the original file, it can be made part of a piping process linking various UNIX utilities. This convenience is, of course, one of the chief justifications of the filter approach to designing programs.

Here's one more example. Suppose that you want a program that sorts one or more files alphabetically and prints the first 10 lines. You can use the following script:

```
sort $* ¦ sed 10q
```

After you start using UNIX tools in this fashion, you are on the road to being a true UNIX user. Well, enough said about **sed**—it's time to inspect **nroff**.

Text Formatting with nroff and troff

A *text formatter* handles such tasks as setting up margins, line spacing, paragraph formats, and so on. The UNIX text formatters are **nroff** and **troff**. The **nroff** (*new runoff*) command formats material for a line printer, whereas **troff** formats material for a typesetter. The **troff** command is the more versatile of the two, for it can select different types of styles and sizes and draw boxes. Aside from a few matters like that, the two accept the same instructions. We will use **nroff** as an example, but what we say applies equally to **troff**.

You have three levels of simplicity and power on which to use **nroff**:

- The simplest and least powerful level is to use `nroff` unadorned on an ordinary file.

- The next level, which brings a great leap in power, is to use an `nroff` macro. This involves placing a few `nroff` commands into a text file.

- The most powerful level, which brings a great increase in complexity, involves putting many `nroff` commands into a file.

We'll start with the simplest level, look a bit at the second level, and then touch on the third.

Level 1: `nroff`

First, get a file with some text. Here are the contents of the **speachify** file:

```
Eighty-seven years before the present time,
a group of men
who could be termed,
with some degree of appropriateness, the ancestors of us here
today and of this distinguished nation, assembled
themselves with the intention, a great intention, we might
add, and one that proved successful,
of modifying for the purpose of improvement our already noble and
notable nation.
```

Now feed this file to `nroff`:

```
nroff speachify
```

Oops! The output runs off the screen!

Like `pr`, `nroff` formats the text to a printed page of 66 lines, so enough blank lines are added to our input to bring the total to 66. We can use **sed** to look at the beginning:

```
% nroff speachify ¦ head -10
Eighty-seven years before the present time, a group  of  men  who
could  be termed, with some degree of appropriateness, the ances-
tors of us here today and of this distinguished nation, assembled
themselves  with  the intention, a great intention, we night add,
and one that proved successful, of modifying for, the  purpose of
improvement our already noble and notable nation.
```

Now we can see what `nroff` hath wrought:

- It has *filled* each line. That means it tries to use enough words in each line to make it as close as possible to the maximum line length without exceeding it. For `nroff`, this maximum length is 65 characters by default, including spaces.

- It has *right-justified* or "adjusted" the text. This means spacing the text so that the right margin is even.

- It has hyphenated a word to get a better fit.

That's about all this simple usage does, so let's move on to the next level.

Level 1.5: Messing Around

We didn't mention this level in our introduction because it's not really a level of using `nroff`. Rather, it's a level of *experimenting* with `nroff`—seeing how `nroff` commands (or "requests") are made and finding out what they do.

First, what does a typical `nroff` command look like? Here are a few:

```
.ce
.sp 3
.ti 8
```

That's the typical appearance: a period followed by two lowercase letters followed (possibly) by an argument.

Next, how are they used? They are placed in the text file. Each command is placed on a line of its own and at the beginning of the line (see Figure 10.3). When `nroff` reads the file, it assumes that any line beginning with a period is an `nroff` request. If it doesn't recognize what follows, it ignores that text. Otherwise, it implements the request when it outputs the following text. For example, let's add **ce** to our text and see what happens. First, here's the new text:

```
.ce
Eighty-seven years before the present time,
a group of men
who could be termed,
with some degree of appropriateness, the ancestors of us here
today and of this distinguished nation, assembled
themselves with the intention, a great intention, we might
add, and one that proved successful,
of modifying for the purpose of improvement our already noble and
notable nation.
```

FIGURE 10.3

Positing an `nroff` request.

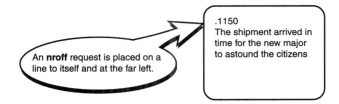

An **nroff** request is placed on a line to itself and at the far left.

```
.1150
The shipment arrived in
time for the new major
to astound the citizens
```

Let's submit it to `nroff`:

```
nroff speachify ¦ head -10
```

We get this output:

```
        Eighty-seven years before the present time,
a group of men who could be termed, with some degree of appropri-
ateness, the ancestors of us here today and of this distinguished
nation, assembled themselves with the intention, a  great  inten-
tion,  we might add, and one that proved successful, of modifying
for the purpose of improvement our already noble and notable nation.
```

The result is that the line following the request was centered. Perhaps that is why `.ce` is called the centering request.

Of course, you can read in the manual what these embedded commands do, but actually using them makes it clearer. To save you the time of constantly reediting a file to insert new requests, here's a shell script that lets you test one request at a time:

```
sed '1i\
'$2 $1 ¦ nroff ¦ head -20
```

This script inserts its second argument at the beginning of the file named by the first argument. The output is filtered through **head** so that you get just the first 20 lines (about a screen).

Let's put the script in a file called **nrtest** and use it to see the effect of adding an argument to the **ce** request:

```
% nrtest speachify ce2
        Eighty-seven years before the present time,
                    a group of men
who   could   be termed,   with some degree of appropriateness,   the
ancestors   of   us   here today and of this   distinguished   nation,
assembled themselves with the intention,   a great   intention,   we
might add,   and one that proved successful,   of modifying for the
purpose of improvement our already noble and notable nation.
```

Now two lines are centered! (The **nroff** command will accept either **ce2** or **ce 2**; we use the first form so that our shell script will take the whole request as $2.)

Not all **nroff** requests produce discernible results when inserted at the front of a file, but Table 10.4 consists of some that do. We've included a brief description, but it's fun to try them out yourself. Try, for instance, a **tra#e\$o%** request.

TABLE 10.4   Some nroff Requests

Request	Action
.ce N	Centers next N lines
.in N	Indents text N spaces
.hy N	Turns on auto-hyphenation if N is greater than or equal to 1, off if N equals 0.
.ll N	Sets line length to N characters
.ls N	Sets line spacing to N (2 = double-spaced, and so on)
.na	Doesn't justify right margin ("no adjust")
.nf	Doesn't fill text
.sp N	Puts in N blank lines
.ti N	Temporarily (next line) indents N spaces
.tr abcd..	Replaces a with b, c with d, and so on. The space between request and argument can be omitted.

Level 2: mm Macros

The term *macro* signifies a command or instruction constructed from several more basic units. The `nroff` command lets you construct your own macros from the basic instructions. The chief tool is the `.de` request that lets you define a single symbolism to represent several requests. For example,

```
.de PG
.sp
.ti5
..
```

defines `PG` to mean "space one line and temporarily indent five spaces." The `..` marks the definition's end.

You could study `nroff` assiduously and create your own set of macros, but most users use a *macro package*. This is just a set of predefined macros designed to handle common situations, such as creating paragraphs and making footnotes. BSD UNIX features the **ms** and **me** macro packages. We'll take a brief look at **ms**, the older and smaller of the two packages.

Macros are used the same way ordinary requests are. Here, for example, we will insert the **ms** macro for an indented paragraph (`.PP`):

```
.ce
A Stirring Speech by Senator Phineas Phogblower
.sp
.PP
Eighty-seven years before the present time,
a group of men
who could be termed,
with some degree of appropriateness, the ancestors of us here
today and of this distinguished nation, assembled
themselves with the intention, a great intention, we might
add, and one that proved successful,
of modifying for the purpose of improvement our already noble and
notable nation.
```

Now that we have the instructions in place, how do we get them noticed? This way:

```
nroff -ms speachify
```

If you use `troff` for typesetting, the corresponding command is this:

```
troff -ms speachify
```

Evoking `nroff`, we get this output:

```
        A Stirring Speech by Senator Phineas Phogblower

    Eighty-seven years before the present time, a group  of
men  who  could  be termed, with some degree of appropriate-
ness, the ancestors of  us  here  today  and  of  this  dis-
tinguished  nation, assembled themselves with the intention,
a great intention, we might add, and one  that  proved  suc-
cessful,  of  modifying  for  the purpose of improvement our
already noble and notable nation.
```

Here we've suppressed several blank lines at the beginning and the end of the text. As you can see, the .PP macro produced a paragraph with the first line indented five spaces.

There you have the essence of ms: embed appropriate macros in the text. The next step would be to learn all of ms's macros. We'll just look at some of the more common commands. Table 10.5 lists a few.

Note
If you use any of the first five from the table, they should be used in the order given. Also, the first line in a file should be an **nroff** or **ms** command.

TABLE 10.5   Some ms Macros

Macro	Meaning and Typical Usage
.TL	Use the next line for a title.
.AU	Use next line(s) to specify author(s).
.AI	Use next line(s) to specify author(s) institution(s).
.AB	**Abstract** begins next line.
.AE	Comes after end of **Abstract**.
.PP	Begin a paragraph with first line indented.
.LP	Begin a block paragraph aligned left.
.IP L	Begin an indented block paragraph. If the optional L is used, the paragraph is labeled L. This label can be a number, letter, symbol, or combination thereof.
.FS L	Start a footnote. The optional label L will be used to label the footnote.
.FE	End a footnote.

Making a Report

Let's use some macros to put a simple report together. Here's the original text:

```
.TL
Canine Behavior
.AU
I.M. Wright
.AI
Wufus Institute of Mammalian Psychology
.PP
Several years of intensive research*
.FS *
```

```
Ten at WIMP and five more earlier at the VitaBita Research
Center.
.FE
into canine behavior have led to a number of interesting
conclusions.
A few are presented below.
.IP 1
Many dogs display a noticeable interest in food.
Regularly scheduled feedings are anticipated with growing
excitement.
Food is eaten rapidly.
.IP 2
The majority of dogs prefer four-footed locomotion.
While it is possible to teach dogs to walk on two legs
(usually the rear two),
they quickly revert to quadrupedal form,
particularly when in a hurry.
.PP
Additional funding has been requested to continue these
fascinating studies.
```

Figure 10.4 shows the output. We've removed several blank lines to conserve space. As you look at the input and output, note these points:

- We followed the prescribed order for using the `.TL`, `.AU`, and `.AI` commands.

- We started each new sentence on a new line. This isn't necessary but makes it simpler to add or remove sentences later.

- The material marked as being a footnote was saved and then printed at the bottom of the page below a horizontal line.

- The indented block paragraphs were labeled 1 and 2, as directed.

- The date was added at the bottom.

FIGURE 10.4

Output from `nroff -ms`.

Canine Behavior

I.M. Wright
Wufus Institute of Mammalian Psychology

Several years of intensive research* into canine behavior have led to a number of interesting conclusions. A few are presented below.

1   Many dogs display a noticeable interest in food. Regularly scheduled feedings are anticipated with growing excitement. Food is eaten rapidly.

2   The majority of dogs prefer four-footed locomotion. While it is possible to teach dogs to walk on two legs (usually the rear two), they quickly revert to quadrupedal form, particularly when in a hurry.

Additional funding has been requested to continue these fascinating studies.

_____

*Ten at WIMP and five more earlier at the VitaBita Research Center.

September 9,1992

This just touches on the **ms** capabilities. For instance, we simply accepted the **ms** default values for many things, such as line width, lines per page, amount of indention, and the like. To go further, you'll have to burrow into the manuals yourself or buy an **nroff** reference. Be aware, however, that System V and BSD UNIX don't use the same macro packages.

Level 3: Naked `nroff`

On this level you are free to use the basic **nroff** requests as you want. Probably, the most profitable way would be to create your own set of macro definitions. However, note that the **mm** macro package can deal with most situations. Most typically, the basic **nroff** requests supplement the macro commands.

We haven't reached the end of the text formatter story yet. UNIX has two more utilities designed to work with **nroff** and **troff**.

Formatting Helpmates: `tbl` and `eqn`

Document preparation often involves putting together tables of data, and technical documents often use equations. The **tbl** and **eqn** programs use their own instruction set to convert descriptions of tables and equations into **nroff** and **troff** requests. We'll outline how to use them without going into detail.

Suppose that you're creating a table. You would include the material for the table between the **TS** (table start) and **TE** (table end) macros. The enclosed material would include the **tbl** instructions and the data to be used. Before and after this material would be the normal text of the document. Because **tbl** should act on the table before **nroff** reaches it, you could use a command like this, assuming the document in the file **Report**:

```
tbl Report ¦ nroff -ms
```

The **eqn** program is used similarly.

Summary

This chapter has taken you further into the world of text processing and filters. You've seen how **join**, **sed**, and **nroff** all stake out their own territory in the business of modifying and shaping text. Because these programs can be linked to each other and to other programs using pipes, they become tools that can be combined in numerous ways to accomplish a multitude of tasks. Suppose that you want to join two files and then replace the separating tabs with colons. The **join** command won't do that alone. But you can pipe **join**'s output to **sed**, thus using one program to do the joining and one to do the replacing.

So when you have a job to do, first ask yourself if there's a UNIX command that will do it. If the answer is no, ask if there's a combination of UNIX commands that will do the task. The more you learn about UNIX, the more likely it is that your answer will be yes.

Review Questions

1. Devise commands to do the following:

   a. Find the misspelled words in the `piffle` file.

   b. Join the sorted files `flip` and `flop` using the # character as a separator.

   c. Run `nroff` on the staid file, which contains `ms` macros.

2. Devise a `sed` command to do each of the following tasks to the file essay:

   a. Replace every instance of `Edgar` with `Elgar`.

   b. Print lines 10 through 15 of the file.

   c. Put every occurrence of `San Francisco Treat` in double quotes.

   d. Delete lines containing the sequences `ude` or `aked`.

Exercises

Experiment with some of the other `ms` macros.

CHAPTER 11

INFORMATION PROCESSING: GREP, FIND, AND AWK

You will learn about the following in this chapter:

- Searching files with grep
- Using find to find files
- Performing more complex sorts
- Understanding awk, in a nutshell

*I*n the cool confines of the Programming Division of Dray Conglomerate, Delia Delphond took off her softball cap and shook her auburn curls loose. She had just finished updating the statistical files for her softball team, the Byte Boomers. Now she copied the files for the other teams in the company league; it was her turn to prepare the league stats. First, she used **sort** to put together a league master file of batting statistics arranged alphabetically by player. Then, by using **sort**'s field-specification option, she created a file listing the players in descending order of batting averages. Next, again by using the field-specification **sort** option and piping it through **head -10**, she created files giving the top 10 players for each of several categories: home runs, RBIs, hits, runs, triples, doubles, walks, stolen bases, and strikeouts.

Curious about how her team was doing, she used **grep** to find Byte Boomers on the top 10 lists. Good, they were making a fine showing. The name D. Delphond, in particular, appeared in several lists. Smiling, she turned her attention to the team statistics. Using **awk**, she had UNIX sum up the at-bats, the hits, and so forth, for each team and calculate the team averages. Then she went on to handle the pitching stats.

Delia enjoyed going through the statistics, but she didn't care much for her next task—preparing a press summary for the company paper, *Draybits*. She'd much rather bat than write. However, with the help of a UNIX editor, she put together a blurb of rather irregular line length. She spell checked the file and corrected the errors that had shown up—words such as "avarage" and "notewordy." Next she invoked a shell script of hers that first sent the file through **nroff** to tidy it up and then forwarded the result through mail to the *Draybit*'s editor.

She leaned back in her chair and relaxed for a few moments. Not for too long, however, because she had her regular work to do, too. Besides being a nifty shortstop, Delia was a prolific C++ programmer. She had scattered her program files through several subdirectories, and now she decided to gather them in one place. She created a directory for that purpose and then set up a `find` command that would locate all her files with names ending in `p` and move them to the new directory.

Delia checked the time (using `date`, of course). It was time for her next project, the long-awaited salary raise! She put her cap on at a jaunty angle, picked up the analysis she had prepared using the UNIX system, and set off for the president's office; Dray wouldn't have a chance...

As you can tell from the preceding scenario, UNIX can be an important tool for information processing. So far, we have concentrated on the more basic operations for information processing. Now we will turn to a few UNIX commands and utilities that take you beyond the basics. Many of them are really useful only when you deal with large numbers of files and directories. (Both commands and utilities are programs run by UNIX. We use the word *utility* to indicate a program more elaborate than a command.) We will describe some of the simpler examples, such as `grep`, in detail. Others, such as the powerful `awk`, are rather extensive in scope and rules, and we will give them just a brief introduction.

Finding Stuff: `grep` and `find`

The `grep` and `find` commands are useful when you have to look through several files or directories to find a particular file entry or file. `grep` lets you find which files contain a particular word, name, phrase, and so forth. `find` lets you find files that satisfy some criterion of yours (a certain name, a certain suffix, not used for two months, and so on) and then lets you do something to those files (print the names, move them to another directory, remove them, and so on). We introduced `grep` in Chapter 7, "Manipulating Files and Directories: `mv`, `cp`, and `mkdir`." Now let's take a more complete look.

File Searching: `grep`

Sometimes, through necessity or curiosity, you may want to search one or more files for some form of information. For example, you may want to know which letter files contain references to the Wapoo Fruit Company. Or you may have a set of files constituting a large C program, and you want to know which ones use a certain function. Let's look at a simpler example using just one file. On most systems, there is a file called `/etc/passwd` that contains information about the system users. (See the following sidebar.) Suppose that you want to find out more about someone using the login name of `physh`, and your system doesn't have the finger command. Then you can have the `/etc/passwd` file searched for the word `physh`, and the line(s) containing that word will be printed. To do this, give the command

`grep physh /etc/passwd`

The response might look like the following:

```
physh:x:201:10:Physh Foreman:/home/physh:/bin/sh
```

This line from the `/etc/passwd` file is interpreted in the following sidebar; the important point is that the pattern of the command was

```
grep pattern filename
```

The `/etc/passwd` File

The UNIX system must keep track of who's allowed to use the system. It must also keep track of login names, group memberships, passwords, and user identification numbers. UNIX may want to know your phone number and, on multiple shell systems, which shell you use. All this information is kept in the /etc/passwd file. Let's look at the sample line used in the previous grep example and see how such a file can be set up:

```
physh:x:201:10:Physh Foreman:/home/physh:/bin/sh
```

The line is divided into seven fields, with each field separated from the adjoining fields by a colon (`:`).

- The first field contains the user's login name (**physh**).

- The second field contains either the user's password (**xKyUrR**) or a symbol such as **x** or **!**.

- The third field contains the user identification number (**201**).
- Next comes the user's group number (**10**).
- Then comes a comment field (**Physh Foreman**).
- The sixth field contains the user's home directory (**/home/physh**).
- The final field gives the user's login shell (**/bin/sh**).

As you can see, the basics of using **grep** are pretty simple. On the other hand, the following explanation will be a little lengthy. That's because we will describe some additional features of **grep** you may want to use.

More generally, **grep** is used as follows:

grep [*options*] *pattern* [*filename(s)*]

Let's look at each part of this form, starting with the *filename(s)* and working backward.

Filenames

You can have **grep** search one filename or several. When you use more than one filename, **grep** tags each line that it finds with the name of the file that the line was in. For example, if you type

grep dentistry boyd carson douglass ernst

the response might look like the following:

```
boyd: will be studying in the school of dentistry.
boyd: me luck in the pursuit of a career in dentistry and
boyd: your soon to be dentistry professional,
douglass: no clue where he studied dentistry and my tooth is still
```

Here, three lines containing **dentistry** were found in the **boyd** file, and one was found in the **douglass** file. None were found in the remaining files.

You can use wildcard substitution for filenames when using **grep**. Consider the commands

```
grep reverse *.c
```

and

```
grep Renaldo /usr/phoebe/*
```

The first would search for **reverse** in all files ending in **c** (that is, files written in C) in your current working directory. The second would search all files in the **/usr/phoebe** directory for **Renaldo**.

If you don't specify any filename with **grep**, it will look to the standard input.

Patterns

So far, we've used single words for the pattern. In general, the pattern can be a string or a limited form of a regular expression. A string is just a sequence of ordinary characters. All the examples that we've used so far for **grep** patterns are strings. A regular expression, on the other hand, may include characters with special meanings. For example, you will see that **grep** recognizes the pattern **b.g** as representing any three-character string beginning in **b** and ending in **g**. The pattern **b.g** is a regular expression, and the **.** in it is a special character playing much the same role that a **?** does when used in a shell command. Like the shell, **grep** recognizes certain regular expressions for patterns, but the rules it uses, as you will see later, aren't the ones used by the shell.

Strings merit a closer look because most of the time you use **grep**, you probably will use strings. If the string is only a single word, you can use it just as in the previous examples. But, what if you want to find something like Los Angeles? The command

```
grep Los Angeles cityfile
```

won't work, because **grep** will think that the pattern you sought was Los and that Angeles was the name of the first file to be searched. To avoid this confusion, you can place the pattern in single quotes—that is, use

```
grep 'Los Angeles' cityfile
```

and all will be well.

When **grep** looks for a string, it doesn't care whether it finds the string by itself or embedded in a larger string. For example, the command

```
grep man moon
```

will find not only the word **man** in the **moon** file but also such words as *woman*, *mantra*, and *command*, because they all contain the string **man**. Depending on which UNIX implementation you are working with, you may be able to use a **-w** option (whole words only) that picks up only lines that contain the pattern as an isolated word. If your system lacks that option, you might try putting spaces in the pattern, as in **' man '**, but that will fail to pick up lines in which **man** is the first or last word. It will also fail to pick up constructions such as **man.** or **man,** because these all lack one of the specified spaces. (Remember, a space is a character too.)

You may run into problems if the pattern string you use contains some of the special characters used by UNIX (for example, `*` or `?`) or by `grep` regular expressions (for example, `.` or `[`).

Sometimes, it's sufficient to enclose the pattern in single quotes. For instance, the command

`grep * froggy`

will confuse UNIX, but the command

`grep '*' froggy`

will cause the system to search the `froggy` file for lines containing an asterisk.

You also can use the backslash (\) to turn off the special meaning of a character, as described in Chapter 8, "The UNIX Shell: Command Lines, Redirection, and Shell Scripts":

`grep \? Dinnerreview`

By using the backslash, the question mark is escaped and treated literally. This command will use `grep` to search for a question mark in the file `Dinnerreview`. Without the backslash, the question mark would be expanded to any single character, which is not what we want.

Forms of Regular Expression

Now we can look at the forms of regular expressions recognized by `grep`. Basically, these forms (with some omissions) are the same as those used by `ed` and `ex`. The following is a rundown of the most important rules:

- A period (`.`) in a pattern stands for any one character. It plays the same role in `grep` patterns as the `?` does in UNIX shell wildcard substitution. Thus, the command

  `grep 'c.n' horply`

  will find such strings as *can* and *con*, but not *coin*, because *coin* has two characters, not one, between the c and the n.

- A string in brackets (that is, enclosed in `[]`) matches any one character in the string. (This is the same as the UNIX shell's use of brackets.) Thus, the pattern

  `[wW]easel`

  will match *weasel* or *Weasel*. You can use a hyphen to indicate a range of characters. For example,

  `[m-t]ap`

  would match the strings *map*, *nap*, and so forth, up to *tap*.

- Preceding a string in brackets with a caret (`^`) causes `grep` to make matches using the characters not in the list. For instance,

  `[^AM-t]ap`

  would match strings like *yap* and *zap*, but not strings like *map* and *tap*.

- A regular expression preceded by a `^` will match only those lines that begin with the expression. Thus, the command

```
grep '^James' jameslist
```

would find the first of the following lines and would skip the second:

```
James Watt
Henry James
```

- Similarly, a regular expression followed by a `$` will match only those lines with the expression at the end. Therefore,

```
grep 'James$' jameslist
```

would find *Henry James* but not *James Watt* in the preceding example.

Tip

You can use both the `^` and the `$` if you want to find only lines that match the pattern in their entirety. For example, the command

```
grep '^The King of Red Gulch$' oddfile
```

would find the line `The King of Red Gulch` and skip over the line `The King of Red Gulch sauntered over to Doc Buzzard's table.`

- A backslash (\) followed by any character other than a digit or parenthesis matches that character, turning off any special meaning that character might have. For instance, suppose you want to search a file for mentions of C++ programming files, which have names ending in `.c`. You can type

```
grep '\.c' ctext
```

If you omit the `\`, **grep** will interpret the period as described in the first rule in this list.

Options

The options for **grep** are indicated in the usual way by using flags. We have already mentioned the `-w` option. The following are some others that you may find useful:

- The `-n` option precedes each found line with its line number in the file. The following is a sample command and the response:

```
grep -n JavaScript JohnLetter

15:Reading about JavaScript a lot lately and I really like it.
17:So what do you think about JavaScript?
```

- The `-v` option causes **grep** to print those lines that don't match.

- The `-c` option prints a count of the number of lines that match but doesn't print the lines themselves. If you are searching several files, it prints the name of each file followed by the number of matching lines in that file.

- The `-i` option allows **grep** to return all lines that match without being case-sensitive. This very useful if you are looking for a string in a file that may have sentences beginning with *string* in which the first letter happens to be capitalized.

---

grep: Searches a File for a Pattern

Name	Options	Arguments
grep	[-n, -c, -v, -w]	*pattern filename(s)*

Description: The grep command searches the named files for lines containing the given pattern and then prints the matching lines. If more than one file is searched, the name of the file containing each line is printed too. If no filename is given, grep looks to the standard input; thus, grep can be used with pipes. The pattern can be a single string, or it can be a limited form of regular expression as described in the text. A pattern containing spaces or special characters, such as *, should be set off by single quotes. Normally, grep will match any string containing the pattern—for example, hose matches whose.

Options:

-n	Precedes each matching line with its line number
-c	Prints only a count of matching lines
-v	All lines but those matching are printed
-w	Finds only complete words
-i	Ignores case-sensitivity

Example: The following command searches the files **peter** and **bugs** for occurrences of the string **hop**. It prints the matching lines along with line numbers.

```
grep -n hop peter bugs
```

Finding Files: find

The find command searches for files that meet some criterion. You can search for files that have a certain name, files of a certain size, files not accessed for a certain number of days, or files having a certain number of links, and this is just a partial list. Once the files are found, you can have the pathnames printed, and you can have the files themselves printed or removed or otherwise acted on. The search will begin at the directory you specify and will then descend through all its subdirectories and all their subdirectories, and so forth, leaving no nook or cranny unexplored (except, of course, for forbidden nooks and crannies). A branching search such as this is termed *recursive*.

It would be difficult to fit the capabilities of the find command into the usual format for commands, so find has its own unique structure. The basic sequence is as follows:

```
find directory_pathname search_criterion action
```

The *directory_pathname* is the pathname of the directory that will be recursively searched (all subdirectories, and so on) for the desired files. The *search_criterion* identifies the files that are sought. The *action* tells what to do with the files once they are found.

The following is an example of a `find` command:

```
find /usr -name calendar -print
```

The directory pathname is `/usr`, so the search starts here and proceeds recursively through all directories branching off this directory. The search criterion is `-name calendar`; this means that UNIX will search for files bearing the name `calendar`. Finally, the action is `-print`, meaning that each time a file is found that meets the search criterion, its pathname is displayed. The output might look like the following:

```
/usr/flossy/calendar
/usr/nark/calendar
```

This output would tell us which users were using UNIX's `calendar` feature.

Naming the directory is straightforward, but the search criteria and action sections need further discussion.

Search Criteria

The `find` command recognizes several search criteria. They take the form of an identifying flag word (a hyphen joined to a word—for example, `-name`) followed by a space and a word or number. The following are the more common ones:

- *Finding a file by name*—Use the `-name` flag followed by the desired name. The name can be a simple word, as in the preceding example, or it can use the shell wildcard substitutions: `[ ]`, `?` and `*`. If you use these special symbols, place the name in single quotes. The following are some examples of acceptable uses:

Criterion	Files Sought
`-name nail`	Files named `nail`
`-name '*.c'`	All files whose names end in `.c`
`-name '*.?'`	All files for which the next-to-last character is a period

- *Finding a file by last access*—Use the `-atime` flag followed by the number of days since the file was last accessed. Plus and minus signs can be used to indicate greater than or less than.

Criterion	Files Sought
`-atime 7`	Files last accessed exactly 7 days ago
`-atime -14`	Files accessed more recently than 14 days ago

- *Finding a file by last modification*—Use the `-mtime` flag followed by the number of days since the file was last modified. Plus and minus signs can be used to indicate greater than or less than.

Criterion	Files Sought
`-mtime 20`	Files last modified 20 days ago
`-mtime +45`	Files modified more than 45 days ago

- *Finding files modified more recently than a given file*—Use the `-newer` flag followed by the name of a file.

Criterion	Files Sought
`-newer slopware`	Files modified more recently than `slopware` was

- *Finding files based on who owns the file*—Use the `-user` flag followed by the account name of the user whose files you are looking for.

Criterion	Files Sought
`-user physh`	Files that the `physh` user owns

Actions

For the action section of the command, you can choose from three flag options:

- The `-print` option prints the pathname for every file found that matches the criterion. On many systems, such as Sun Solaris, the `-print` option is assumed if you don't provide an action option.

- The `-exec` option allows you to give a command to be applied to the found files. The command should follow the flag and should be terminated with a space, a backslash, and then a semicolon. Braces (`{}`) can be used to represent the name of the files found. For example,

```
find . -atime +100 -exec rm {} \;
```

would find and remove all files in your current directory (and its offshoots) that haven't been used in more than 100 days. The braces are essentially taking the list generated by the first part of the command and substituting them into the **exec** command one at a time. This type of list expansion could be achieved through shell programming, but the braces save this effort.

- The `-ok` option is just like the `-exec` option except that it asks for your "ok" for each file found before it executes the command. For instance, if you gave the command

```
find . -atime +100 -ok rm {} \;
```

and the system found a file called `first.prog` that satisfied the criterion, the system would then query you:

```
< rm ... ./first.prog >?
```

If you reply with the letter **y**, the command is executed; otherwise it's not. A command along the lines of this example is a handy aid in cleaning up your file systems.

For Advanced Users: More Complex Forms of `find`

You can expand each of the basic sections of the `find` command to pinpoint more exactly what you want done.

The Directory Pathname

You actually can give a list of directories to be searched. For instance,

```
find /usr/lester /usr/festus . -name '*.pl' -print
```

would search **lester**'s home directory, **festus**'s home directory, and your current directory for files whose names end in `.pl` and would then print the pathnames of those files.

Primaries

The search criteria we have given are called *primaries*. You can combine them or act on them in the following three basic ways:

- The **!** operator negates a primary. It should precede the primary and should be isolated by spaces on either side.

Criterion	Meaning
-newer fops	Files revised more recently than fops
! -newer fops	Files not revised more recently than fops
! -name '*.c'	Files whose names don't end in c

- Listing two or more criteria in a row causes `find` to seek those files that simultaneously satisfy all criteria.

Criteria	Meaning
-name calender -size +2	Files named calendar having a size greater than two blocks
-size +2 -size -6	Files whose size is greater than two disk blocks and less than six disk blocks (block sizes depend on the version of UNIX but generally are either 0.5KB or 1KB)

- Separating two criteria with an `-o` flag (a space on either side) causes `find` to search for files that satisfy one or the other criterion.

Criteria	Meaning
`-name turk -o -name terk`	Files named `turk` or `terk`
`-atime +7 -o -mtime +14`	Files that haven't been accessed within 7 days or modified within 14 days

---

`find`: Searches Designated Files and Acts on Them

Name	Options	Arguments

find	None	`directory_pathname(s)`
		 `search_criteria`
		 `action(s)`

Description: The `find` command searches the named directories recursively for files matching the specified criteria. It then performs the specified actions on the files.

Search Criteria: In the following list, *n* represents a decimal integer. It can be given with or without a sign. With no sign, it means *n* exactly; +*n* means greater than *n*, and -*n* means less than *n*.

`-name filename`	Files named `filename`
`-size n`	Files of size *n* blocks
`-links n`	Files with *n* links
`-atime n`	Files accessed *n* days ago
`-mtime n`	Files modified *n* days ago
`-newer filename`	Files modified more recently than the file `filename`

Actions:

`-print`	Print the pathnames of the found files
`-exec command {} \;`	Executes the given command on finding a file; the braces (`{}`) represent the found file
`-ok command \;`	Same as `-exec`, except that your approval is requested before each execution; reply with a `y` to have the command executed

Note: There's a procedure for combining criteria. A ! before a criterion negates it. Giving two or more criteria means that all must be satisfied by the file. Separating two criteria by an -o (isolated by spaces) means one or the other. Escaped parentheses or beginning and ending back slashes (\ and \) can be used to clarify groupings.

Examples: This command searches through the current directory and all its offshoots for a file named `boobtube`:

```
find . -name boobtube -print
```

The following command finds all files in the current working directory (and its offshoots, and their offshoots, and so on) that have been used within 60 days but not within 30 days. These files then are moved to the directory `./old`.

```
find . -atime +30 -atime -60 -exec mv {} ./old \;
```

Revisiting sort: Using Fields

In Chapter 8, you saw that **sort** sorts files on the basis of the beginning of each line. This is useful, for example, if you have a mailing list in which people are listed last name first. But you might want to sort that same list on the basis of city or state. You can do that, providing you have set up your file accordingly. The key is to break each line into fields. As you will see, you can instruct **sort** to look only at certain fields when sorting. Thus, you can set up the file so that last names are in the first field and states in, say, the sixth field. Having the file sorted by the sixth field would then sort the file by state.

Fields and Field Separators

What makes up a field is a matter of definition. If you don't specify differently, fields are nonempty, nonblank strings separated by blanks. (A blank is a space or a tab.) For example, in Figure 11.1 the first field in the line is `McHaggis`, the fifth field is `Drive`, and the last field is `94889`.

FIGURE 11.1

Fields in a line.

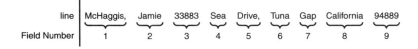

For some types of files, the blank is a fine field separator, but not for a mailing list. The reason is that a metropolis such as "Hogback" uses one field, but a town like "San Luis Obispo" uses three fields, and this would throw off the numbering of the field containing the state (see Figure 11.2).

FIGURE 11.2

The problem that occurs when a blank is used as a field separator.

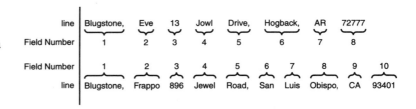

To get around this sort of problem, you can choose your own field separator. A common choice is the colon (Figure 11.3). You could make a file entry look like the following:

```
McHaggis:Jamie::33883 Sea Drive:Tuna Gap:California:94888
```

FIGURE 11.3

Using a colon as a field separator.

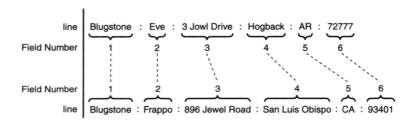

In this case, the first field is the last name, the second field is the first name, the third field (empty) is the middle name or initial, the fourth field is the street address, the fifth field is the city, and so on.

Note

A field now can have spaces within it, as the fourth field does in `McHaggis:Jamie::33883 Sea Drive:Tuna Gap:California:94888`, or it can be empty, as is the third field. The value of the empty field is that it's a placeholder; even though a middle name is missing in this case, the address is still in the fourth field. Also notice that we haven't left any spaces at the beginnings or ends of the fields. This, as you may remember, is because a space itself is a character. Therefore, `: Wickley :` is a field containing nine characters (the first and last being the space character), and it would be sorted differently from the seven-character field `:Wickley:`. The `-b` option of **sort** would ignore leading blanks but not the trailing blanks in a field, so it's simpler to just leave out extra blanks in the first place. Of course, there is another possibility: you also could carefully use the exact same number of blanks for each entry.

Using Fields with sort

But how does **sort** know to use a colon instead of a blank as a field separator? You have to use the `-t` option to tell it so. When you use this option, you follow the `-t` with the symbol that is to be the field separator. The symbol follows the **t** directly with no spaces. Thus, to use the colon as a separator, you would use `-t:` as the flag.

Next, how do you tell **sort** which fields to use? You include a flag consisting of a plus sign followed by a number. This tells **sort** how many fields to skip. For example, the command

```
sort -t: +4 maillist
```

tells **sort** to recognize colons as a field separator and to skip four fields before comparing lines in the **maillist** file. The comparison thus will start with the fifth field, which, in the preceding address example, corresponds to the city, and will proceed to the end of the line.

When you run the previous command, suppose that two lines are identical from the fifth field onward to the end of the line. How does **sort** decide to arrange these two lines? It bases the **sort** on the complete line. A definite example will help clarify this and later points, so let's suppose that **maillist** contains the following entries:

```
Paswater:Angie::7272 Dependeau Lane:Indianapolis:Indiana:46237
Carlisle:Erica::4357 Howard Lane:Indianapolis:Indiana:46237
```

Then the result of **sort -t: +4 maillist** is

```
Carlisle:Erica::4357 Howard Lane:Indianapolis:Indiana:46237
Paswater:Angie::7272 Dependeau Lane:Indianapolis:Indiana:46237
```

The two lines in the sorted list have the same city, state, and ZIP code, so the tie was decided by looking at the rest of the line and, alphabetically, Carlisle precedes Paswater.

You also can tell **sort** where to stop the comparison by using a flag consisting of a minus sign followed by a number. This tells **sort** to stop at the end of the numbered field. Thus,

```
sort -t: +4 -6 maillist
```

would mean to sort the file based on the fifth and sixth fields. If two or more lines have identical fifth and sixth fields, they are sorted further based on the whole line as before.

Multiple Fields

With **sort**, you can create your own sorting scheme by using multiple fields. The **sort** command will first sort the file using the first field pattern you give it.

Then, within a block of lines that are identical for those fields, it will sort further using the next field pattern you give. For example, consider the following command:

```
sort -t: +0 -1 +5 maillist
```

The first field pattern is **+0 -1**, which is simply the first field—in this case, the last name. So, first, the file is sorted by last name. The second field pattern is **+5**, which means field six to the end of the line. (Whenever a plus (+) field option is given without a minus (-) field option, the pattern comparison goes to the end of the line.) In this case, the second pattern corresponds to state and ZIP code. Thus, all those address lines containing the same last name are further sorted on the basis of state and ZIP code. This command would yield

```
Carlisle:James::6345 East Burn Ave.:Los Angeles:California:92832
Carlisle:Mike::5821 Citation Blvd.:Milpitas:California:92838
Carlisle:Erica::4357 Howard Lane:Indianapolis:Indiana:46237
```

Notice how the various Carlisles are arranged in order of state, not city.

On the other hand, the command

```
sort -t: +5 -6 +1 maillist
```

sorts the file first by state. Then those with the same state would be sorted by field two (first name) to the end.

To repeat the main point of this section, when you give a series of field ranges by which to sort, the initial sorting is done according to the first range. Then any ties are resolved by the next range, and so on. Any remaining ties are resolved by looking at the whole line; **sort** always has a reason for putting lines where it does.

Subdividing a Field

You can refine the sorting process even further. Within each field, you can have **sort** skip a certain number of characters. This is done by adding a decimal point to the field number and following it with the number of characters to be skipped. For example,

```
sort +2.3 inventory
```

would skip the first two fields and three characters when sorting the file **inventory**—that is, it would start at the fourth character of the third field.

Flag Options and Fields

Several **sort** options discussed in Chapter 7 can be applied globally or just for certain fields. The choice is controlled by the placement of the option letter. Consider the following commands:

```
sort -r +4 -5 somefile
sort +4r -5 somefile
```

In the first command, the r (reverse) option is invoked universally. Lines will be in reverse order on the basis of field five, and ties will be resolved by applying reverse order to the whole line. In the second command, the r option applies only to the initial ordering using field five; ties are resolved by applying normal order to the whole line. If a field locator option has any additional options appended, all global options are overridden for that field. That is, if the instruction is

```
sort -n +4 -5 +6r somefile
```

the -n option will apply to field five but not to field seven. (Remember, the **+6** means to skip six fields, so the r option will begin with field seven.)

Of the **sort** options discussed in Chapter 7, the following options can be used but are limited to a field: b, d, f, n, and r. The method is (as in the preceding discussion) to append the letter to the field number.

The **sort** command is so flexible and has so many options that you should be able to tackle almost any sorting problem except, perhaps, multiple-line records (where the information for each entry is spread over more than one line) and your laundry.

	sort: Sorts Files	
Name	Options	Arguments
sort	[-tc, -b, +*n*.m, -*n*.m]	[*filename(s)*]

Description: The **sort** command, used with its options, allows you to sort files on the basis of chosen fields within a line.

Options:

-tc the	Sets the field separator to be the character c. (A blank is default.)
-b	Ignores leading blanks when comparing fields.
+n.m	Skips *n* fields and then *m* characters before beginning comparisons. A +n is the same as +*n*.0.
+n.m and -n.m	Stops comparison after skipping n fields from the beginning plus *m* characters. A -n is the same as *n*.0.

Notes: The b, d, f, n, and r options can be appended to the field locator flags; this causes the option to apply to just that field. Options appearing before the field locators apply globally, except that all global flags are turned off for fields with a local flag.

If multiple fields are specified, sorting is done by the first field given. Lines in which those fields are identical are then sorted by the second specified field, and so forth. Remaining ties are resolved by looking at the whole line.

Example: In the following command, the field separator is declared to be a colon. The file **sauerbrot** is sorted in reverse order by field three. Lines having the same field three are further sorted numerically by the sixth field to the end of the line; the numerical sorting isn't in reverse order. Lines identical to this point are then sorted on the basis of the whole line, again using reverse order.

```
sort -t: -r +2 -3 +5n sauerbrot
```

A Quick Peek at awk

Suppose that you have a file in which the first column is the name of an item, the second column is its price, and the third column is the number sold. You want to add a fourth column giving the money value of the sales, but you don't want to make the calculation yourself. (Why get a computer if you have to do the work yourself?) Can you get UNIX to help? You have a file of names, debts, and last payment dates. You want to create a file containing information about everyone who owes more than $50 and hasn't paid in two months. Can UNIX help you? The answer to both questions (surprise!) is yes, providing you know how to use **awk**.

The **awk** program was created by Alfred Aho, Brian Kernighan, and Peter Weinberger of Bell Labs. Some suspect an awkward connection between the name of the utility and the names of the authors. In any case, **awk** is one of the most interesting of the UNIX utilities, and although we don't have space here to explain it completely, we wanted to give you an idea of what it can do and how it works.

In UNIX-speak, **awk** is a pattern scanning and processing language. *Pattern scanning* means that awk can look through a file for certain patterns. In this, it is like **grep**, except that **awk** is both more general (the patterns can be rather sophisticated) and more specific (the patterns can be limited to particular fields within a line). *Processing* means that once **awk** finds an appropriate line, it can do something with it—for example, print it, change it, or sum numbers in it.

One important use of **awk** is as a file processor. Given a file consisting of three columns of numbers, for example, **awk** can produce a new file consisting of the original three columns plus a fourth that is the arithmetic product of, say, the first two columns. Indeed, **awk** can do many of the same things that a spreadsheet program can. The **awk** command works with text as well as numbers. For example, a simple **awk** program can scan an address list and print those people who live on a certain street. (The **grep** command could do something similar, but grep would be fooled by entries containing people with the same name as the desired street.)

There are two methods of using **awk**. One method is to type something in the form

awk *program* *filename*

where *program* consists of the instructions and *filename* is the name of the file **awk** is to act on. The second method is to type

awk -f *file* *filename*

where *file* is the name of the file containing the program instructions. This second method is, perhaps, a bit more difficult, but it's much less likely to produce syntax error messages when you use symbols in the program that also have special meaning to the shell. We will confine our examples to the second method.

A program consists of one or more program lines. A program line consists in general of two parts: a pattern and an action enclosed in braces. The following is one possible line:

`/rotate/ {print}`

The pattern is **rotate** (simple string patterns are enclosed in slashes) and the action is **print**. Using this, the **awk** program finds lines containing the string **rotate** and prints them; it's equivalent to using **grep** *rotatefilename*.

Learning to use **awk** consists of learning the many possibilities for defining patterns and learning the possible actions.

Note

Actually, the **print** action isn't needed here because a line that matches a pattern is printed automatically if you omit giving any action. Also, if you give an action without a pattern, that action is performed on all lines.

We won't go into the many pattern-defining options, but we will let you in on the secret of using fields. Fields are defined as they are for sort—that is, fields are strings separated by blanks. Again, as in sort, you can choose some other character to be a field separator, but the method of doing so is different. (One way is to use the -F option followed immediately—with no spaces—by the chosen character.)

The awk program has a labeling system for fields: $1 is the first field, $2 is the second field, and so forth. The label $0 has a special meaning; it stands for the entire line. These field labels can be used in patterns and actions both. The following are some examples:

Pattern	Meaning
/fish/	Any line containing the string fish
$1 ~/fish/	Any line whose first field contains the string fish
$3 ~/fish/	Any line whose third field contains the string fish
$1 !~/fish/	Any line whose first field doesn't contain the string fish

Action	Meaning
{print $2}	Print only the second field
{print $4,$2}	Print the fourth field and then the second field
{s=$2+$4;print s}	Add the second and fourth fields, and print the sum

Notice the use of ~ and ! in the patterns. The tilde (~) means that the pattern to the right is contained in the field to the left. The !~ combination means that the pattern to the right isn't contained in the field to the left. Also note that the print instruction can be used with individual fields and with combinations of fields.

You can do arithmetic in the action parts: + is addition, - is subtraction, * is multiplication, and / is division. You can include more than one action by separating them with a semicolon, as in the preceding example.

Let's look at a simple example using some of these ideas. The file sales contains six columns of information. The first column is the name of an item, the second column is the selling price of the item, and the next four columns are quarterly sales figures for the item. (This is such a simple example that the prices remain constant for a year.) The file looks like the following:

```
TV       595.00   178500.00   206465.00   177310.00   224317.00
VCR      237.00    94800.00    91956.00    47400.00   108309.00
STEREO   399.00   100947.00   159600.00   134463.00   164388.00
DRYER    789.00   199617.00   315600.00   265893.00   325068.00
WASHER   890.00   225170.00   356000.00   299930.00   366780.00
```

We want to add two more columns: total items sold and total cash sales. We create a file called, say, addup that looks like the following:

```
{total=$3+$4+$5+$6; print $0, total, total*$2}
```

This action contains two parts separated by a semicolon. The first part sums the sales and cleverly calls the total **total**. The second part prints the original line (**$0**), followed by the total, and then **total*$2**, which means "total" times the second column.

The command

```
awk -f addup sales
```

produces the following output:

```
TV       595     178      206465   177310   224317 608270 361920650
VCR      237     94       91956    47       108309 200406 47496222
STEREO   399     947      159      134463   164388 299957 119682843
DRYER    789     199617   315      265893   325068 790893 624014577
WASHER   890     225170   350      299930   366780 892230 794084700
```

You could save the output in a file called **sumsales** by using redirection:

```
awk -f addup sales > sumsales
```

This introduction just scratches the surface of **awk**. The online manual has a concise summary of **awk**, but the classic Bell Labs publication "Awk—A Pattern Scanning and Processing" Language (also published in the Support Tools Guide), by A.V. Aho, B.W. Kernighan, and P.J. Weinberger, is easier to read and much more informative. It's also much longer.

Summary

In this chapter you've seen a lot of advanced features of UNIX that you will find useful. The **grep** command is very handy when you want to find a file that contains a particular string. We've all saved a document and then can't remember what we called the one with a particular name or sentence in it; **grep** finds it quickly. You've also seen **awk**, one of the most useful pattern-matching tools available in UNIX. When you combine **awk** with shell scripts, you have an amazingly powerful programming language.

Review Questions

Using grep to Match Patterns

For each **grep** pattern on the left, indicate which pattern(s) following it would be matched:

1. 'to'   a. hot   b. to   c. toad   d. stool   e. Top

2. 't.n'   a. tin   b. stun   c. nation   d. stony   e. tnuch

3. 'a[o-t]'   a. art   b. act   c. task   d. tort   e. at

Using `find`

Describe what each of the following `find` commands would do:

1. `find $HOME -name '*.c' -exec mv {} $HOME/cdirect \;`

2. `find . -name '*.c' -size +3 -ok rm {}\;`

3. `find /usr \(-size +10 -atime +20 \) -o -size +30 -print`

Questions

The following questions all refer to a file named `maillist`, whose contents are

```
Morgan:Joe::315 Second Street:Riesenstadt:CA:94707
Vegetable:Joe:Fritz:1002 Market Pl.:Riesenstadt:CA:94707
Morgan:Joe::315 Second Street:Redville:OH:40817
Morgan:Joe::315 Second Street:Hot'n'wet:TX:72727
Antibody:Aristotle:Asis:26 Furtz Way:Redville:OH:40822
Zircon:Bilbo:Nagy:1313 Ratgut Blvd.:Hot'n'wet:TX:72702
```

1. What order would each of the following commands produce?

   a. `sort -t: +3n -4 +6n maillist`

   b. `sort -t: +3n -4 +6nr maillist`

   c. `sort -t: +6.3n maillist`

2. What instruction will sort `maillist` by state, and then by city within state, and then by name within city?

Exercises

1. Duplicate as many features as you can of those described in the introductory story.

2. Write an **awk** command that sums fields 2 through 5 on a line and computes their average.

CHAPTER 12

ADVANCED EDITING TECHNIQUES

You will learn about the following in this chapter:

- Extending your editing abilities with vi
- Using the search-and-replace capabilities
- Using yank buffers

- Running shell commands from inside v
- Customizing your vi editor's behavior

After you become comfortable with the vi editor, you may want to add more editing power to your repertoire. In this chapter we'll assume that you are editing with vi. The following are some of the advanced features available with vi:

- Repeat or undo the last command.

- Use abbreviations for faster typing.

- Create command macros for repetitive changes.

- Edit multiple files.

- Run shell commands while in the editor.

- Use advanced search and replacement commands.

- Customize vi to fit your requirements and needs.

Most of these features come directly from the ex editor. Because vi is part of ex, vi may access all ex commands. You must be in vi and in command mode to execute any of the ex commands. Press the colon and at the bottom of the page a colon prompt (:) will appear.

Some vi commands have already been described: w, :wq, and :q!. Most vi commands (except those just mentioned) return you to the vi editor's command mode following execution.

The Last Command

One handy `vi` feature is the ability to repeat or undo the last command executed. Just as the undo command (u), described in Chapter 5, will undo the last text change, the dot command (.) will repeat the last text modification. The dot command can be used to repeat insertions, deletions, and changes.

The following example shows the undo and dot commands in use in an editor buffer. The file itself won't be shown, only the sequence of commands. The dot command is used to repeat a deletion, and then we use the u command to undo the last dot command.

j	Move the cursor down to a specific line
3dd	Delete three lines
j	Move the cursor down to another line
.	Repeat last text change, deleting three lines
u	Undo last text change; restore three lines

The next example demonstrates a more powerful use of the dot command with the search operator (/). In this example, the search operator is used to find the word **country**, and then we change the word to **County**. The n operator repeats the search (as described in Chapter 5, "The `vi` Screen Editor,") and the dot command repeats the correction.

/country	Find the next occurrence of country
country	Cursor is on the c in country
cw<Esc>County	Type **cw** and then press Esc to change word; then retype word correctly
n	Find next country
.	Repeat last text change—make country **County**
n	Find next country
.	Repeat text change

These shortcuts for repeating the last command are great for making identical changes to a file. It's not necessary to use the dot command after each operator. If there's a **country** that you want to leave unchanged, just type n to continue searching.

Using Abbreviations for Faster Typing

This section uses the word *abbreviation* several times. We've simplified our typing requirements by creating an abbreviation for the word *abbreviation*. Here are some examples given from command mode:

```
:ab abb abbreviation
:ab mse math, science, and engineering
:ab lo longing for you
:ab word rhs
```

The last example shows the general form of the command. After the command `:ab`, enter the abbreviation or word and what it stands for. Abbreviations are used only in `vi`'s text input mode. As you type, just enter the abbreviation (`lo`, `mse`, or `abb`) followed by a space. The `vi` editor expands `lo` to `longing for you`, and so forth. If you type `lo` as part of a word—say, "long, low, and sleek"—no substitution is made because there's no space after `lo`.

To remove an abbreviation or to see which abbreviations have been created, use these two commands:

`:una word` (to unabbreviate word)

`:ab` (to see which abbreviations are set)

Abbreviations given while in `vi` are temporary only for the duration of that `vi` session. Abbreviations may be made permanent by placing them either in the `.exrc` file in your HOME directory or in a local directory, as described later.

Using the `map` Command to Create Macros

When you start up the `vi` editor, you enter command mode. The `vi` editor has dozens of commands available, such as `h` and `k`. These commands are used for movement and positioning so that file modifications are possible.

The `map` command can be used to save command sequences for repeated use. Just as abbreviations give you a shorthand in input mode, `map` macros give you a shorthand in command mode. The `map` command has a format similar to the abbreviation command:

`:map [x] [editing_commands]`

One difference between the two commands is that the *x* of the map command is limited to specific single characters. The following is a list of keys available for use in defining `map` keys:

- Symbols available: `_ * \ =`

- Characters available: `K V q g v`

- Control keys available: Ctrl-a, Ctrl-k, Ctrl-o, Ctrl-t, Ctrl-w, Ctrl-x

So few characters are available as `map` symbols because `vi` uses for commands most of the letters, symbols, and control characters on the keyboard. On some terminals, the *x* may be set to a function key with the sequence *#n*, where *n* refers to the function key number. You can use any key if you are willing to forfeit its normal command mode use. A good reason for you to become familiar with `vi`'s functionality is to determine what key(s) can be surrendered to increase your `map` capabilities.

To the right of a `map` macro are command-mode commands. These commands can include cursor positioning, insertions, changes, and deletions. To include an Esc or Return in the macro, press Ctrl-v, which serves as an escape sequence to turn off the special meaning of the character that follows. Here are some examples of `map` commands given from `vi`'s command mode:

- Replace the character under the cursor with the letter G:

  `:map q rG`

- Place **AA** at the start and end of a sentence (note that a comma (,) is used as the delimiter in the command):

  `:map v :s, .*; AA & AA; ^M`

- This complicated `map` macro does simple text formatting by inserting Return before the first word following the 67th character on a line:

  `:map ^ 067lwi<Ctrl-v><Return><Ctrl-v><Esc>`

  The initial zero (**0**) sets the cursor to the beginning of the line. The **67l** uses the letter l key to move the cursor 67 spaces to the right. The **w** key moves to the beginning of the next word, and then we insert an **i**, a Return, and an Esc.

The best way to create a `map` macro is to do the editing once manually, write down the keystroke sequence, and then enter the `map` command. Remember, you can always undo or repeat the last command given, which includes `map` macros. Maps created while in `vi` are temporary only for the duration of that `vi` session. To make maps permanent, place them either in the `.exrc` file in your `HOME` directory or in a local directory, as described later.

Editing Multiple Files

The `vi` editor lets you edit more than one file during an editing session. Editing multiple files has three major advantages:

- It's much faster to start the `vi` editor once rather than several times.

- Abbreviations and `map` macros created temporarily while in `vi` can be used for several files.

- You can yank and store lines from one file for insertion into a second or a third file.

Multiple files to be edited are called sequentially; the editor works on one file at a time. Before going to the next file, changes should be saved with the `:w` command.

There are two ways to edit multiple files. One method is to start `vi` on one file and then call in a second file with the `:e` or `:r` command. The second method is to list all the files to be edited when starting `vi` (we'll describe this first). To edit multiple files at the beginning of an editing job, give the command

```
$ vi file1 file2 file3
```

to edit the three named files or

```
$ vi ch*
```

to edit all files beginning with `ch`. The `vi` editor responds by telling you how many files are to be edited, and then displays the first file for editing. After you make your changes, type `:w` to write the changes and then type `:n` to display the next file as shown here:

`$ vi file1 file2 file3`	Edit these three files
`3 files to edit`	vi responds
`"file1" 12 lines, 456 characters`	
`cw, etc`	Enter changes in the first file
`:w`	Save changes by writing
`"file1" [Modified] 13 lines 512 characters`	
`:n`	Go to the next file
`"file2" 45 lines, 2014 characters`	
`cw, etc`	Enter changes in the second file
`:w`	Save changes by writing
`"file2" [Modified] 43 lines, 1977 characters`	
`:n`	Go to the next file
`"file3" 6 lines, 289 characters`	
`:wq`	Write and quit the editor
`"file3" [Modified] 6 lines, 289 characters`	
`%`	The shell prompt

Another way to edit multiple files is to call in a new file by using the `:e` command while still in `vi`. Here's an example in which we call in a second file, yank eight lines, and put them into the first file. We'll assume that we are editing a file called `chapter4`:

`:w`	Write changes to the first file
`"chapter4" [Modified] 987 lines, 23078 characters`	
`:e appendix`	Call in new file
`"appendix" 98 lines, 4555 characters`	
`8H`	Move to 8th line from top of screen
`"a5yy`	Yank five lines and store in buffer **a**
`:e chapter4`	Return to first file
`44G`	Go to line 44
`"ap`	Put contents of buffer **a** following cursor
`:wq`	Write and quit
`"chapter4" [Modified] 995 lines, 23478 characters`	

When using the `:e` command, you can give the abbreviation `:e#` (using the pound symbol) to switch back to the other file. Remember to *save before you switch*. You must save the file with `:w` before switching to another file, unless you have made no changes; otherwise, you'll lose all your changes.

In addition to editing a second or third file, the `vi` editor lets you read a file into the current editor by using the `:r` command. The command, given while in `vi`'s command mode, looks like this:

`:r filename`

The `:r` command places the named file into the editor at the cursor's location. Using the `:r` command like this isn't really editing two files; the `:r` command involves placing a copy of the second file into the editor buffer where it can be edited as part of the first file. (No change is made to the original of the second file.)

Running Shell Commands

The shell command-line interpreter is a powerful programming language. The `vi` editor provides four ways to use the shell while in the editor. You can

- Run a shell command.
- Temporarily escape to the shell.
- Read in the results of shell commands.
- Filter text through a shell command.

Most of these "escapes" to the shell start with a colon and an exclamation mark as shown here:

`:!ls`	Runs the command `ls` to list files
`:!who`	Runs the command `who`

After the command is run, you are returned to the `vi` editor. If you want to run more than one command, you can create a shell with the command

`:sh`	Create a shell
`%`	Shell prompt
`<Ctrl-d>`	Leave the shell and return to the editor

If you want to read in the results of a shell command, use the command combination `:r` and `!` like this:

`:r !who`	Read in a `who` listing into the buffer
`:r !cal 1 1999`	Read the month of January 1999 into the buffer
`:w`	Write buffer to file being edited before spelling check
`:r !spell filename`	List all misspelled words in file

The last two lines show how to write the `vi` buffer contents to a file and then run the file through a spelling checker. (The **spell** command is optional on UNIX, so this example will work only if you have it on your system.) All misspelled words are listed in the file for handy reference. After correcting misspelled words, you would delete this listing.

In addition to reading the results of a shell command into the current editing buffer, you can write parts of the editing buffer to a shell command—for example,

`:w !sort`

runs the command **sort** with the current editing buffer as input. Output of the command goes to the terminal, not to a file.

Note

The current editing buffer remains as it was before the command. Later you will learn how to replace the current editing buffer with the results of the shell command.

Writing the editing buffer to a shell command is useful for getting information about the file you're editing (with your modifications) without having to save the buffer first. For example,

`:w !wc -lw`

runs the command **wc** to find out how many lines and words are in the current editor buffer, and

`:.w !spell`

runs the spelling checker on the current line (line dot). This is useful for quickly checking the spelling of one or more words on the current line.

You can also filter lines of text in the **vi** buffer through a shell command. The most common commands used for filtering are **sort** and **nroff**, both described in Chapters 9 and 10. Here are several examples of their use:

`:7!! sort`	Sort seven lines including the current line.
`:!7! sort`	Sort seven lines including the current line. The second ! is a special text object that designates the use of the current line.
`:5,10!nroff`	Format lines 5 to 10 with **nroff**.
`:5)!nroff -ms`	Format the next five sentences, starting with the current line, with **nroff**'s **ms** option. The) states that the unit of work will be accomplished on a sentence. Other options could be a word, character or number of characters.
`:!)!tr '[a-e]' '[A-E]'`	Change all lowercase a through e to uppercase. The) states that the unit of work will be accomplished on a sentence.

If a file gets messed up beyond the last command, there are two forceful ways of undoing changes that involve returning to the original file:

- Give the command **q!** to quit the editor without writing.

- Give the command **e!** to re-enter the original file into the buffer, eliminating all changes made since the last write (`:w`).

Using Advanced Search-and-Replace Commands

One earmark of a powerful editor is the capability to conduct both large-scale and detailed search-and-replace operations. There are two general approaches to searching with the **vi** editor. One approach is to use the **vi** search operators, **/** and **?**, to find patterns. The other approach is to use the search format *:nm/pattern/* to find lines and patterns on lines. We'll begin this section by describing the search format.

The key to the search capability lies in the address part of the command format, as shown here:

`:address/command/parameter`

The *address* can have two parts—lines and patterns—as shown in the following examples:

- For lines one to seven, find the first occurrence of **man** and substitute for that word (**s//**) the word **person**:

  `:1,7/man /s//person /`

Tip

The space following **man** in the preceding example is used to avoid matching up *man* within words such as in *mandate*.

- Often, we are interested in searching all lines and finding all occurrences:

  `:g/man /s//person /g`

The first global (**g**) searches all lines, whereas the last global means to apply the substitution to all occurrences on a line.

Caution

Global replacements occur throughout the text. If unwanted changes are made, they can be undone with the undo command. However, it can easily happen that unwanted changes aren't discovered soon enough to undo them. To protect yourself, write the buffer contents to disk with the command `:w` before making any global changes. If problems are discovered later, you can return to the last written version of the file by using the command `:e!`. One way to double-check global substitutions is to use the confirm parameter, **c** (see the "Remove all tab stops but confirm each occurrence before removing" example in the upcoming list).

What makes **vi** search operations very powerful is the use of special characters called *metacharacters* that can be used to form search patterns called *regular expressions*. Here is an example:

`:g/ occ[a-z]*ces /s// occurrences /g`

The metacharacter combination **[a-z]*** stands for any letters. This command will correct various spellings of the word occurrences. Table 12.1 shows some metacharacters used by **vi**.

TABLE 12.1   Metacharacters Used for Pattern Matching

Character	Description
\	Turns off the special meaning of the following character; this character is called an *escape* character.
^	Matches the beginning of a line.
$	Matches the end of a line.
.	Matches any single character except a newline.
*	Matches the preceding character (or expression) any number of times, including zero.
[string]	Matches any one of the enclosed characters. A dash (-) between characters specifies a range—thus, [a-d] is the same as [abcd].
[^string]	Matches any character not enclosed. Thus, [^a-d] is the same as all other characters—e-z, A-Z, 1-9, and so on.
&	Used in a substitute command to stand for the text in a search. For example, /giant/s//&s/ replaces giant with giants.
\(pat\)	These escaped parentheses can be used to define a regular expression or pattern for substitution.
\n	The number *n* refers to previous patterns defined by parentheses.
Ctrl-v	Escapes an Esc or Return in the replacement part of the command.

The best way to understand these special characters is to see them in action:

- Delete all blank lines:

    `:g/^$/d`

    Find all lines (g) that have a beginning (^) and an end ($) with no characters between and delete (d) them.

- Change county or County to COUNTY:

    `:g/[cC]ounty/s//COUNTY/g`

    Find all lines with county or County and substitute for this pattern (s//) the word COUNTY. The last character (g) means to replace all patterns, not just the first one on each line.

- Double-space all lines:

    `:g/$/s//<Ctrl-v><Return>/g`

    Find the end of each line ($) and substitute for it (s//) a Return. The Ctrl-v is required to enter a Return. If you want to double-space all lines of text only, delete all blank lines and then double-space all lines.

- Shift the beginning of each line three spaces to the right:

  `:g/^/s//   /`

  Find the beginning of each line (`^`) and substitute for it (`s//`) three spaces.

Tip

You can also use the shift operator in `vi` (`>L`) to do the same thing, assuming `shiftwidth=3`.

- Remove all tab stops:

  `:g/<Tab>/s///g`

  If the keyboard doesn't have a Tab key, you can use Ctrl-i to insert the tab:

  `:g/<Ctrl-i>/s///g`

  Find Tab or Ctrl-i and substitute for it the empty space. If you don't want to remove all tab stops, but just some of them, use the confirm (c) parameter.

- Remove all tab stops but confirm each occurrence before removing:

  `:g/<Tab>/s///gc`

  or

  `:g/<Ctrl-i>/s///gc`

  The confirm parameter, `c`, will cause the editor to display each line and mark each substitution requiring a change. You are prompted for a yes or no, y or n. This isn't as convenient as it sounds because the line displayed is taken out of context. Another way to do the same thing is to use the dot command (`.`) and the search operator (`/`) as described in the following section, "Search and Replace with `vi`."

- Replace one or more spaces following a period with one space for lines 20 through 33:

  `:20,33/\.   */s//\. /g`

  The search is now restricted to lines 20 to 33. Find a period followed by a space (`\.`), followed by zero or more spaces (`*`), and replace with a period and one space (`\.`).

- Reverse the strings on either side of a hyphen and confirm the substitution:

  `:g/\(.*\) - \(.*\)/s//\2 - \1/gc`

  Find the pattern (*string1* - *string2*) and put down the pattern (*string2* - *string1*). Notice that the pattern

  `x y z - A B C`

  is replaced by

  `A B C - x y z`

and not x y A - z B C because the .* matches as much of the line as possible, not limiting itself to a single word. If you want to find all the hyphenated *words* and swap either half, you can use

```
g:/\([^ -]*\) - \([^ ]\)/s//\2 - \1/gc
```

where the two spaces inside the brackets [^] are the spacebar and a tab. This command finds the pattern *string1* - *string2*, where *string1* has no space or tab (recall that the caret inside the bracket—[^]—means *all but* the following characters) and the same pattern for *string2* and reverses them.

Search and Replace with vi

All the previous search-and-replace expressions are formed by using vi editor commands. The other way to search for patterns is to use the vi editor search operators / and ?. The search commands are

/pattern
?pattern

The / searches for *pattern* forward from the cursor, whereas the ? operator searches backward from the cursor. In both cases, the key n is used to repeat the search. The vi editor can use regular expressions to conduct searches. Here are a few examples:

- Find the beginning of each line:

/^	Find the beginning of the next line
n	Continue the search

- Find the word county or County and change to COUNTY:

/[Cc]ounty	Find County or county
cwCOUNTY	Change to COUNTY
n	Repeat the search
.	Repeat the change

- Find the misspelled word occurance and correct:

/?occ[a-z]*nce	Find the word beginning with occ and ending with nce
cwoccurrence	Change to occurrence
n	Repeat the search
.	Repeat the change

- Find the word `Section` and remove:

/Section	Find the word `Section`
dw	Delete the word
n	Repeat the search
.	Repeat the deletion

You can see that the search operators are used to find the patterns but not replace them. Then the change (`cw`), delete (`dw`), or other operators are used to make changes. The advantage to using `vi`'s search-and-replace method is that patterns are displayed in context and can be selectively replaced.

Customizing the `vi` Editor

`vi` has a number of options that can be set to change its behavior. You've already seen two of those options in Chapter 5: the wrap margin and redraw options. Altogether, more than 30 options are available and, fortunately, all have default or preset values. Thus, you can work in the default environment, or you can create a custom environment to fit your special needs.

The `set` command is used to change `vi` options and allows the customization of `vi`. Options may be set temporarily by using the `set` command while in the editor, or options may be created permanently by placing them in files, such as the `.exrc` file in the HOME directory or a subdirectory. Options placed in a subdirectory let you customize the editor for particular jobs. For example, when you use the editor to write programs in C, you can create a subdirectory for those programs and then set the `autoindent` option to simplify program indention.

In all the following examples, we'll assume that you are working in `vi`'s command mode. You start each options with a colon (:). The `vi` editor responds by displaying the colon prompt on the bottom line and waits for you to enter the option. After giving the option and pressing Return, you are returned to `vi`'s command mode.

Three types of options are available:

- Numeric options have this format:

Syntax	Example
:set *option=value*	:set wrapmargin=15

- Toggle options have this format:

Syntax	Example
:set *option*	:set redraw

Turning off a toggle option has this format:

Syntax	Example
`:set nooption`	`:set noredraw`

- String options have this format:

Syntax	Example
`:set option=string`	`:set term=vt100`

- To see the current value of any option, use this format:

Syntax	Example
`:set option?`	`:set columns?`

- To see what options `vi` is using, use this command:

  `:set all`

- To see what options have been changed or set during this `vi` session, use this command:

  `:set`

Here is a list of the `:set all` options. These options may vary some from one computer to another, but the ones described here are the most common:

noautoindent	mesg	noshowmatch
autoprint	nonumber	noslowopen
noautowrite	nooptimize	tabstop=8
nobeautify	shiftwidth=8	length=0
directory=/tmp	prompt	tags=tags /usr/lib/tags
noedcompatible	noreadonly	noterse
errorbells	redraw	window=23
hardtabs=8	remap	wrapscan
noignorecase	report=5	wrapmargin=10
nolisp	scroll=11	nowriteany
nolist	sections=NHSHH Hunhsh	
magic	paragraphs=IPLPPPQPP Lipplpipnpbp	

This is an impressive list of options. Experimenters and tinkerers will have a field day exploring combinations of options. For those who are more discriminating, Table 12.1 lists the more useful options.

TABLE 12.2 Useful `:set all` Options

Option	Abbreviation	Definition
autoindent	ai	Indents the new line to align with the previous line. Use Ctrl-d one or more times to backspace one or more indents (see `shiftwidth`). Useful for writing structured program text in C and other languages. Also useful for indenting tables and text. Default: `noai`
ignorecase	ic	Ignores letter case in searching and in regular-expression matching. Most useful for finding and rearranging text, but not to correct spelling. Default: `noic`
magic	None	Creates the magic characters ., *, and [ ] for use as wildcards or metacharacters in searching and in regular expressions. If `nomagic` is set, only ^, $, and \ have special meaning. Default: `magic`
number	nu	Each line in the editor buffer is numbered. This option displays line numbers on the left side of the screen and is useful with the `move` and `copy` commands. Default: `nonu`
redraw	re	This option makes the editor simulate an intelligent terminal by displaying each character in its proper location at all times. The `nore draw` option is useful for terminals operating at slow speeds like and 1200bps. Default: `redraw`
shiftwidth	sw	Sets the number of spaces used by Ctrl-d in `autoindent` and by the shift operators. Default: `sw=8`
showmatch	sm	When a) or } is typed, the cursor is moved to the matching { or (for 1 second. It's useful for programming, especially in C. Default: `nosm`
slowopen	slow	Prevents update of the screen during input and is essential for terminals operating at slow speeds. The default value depends on line speed and terminal type. Default: varies.
tabstop	ts	Sets the number of spaces that a Tab or Ctrl-i uses to expand tab stops for a file. Default: `ts=8`
terse	None	When set, `terse` error messages are shorter. It's useful for fast typists and slow terminals. Default: `noterse`
window	w	Sets the number of lines of text in the `vi` editor, which generally ranges from 8 lines for slow terminals to 16 to 24 lines for faster terminals. Default: varies.
wrapscan	ws	When set, allows searches by using a / or ? to proceed from the cursor around the end of the file and back to the cursor. Default: `ws`
wrapmargin	wm	Defines a right margin for automatic wrapping of text (by inserting Returns). A typical value of `wm=15` would create text lines having 80 minus 15 (that is, 65) or fewer characters long. Default: `wm=0`

Remember that options set while in the editor are lost when you leave the editor. The `.exrc` file is normally used to create semipermanent options.

The `.exrc` File

The `.exrc` file is used to create customized editing environments. When the **vi** editor starts up, it looks at the `.exrc` file for instructions, which may be set options, abbreviations, or maps. You can enter these instructions into the `.exrc` file just like any other file by using the **vi** editor. Give the command **vi** `.exrc` in the HOME directory or a different directory. A typical file might look like this:

```
set wm=15
set redraw
set ai
ab nyc New York City
ab abb abbreviation
map ^ 067wi<Ctrl-v><Return><Ctrl-v><Esc>
```

The last line, **map**, helps do simple formatting as described in a previous section. You can copy the `.exrc` file in your HOME directory to put in any subdirectory and then modify it to fit the editing jobs of that subdirectory. If you want to have more than one custom editor file in a directory, **vi** lets you read in an editor file of instructions by using the source command. Just give the command:

```
:source filename
```

where *filename* contains the appropriate options, abbreviations, and maps. The advantage of the `.exrc` file is that **vi** "sources" that file automatically.

Summary

After you master the techniques in this chapter, as well as the techniques in Chapters 5, you are well on your way to becoming a **vi** expert. We've left out a few odds and ends for brevity: more options, more scopes, more commands, and so on. These can be added to your editing routine by consulting the man pages, as you feel ready, on the **vi** editor.

Review Questions

1. Will the dot command repeat cursor movement? How about the undo command?

2. Will the dot and undo commands repeat only the last command or can they be used to sequentially repeat and undo commands?

3. Why are two- and three-letter word abbreviations better than single-letter word abbreviations?

4. What's the major difference between an abbreviation and a **map** macro?

5. Can a macro perform the same tasks as a substitute command?

6. Why do Return and Esc need to be escaped in a **map** macro?

7. What key is used to escape a Return in a **map** macro? What key is used to escape metacharacters in a regular expression?

8. In creating regular expressions for search and replacement, what does `.*` mean? Why would the following command *not* be a good way to correct the spelling of `receive`?

   `:g/rec.*ve/s//receive/g`

9. What's the difference between `.` and `\.` in a regular expression?

10. What does the confirm parameter, `c`, do in a search expression?

11. Why is the `.exrc` file a good place to put abbreviations, maps, and option settings?

12. If you set the option **ai** and indent several lines of text in a row, how can you start a new line, not indented, without leaving text input mode?

Exercises

There are lots of examples in this chapter to try. We suggest that you make a copy of a file with about 20 lines of text in it to use as a practice file.

1. In your practice file, do each of the following:

   a. Delete three lines of text. Move the cursor and use the dot command to repeat the deletion.

   b. Find the word **the** and change it to **th#**, using the **cw** operator. Now use the search repeat key, **n**, and the command repeat key (dot) to change all **the**'s to **th#**.

   c. To return the file to its original state, type `:e!`.

2. Create an abbreviation for a friend of yours and type a short letter of recommendation for him or her.

3. Create a **map** macro that changes the spelling of the word **the** to **thee**. Use the search operator, /, along with **n**, to find and change every **the** to **thee**.

4. In your practice file, use Shift-j to join several lines of text. Now create the **map** macro, ^, defined in this chapter, to format long lines.

5. In your practice file,

   a. Use the shell command, **date**, to put the date and time at the top of the file.

   b. Escape to the shell to list your files.

   c. Read in a short file by using the command **:r** *filename* into the middle of your practice file.

   d. Filter the editor buffer through the **sort** utility.

   e. Filter the buffer through **nroff**.

   f. Use **:e!** to return your practice file to its original state.

6. In your practice file, do each of the following:

   a. Delete all blank lines. If you had a blank line consisting of a single tab, was it deleted? Why or why not? Try it.

   b. Double-space all lines.

   c. Shift all lines three spaces to the right.

   d. Undo the shift and then tab all lines to the right.

   e. Try some of the other substitute examples in this chapter.

7. Try the **autoindent** and **number** options.

8. In your practice file, do each of the following:

   a. Escape to the shell.

   b. Edit your **.exrc** file. (If you don't have one, create one.)

   c. Enter one or more abbreviations and **map** macros.

   d. Write and quit the **.exrc** file and return to the editor with Ctrl-d.

   e. Now give the command **:source .exrc** and try out the abbreviations and maps.

   f. Try the commands **:ab**, **:map**, **:set**, and **:set all**.

9. What does the following command do?

```
:w !diff %
```

Why is this useful when you're editing a file? Try it.

APPENDIX A

ASCII TABLE

DEC X_{10}	HEX X_{16}	OCT X_8	Binary X_2	ASCII	Key
0	00	00	000 0000	NUL	Ctrl-1
1	01	01	000 0001	SOH	Ctrl-A
2	02	02	000 0010	STX	Ctrl-B
3	03	03	000 0011	ETX	Ctrl-C
4	04	04	000 0100	EOT	Ctrl-D
5	05	05	000 0101	ENQ	Ctrl-E
6	06	06	000 0110	ACK	Ctrl-F
7	07	07	000 0111	BEL	Ctrl-G
8	08	10	000 1000	BS	Ctrl-H, Backspace
9	09	11	000 1001	HT	Ctrl-I, Tab
10	0A	12	000 1010	LF	Ctrl-J, Line Feed
11	0B	13	000 1011	VT	Ctrl-K
12	0C	14	000 1100	FF	Ctrl-L
13	0D	15	000 1101	CR	Ctrl-M, Return
14	0E	16	000 1110	SO	Ctrl-N
15	0F	17	000 1111	SI	Ctrl-O
16	10	20	001 0000	DLE	Ctrl-P
17	11	21	001 0001	DCI	Ctrl-Q
18	12	22	001 0010	DC2	Ctrl-R
19	13	23	001 0011	DC3	Ctrl-S

DEC X_{10}	HEX X_{16}	OCT X_8	Binary X_2	ASCII	Key
20	14	24	001 0100	DC4	Ctrl-T
21	15	25	001 0101	NAK	Ctrl-U
22	16	26	001 0110	SYN	Ctrl-V
23	17	27	001 0111	ETB	Ctrl-W
24	18	30	001 1000	CAN	Ctrl-X
25	19	31	001 1001	EM	Ctrl-Y
26	1A	32	001 1010	SUB	Ctrl-Z
27	1B	33	001 1011	ESC	Esc, Escape
28	1C	34	001 1100	FS	Ctrl-\
29	1D	35	001 1101	GS	Ctrl-]
30	1E	36	001 1110	RS	Ctrl-=
31	1F	37	001 1111	US	Ctrl--
32	20	40	010 0000	SP	Spacebar
33	21	41	010 0001	!	!
34	22	42	010 0010	"	"
35	23	43	010 0011	#	#
36	24	44	010 0100	$	$
37	25	45	010 0101	%	%
38	26	46	010 0110	&	&
39	27	47	010 0111	'	'
40	28	50	010 1000	(	(
41	29	51	010 1001	)	)
42	2A	52	010 1010	*	*
43	2B	53	010 1011	+	+
44	2C	54	010 1100	,	,
45	2D	55	010 1101	-	-
46	2E	56	010 1110	.	.
47	2F	57	010 1111	/	/

DEC X_{10}	HEX X_{16}	OCT X_8	Binary X_2	ASCII	Key
48	30	60	011 0000	0	0
49	31	61	011 0001	1	1
50	32	62	011 0010	2	2
51	33	63	011 0011	3	3
52	34	64	011 0100	4	4
53	35	65	011 0101	5	5
54	36	66	011 0110	6	6
55	37	67	011 0111	7	7
56	38	70	011 1000	8	8
57	39	71	011 1001	9	9
58	3A	72	011 1010	:	:
59	3B	73	011 1011	;	;
60	3C	74	011 1100	<	<
61	3D	75	011 1101	=	=
62	3E	76	011 1110	>	>
63	3F	77	011 1111	?	?
64	40	100	100 0000	@	@
65	41	101	100 0001	A	A
66	42	102	100 0010	B	B
67	43	103	100 0011	C	C
68	44	104	100 0100	D	D
69	45	105	100 0101	E	E
70	46	106	100 0110	F	F
71	47	107	100 0111	G	G
72	48	110	100 1000	H	H
73	49	111	100 1001	I	I
74	4A	112	100 1010	J	J
75	4B	113	100 1011	K	K

DEC X_{10}	HEX X_{16}	OCT X_8	Binary X_2	ASCII	Key
76	4C	114	100 1100	L	L
77	4D	115	100 1101	M	M
78	4E	116	100 1110	N	N
79	4F	117	100 1111	O	O
80	50	120	101 0000	P	P
81	51	121	101 0001	Q	Q
82	52	122	101 0010	R	R
83	53	123	101 0011	S	S
84	54	124	101 0100	T	T
85	55	125	101 0101	U	U
86	56	126	101 0110	V	V
87	57	127	101 0111	W	W
88	58	130	101 1000	X	X
89	59	131	101 1001	Y	Y
90	5A	132	101 1010	Z	Z
91	5B	133	101 1011	[	[
92	5C	134	101 1100	\	\
93	5D	135	101 1101	]	]
94	5E	136	101 1110	^	^
95	5F	137	101 1111	—	—
96	60	140	110 0000	`	`
97	61	141	110 0001	a	a
98	62	142	110 0010	b	b
99	63	143	110 0011	c	c
100	64	144	110 0100	d	d
101	65	145	110 0101	e	e
102	66	146	110 0110	f	f
103	67	147	110 0111	g	g

DEC X_{10}	HEX X_{16}	OCT X_8	Binary X_2	ASCII	Key
104	68	150	110 1000	h	h
105	69	151	110 1001	i	i
106	6A	152	110 1010	j	j
107	6B	153	110 1011	k	k
108	6C	154	110 1100	1	1
109	6D	155	110 1101	m	m
110	6E	156	110 1110	n	n
111	6F	157	110 1111	o	o
112	70	160	111 0000	p	p
113	71	161	111 0001	q	q
114	72	162	111 0010	r	r
115	73	163	111 0011	s	s
116	74	164	111 0100	t	t
117	75	165	111 0101	u	u
118	76	166	111 0110	v	v
119	77	167	111 0111	w	w
120	78	170	111 1000	x	x
121	79	171	111 1001	y	y
122	7A	172	111 1010	z	z
123	7B	173	111 1011	{	{
124	7C	174	111 1100	|	|
125	7D	175	111 1101	}	}
126	7E	176	111 1110	~	~
127	7F	177	111 1111	Del	Del, Rubout

APPENDIX B

GLOSSARY

alias A user-supplied name interpreted by the system to represent a command or program or some combination thereof.

aliasing The process of creating an alias.

argument An item of information following a command. It may, for example, modify the command or identify a file to be affected.

assembly language A mnemonic code representing the basic instructions understood by a particular computer.

background Running the system so that the terminal is left free for other uses.

backup A file copy set aside as insurance in case something happens to the original.

baud rate The rate at which information is transmitted between devices—for example, between a terminal and the computer. One baud is one unit of information (a bit) per second. A hundred baud is about 9 characters a second, or 110 words a minute.

Berkeley Software Distribution UNIX versions developed at the University of California, Berkeley. They bear names such as BSD 4.4.

bit The smallest unit of information or memory for a computer. A bit can have the value 0 or the value 1. It forms the basis of the binary coding used internally by computers.

block A standard chunk of memory used as a unit by the computer; a block typically consists of 512 bytes.

Bourne shell The UNIX shell used by the standard Bell Labs UNIX.

BSD See *Berkeley Software Distribution*.

buffer A temporary work area or storage area set up within system memory. Buffers are often used by programs, such as editors, that access and alter text or data frequently.

bug A design error in the hardware or software of a computer system.

byte A unit of information or memory consisting of 8 bits. A byte of memory will hold 1 character.

call To summon a program into action.

central processing unit See *CPU*.

change mode   To alter a set of parameters that describes a file—telling who can use the file and how it can be used. The `chmod` command is used to do this.

character   A letter, numeral, punctuation mark, control character, blank, or other such symbol.

character string   A series of characters—for example, `gofats` and `hot&#$&23`.

chip   A small chunk of silicon bearing the equivalent of a large number of electrical components; an integrated circuit.

chmod   See *change mode*.

clobber   To wipe out a file.

command   An instruction to the computer. A command typically is a character string typed on a keyboard that's interpreted by the computer as a demand for a particular action.

command interpreter   A program that accepts commands from the keyboard and causes the commands to be executed. The shell is the UNIX command interpreter.

command line   A line consisting of one or more commands, each followed by its arguments, if any.

compiler   A master program that converts a high-level computer language (such as COBOL or C++) into machine language.

concatenate   To string together two or more sequences, such as files, into one longer sequence. The `cat` command, for example, concatenates files.

control characters   Characters typed by pressing a key while the Ctrl key is held down. For instance, a Ctrl-h is typed by pressing the *h* key while pressing the Ctrl key.

CPU   Abbreviation for *central processing unit*, the part of the computer in which calculations and manipulations take place.

C shell   The standard shell provided with all versions of UNIX.

cursor   A marker onscreen—usually a rectangle of light or an underscore—that indicates where the next letter you type will appear.

directory   A file containing a list of associated files and subdirectories.

directory pathname   The complete name by which a directory is known. The pathname gives the sequence of directories by which the directory is linked to the root directory.

dumb terminal   A terminal having no computing power of its own; the opposite of a smart terminal.

echo   To repeat a stream of characters. For example, the commands you type to the computer are echoed onscreen.

editor   A program to assist you in writing material to be stored in files. Editors allow you to modify existing files and create new ones.

email An electronic system of sending messages and data files between computers and their users. These computers can be on a local network or anywhere in the world, depending on their configuration.

EOF Abbreviation for *end of file*. Files are terminated with a particular end-of-file character, usually Ctrl-d, that tells the system it has reached the end of the file.

escape To divest a special character of its special meaning by preceding it with a backslash character. For example, the UNIX shell interprets a ? to represent any single character, but a \? (an "escaped" question mark) is interpreted as just a question-mark character.

event A previous line of input from the terminal, usually either a command line or an attempted command line. The history function maintains a numbered list of the last several events that you've entered.

event identifier A shorthand code used by the user to identify earlier events on the history list.

execute To run a command or program. (Not to be confused with *kill*.)

field A subsection of a line. Programs such as `sort` and `awk` can look at individual fields within a line.

field separator The character used to separate one field from the next. A string of one or more spaces is the usual field separator.

file A sequence of bytes constituting a unit of text, data, or a program. A file can be stored in system memory or on an external medium, such as tape or disk.

filename expansion The process by which UNIX matches filenames with metacharacters to actual filenames—for example, matching `?oo?` to `foot` and `Loop`.

filling Adjusting line lengths in text so that all lines have about the same length.

flag An argument to a command signifying a particular option or modification. UNIX flags usually are indicated by a leading hyphen (-).

foreground Running under direct control of the terminal. The terminal can't be used for anything else until a foreground job finishes or is halted.

Formatting Arranging text or data into a suitable visual form. Also, the process of setting up a system's hard drive to enable it to be partitioned and used on a UNIX file system.

global Having extended or general scope. For example, a global substitution of one word for another in a file affects all occurrences of the word.

graphical user interface A windowing display on the terminal or monitor. GUIs allow the use of a mouse, multiple windows, and more exciting graphics.

GUI See *graphical user interface*.

hardware The mechanical and electrical components of a computer system.

history   A UNIX facility that maintains a numbered list of previous commands and provides shorthand notation that lets you repeat or modify previous commands.

home directory   The directory assigned to you by the system manager, usually the same as your login directory. Additional directories that you create would stem from your home directory.

housekeeping   Keeping track of which files are where, renaming and removing files, monitoring who is doing what on the system, and the like.

input   Information fed to a command, a program, a terminal, a person, and so on.

interactive   Allowing the computer and the user to carry on a dialog.

Internet   A worldwide computer network connecting computers via unique addresses. This allows exchange of data between any two or more computers anywhere in the world. It's growing at an explosive rate in response to business, government, and private entities seeking to use this free, ungoverned electronic resource.

interpreter   A master program that translates a high-level computer language (such as BASIC) into machine language, a line at a time. Interactive languages use interpreters instead of compilers. For example, Java gets converted to byte code on the target machine.

interrupt   To break off a command or other process and thus terminate it; also, a signal that accomplishes this.

job number   An identification number assigned to a job by the C shell. Unlike the process ID, this number is local to the terminal.

kill   To terminate a process before it reaches its natural conclusion.

Korn shell   Also called the K shell or `ksh`. A UNIX shell written by David Korn of AT&T Bell Laboratories. It is compatible with the Bourne shell but has C shell enhancements.

learn   A computer-aided instruction program provided with older installations of UNIX.

line editor   An editor that works on a line as the basic unit. In general, the user identifies the line to be changed and then indicates the change desired.

link   An entry in a directory file that links a user-assigned name for a file or directory to the system's identification number for that file; a name you give to a file or directory.

loading   Putting the machine-language instructions of a program into memory.

local   Having limited scope; the opposite of global.

log in   The process of gaining access to the computer system to begin a session.

login directory   The directory you are placed in when you log in, usually your home directory.

login name   The name by which the computer system knows you.

log out   The process of signing off the system.

Linux   A UNIX-like operating system developed for PCs by Linus Torvalds in the early 1990s. It is increasingly popular because it is freely distributed and can turn any modern PC into a UNIX-like workstation.

machine-collating sequence   An extended alphabetical sequence that encompasses upper-case letters, lowercase letters, numerals, punctuation marks, and the various other characters recognized by the system.

machine language   The basic set of instructions understood by a given computer. These instructions are represented internally by means of a binary code.

macro   A compound instruction put together from simpler instructions.

mail   A computer system facility that allows the sending and holding of messages via the computer.

map   To assign a new interpretation to a terminal key. For example, in vi you can map, say, the @ key to represent the sequence o Esc j.

metacharacter   A character having a special meaning to UNIX. For example, the UNIX shell interprets the ? metacharacter to stand for any single character. See *wildcard* and *special character*.

microprocessor   The essential electronics of a computer miniaturized to a single chip.

modem   Short for *modulator-dem*odulator, a device for connecting a terminal or printer to a computer via a telephone line.

multitasking   The execution of more than one program at a time in such a way that the tasks appear to be carried out simultaneously. This is where UNIX gives the illusion that each user is the only one working on the system. In fact, the operating system gives each process a slice of CPU execution time and executes each job very quickly, one at a time, leading to the illusion of simultaneous execution.

multiuser   Permitting more than one user to use the system at the same time.

network attached storage (NAS)   One of the new Network Appliance type devices that acts as a disk storage array. It's usually accessed via NFS in a UNIX environment.

null character   An invisible character that has an internal code of 0 and occupies no space if printed. Not to be confused with a blank, which is invisible but occupies a space.

object file   A file containing machine-language code.

online   Connected to the system and in operation. Also, connected to the Internet.

operating system   A master program that handles the varied tasks involved in running a computer system, including the user-computer interface.

option   A variation on, or modification to, a command, usually requested by use of a flag.

optional argument   An argument accepted but not required by a command.

output   Information produced by a command, program, and so on, and sent elsewhere—for example, to the terminal, to a file, or to a line printer.

overwrite   To write over an existing file or text block, eliminating what previously was there.

owner   The person who created a file.

page   To advance text onscreen by one screen (or page) at a time.

password   A series of letters, numbers, or special characters held in confidence from others. A password is generally used in combination with a user name to validate your identity to a computer.

pathname   A name for a file or directory specifying the location of the file or directory in the directory system. See *directory pathname*.

peripheral input-output   Input and output devices attached to a computer—for example, terminals, printers, and tape drives.

permission   The yes-or-no specification of what can be done to a file or directory. A file or directory has read permission, write permission, and execute permission.

pipe   To make the output of one command or program into the input of another. Also, the UNIX operator (¦) that accomplishes this.

pipeline   The program linkage established by performing one or more pipes.

POSIX   Commonly used term for *Portable Operating Systems Environment*. The Institute of Electrical and Electronics Engineers (IEEE) developed a series standards with which most modern operating systems vendors attempt to comply. (We use the phrase *attempt to* because vendors sometimes vary their interpretations with standards.)

process   A particular computer activity or job.

process ID   A unique, system-wide identification number assigned to a process.

process status   The current state of the process: running, stopped, waiting, and so on.

program   A sequence of instructions telling a computer how to perform a task. A program can be in machine language, or it can be in a higher-level language that is then translated into machine language.

prompt   A character or character string sent from a computer system to a terminal to tell the user that the system is ready to accept input. Typical UNIX prompts are % and $.

protection   Safeguarding a file from accidental erasure or from the unwanted inspection of others. Protection can be accomplished, for example, by using chmod to deny others the right to read a file.

recursive   In reference to a directory system, the application to a directory, to all its offshoots, to all their offshoots, and so on. In reference to a computer program, the description of a program that calls itself.

redirection   The channeling of output to a file or device instead of to the standard output. The channeling of input from a file or device instead of from the standard input.

regular expression   A pattern representing a class of character strings. The `grep` command, for example, recognizes the regular expression `h.t` to mean any three-character string beginning with `h` and ending with `t`.

root directory   The base directory from which all other directories stem, directly or indirectly.

rubout   An older term meaning to erase.

scope   The range over which an action or definition applies.

scroll   To shift text up or down or left and right onscreen.

search and replace   In word processing, an operation that finds one or more occurrences of a word or pattern and replaces it with another, as stipulated by the user.

shell   A UNIX program that handles the interaction between user and system.

shell script   A file containing a sequence of shell commands. It can be used as input to the shell or declared an executable file.

smart terminal   A terminal possessing some computing power of its own.

special character   A character with special meaning beyond its literal one; a metacharacter.

standard input   Short for *standard input device*. The device from which a program or system normally takes its input, usually a terminal—more specifically, your keyboard or, in the case of a hand-held device, a wand.

standard output   Short for *standard output device*. The device to which a program or system normally sends its output, usually a terminal or console screen.

stopped job   A job that has been halted temporarily by the user and that can be resumed at his command.

string   A sequence of characters.

subdirectory   A directory branching off another directory.

time-sharing   The allocation of computer resources among several users so that the resources can be used simultaneously.

tools   Compact, well-designed programs designed to do a specific task well. Several tools can be linked to perform more complex tasks.

user   A person using the computer system.

visual editor   An editor that shows one screen of text at a time and allows the user to move a cursor to any part of the screen and make changes there.

wildcard   A metacharacter used to represent a range of ordinary characters. Examples include the shell's use of * and ?. See also *special character*.

word processing   The use of editors and other computer programs to prepare, alter, check, and format text.

working directory   The directory in which your commands take place if no other directory is specified.

SUMMARY OF UNIX ABBREVIATIONS

Shell Abbreviations for Files and Directories

The following abbreviations can be used to represent the names of files and directories:

?	Represents (or matches) any single character
*	Matches any number of characters (including none)
[ ]	Matches any one character from the list included between the brackets; a hyphen (-) can be used to indicate a range

Examples:

Abbreviation	Some Matches	No Match
b?t	bit bot bst	bt bout
b*t	bot bout batent bt	bots abbot
b[aou]t	bat bot	bout
b[3-6]	b3 b5	b2 b33
b[3-5][7-9]?	b38q b472	b27n b38

The following can be used in identifying directories:

.	Your current working directory
..	Parent directory to your current working directory
~	Your home directory; if followed by a login name, the home directory of that person (BSD)

Examples:

Abbreviation	Meaning
cp ~boozy/recipe .	Copies the file recipe from **boozy**'s home directory into your current working directory
cd ..	Changes directories to the parent directory of your current working directory
cp hormones ~	Copies the file **hormones** from your current working directory into your home directory

Abbreviations Used by grep, ed, and edit

The following abbreviations are used in search patterns:

.	Matches any single character (works the same as the shell abbreviation ?)
[ ]	Matches any *one* character found in the list between the brackets; a hyphen (-) can be used to indicate a range of characters
^	Matches the beginning of the line—that is, the following pattern must begin the line
$	Matches end of line—that is, the preceding pattern must end the line

Examples:

Abbreviation	Matching Line	Nonmatching Line
car.o	a carton of milk	carts of fish eyes
car[gt]	a cargo of gold	a tub of carp
^car[gt]	cartoon of frog	a fine cartoon
car.o$	a fresh cargo	fresh cargos

Abbreviations Used by the C-Shell History Function

The exclamation mark (!) alerts the C shell that a history reference is about to be made.

References to Complete Events

In the following list, *n* stands for a numeral and *c* for a character string.

!*n*	The *n*th event
!-*n*	The event number that's *n* less than the current event number
!*c*	The most recent event beginning with the string *c*
!?*c*?	The most recent event containing the string *c*

Examples:

!12	Runs the 12th event on the history list
!-2	Runs the event that is two before the preceding one
!ca	Runs the most recent command that began with ca
!?cow?!	Runs the most recent command that contains the pattern cow

References to Words within an Event

These forms are used by appending them to an event reference:

:*n*	The *n*+1 word in the event. (Thus, :0 is the first word, generally the name of the command, and :1 is the second word, usually the first argument of the command.)
:^ or ^	The second word (first argument); the same as :1.
:$ or $	The last word in the event.
:* or *	All the words subsequent to :0; generally the complete argument list of the command.

Examples:

!32:3	The third argument of the 32nd command on the history list
!4$	The final argument of the fourth command on the history list
cat !5* cat	The arguments of the fifth command

Some Additional Conventions

!!	The immediately previous event (the same as !-1)
!	Similar to !!, except that this form must be followed by a word identifier

Examples : Suppose that the last history entry is `ls /usr`.

`!! /bin`	Means `ls /usr/bin`
`cd !$`	Means `cd /usr/bin`

Shell-Script Abbreviations

`$0`	The name of the shell script
`$n`	The *n*th argument of the shell script
`$*`	The complete argument list of the shell script

Suppose that the following command has been given, where `freem` is a shell script:

`freem click clack clock`

Then, within the script,

`$0`	Represents `freem`
`$2`	Represents `clack`
`$*`	Represents `click clack clock`

awk Abbreviations

The following are some abbreviations used by the `awk` utility.

`$n`	The *n*th field of a record (by default, a record is a line)
`$0`	The entire record
`NF`	The number of fields in the current record
`NR`	The ordinal number of the current record
`FILENAME`	The name of the current input file

Examples:

`{print $3}`	Prints the third field
`{print $3/NR >> FILENAME}`	Divides the contents of the third field by the current line number and writes the result at the end of the current file

UNIX COMMAND REFERENCE

This reference is best used for commands with which you are already somewhat familiar. If you are using a command for the first time, read the discussion of the command in the text or refer to your online manual.

- Type the commands (shown in a `computer typeface`) exactly as you see them.

- When a word or letter is printed in the *`italic version`* of the computer typeface, substitute an actual value, filename, range of numbers, or other appropriate parameter for the italicized word.

- Substitute your filenames for *`file, file1`*, and so on.

- Repeatable arguments are followed by an ellipsis (. . .).

- Arguments in square brackets (`[ ]`) are optional. Do not type the brackets.

Note

This appendix isn't meant to be a comprehensive reference for all UNIX commands. Only the commands used most often that are common across all versions of UNIX are listed here.

Starting Up

login   Sign on.

passwd   Change login password.

Manipulating Files and Directories

cat   Concatenate and print.

`cat [-n, -s, -v]` *`file...`*

- Options:

-n	Number lines starting at 1.
-s	Eliminate multiple, consecutive blank lines.
-v	Print invisible characters.

- Example:

  `cat file2`

  displays file2 on terminal.

cd, **chdir**   Change directory.

```
cd
cd directoryname
```

- Example:

  `cd /usr/reggie/foods/carbo`

  places you in the `usr/reggie/foods/carbo` directory.

chmod   Change modes or permissions on files.

`chmod ugo, + -, rwx file... or directory...`

- Who:

u	Login owner (user)
g	Group
o	Other users

- Op-codes:

+	Add permission.
-	Remove permission.

- Permissions:

r	Read
w	Write
x	Execute

- Example:

  `chmod o-rwx private`

  removes read, write, and execute permissions for others from the file named `private`.

cp   Make copy of files.

```
cp [-i] file1 file2
cp [-i] file... (file, file..., directory)
```

- Option:

  `-i`   Prompts for confirmation before overwriting existing files.

- Example:

  `cp flim flam`

  makes a copy of the file `flim` and calls it `flam`.

ln   Make file links.

```
ln file ... file ...
ln file ... directoryname
```

- Example:

  `ln hist /usr/francie`

  links the file `hist` to the `/usr/francie` directory if it exists. Otherwise, it creates a `francie` link to `hist` in the `/usr` directory.

lpr, lpq, and lprm   Use the line printer.

```
lpr file
... lpq
lprm file ...
```

- Options: These vary from system to system.
- Examples:

  `lpr some stuff`

  sends the files `some` and `stuff` to the printer.

  `lpq`

  checks the line printer queue.

  `lprm data3`

  removes the file `data3` from printer queue.

ls   List directory contents.

ls [-a, -c, -l, -m, -r, -s, -F, -R, + *others*] *directory*...

- Options:

-a	List all entries.
-c	List by time of file creation.
-l	List in long format.
-m	List in a stream output.
-r	Reverse the order of the listing.
-s	Give the size in blocks.
-F	Mark directories with a / and executable programs with a *.
-R	List recursively any subdirectories.

- Example:

  ls -c

  will list contents of current directory in order of the time of creation.

mkdir   Make a new directory.

mkdir *directoryname*

- Example:

  mkdir Chapter4

  creates a new subdirectory called **Chapter4** in the present directory.

more   View long files one screen at a time.

more *file*...

- Options: See online manual for many options.

mv   Move or rename files and directories.

mv [-i] filename1 filename2
mv *filename1 directoryname*

- Option:

-i	Prompts for confirmation before overwriting existing files.

- Example:

  mv gappy happy

  changes the name of the file **gappy** to **happy**.

rm   Remove files.

rm [-i, -r] *file*...

- Options:

-i	Prompts for confirmation before removing files.
-r	Delete a directory and every file or directory in it. (Be careful!)

- Example:

  rm rodgers

  removes the file rodgers.

rmdir   Remove empty directories.

rmdir *directory*...

- Example:

  rmdir BUDGET65

  removes directory BUDGET65 if it does not contain any files.

Redirection Operators <, >, >>

- Example:

  cat listA listB >> listC

  appends the files listA and listB to the file listC.

Pipes ¦

- Example:

  cat listA listB ¦ lpr

  joins two files and pipes the result to the line printer.

Communication

finger   Provide information about users.

finger [-m, -l, -s] *name*

- Options:

-m	Search only login names.
-l	Display long form.
-s	Display short form.

- Example:

  ```
  finger -s john
  ```

  finds all users with the login or comment field containing the name of `john`.

mail   Receive mail.

```
mail
```

- Commands:

1, 2, 3, …	Reads message number 1 each time you push 1, and so on.
p	Print the first message.
d2	Delete message number 2.
s3 *filename*	Append message number 3 to *filename*.
q	Quit `mail`.
?	Display help screen.
Plus others	

mail   Send mail.

```
mail loginname(s)
```

- Commands:

~v	Invoke editor.
~?	Display help screen.
Plus others	

- Example:

  ```
  mail rick bob
  text of message here
  <Ctrl-d>
  ```

mesg   Permit or deny message from `talk`.

```
mesg [[-]y¦[-]n]
```

See your systems manual; some systems drop the hyphen.

- Example:

  ```
  mesg n
  ```

  prevents people from using `talk` to interrupt you.

talk   Talk to another user.

```
talk loginname
```

Housekeeping Utilities

cal   Provide a calendar.

cal [*month*] *year*

- Example:

  cal 05 1942

  will provide the calendar for May 1942.

calendar   A reminder service.

You create a file in your home directory called `calendar`. UNIX sends you reminders by mail.

- Example: Your calendar file might look like the following:

  Buy goose March 19
  call gus mar.20 at 3 pm
  3/23 Report due

date   Give date and time.

pwd   Print working directory.

who   List who is on the system.

who [am i]

- Example:

  who

  tells who is on the system.

Online Help

learn   Computer-assisted lessons available on a few older UNIX systems.

Type `learn` to start these lessons.

man   Find manual information by keywords.

man [-k] [*keyword*]

- Option:

  -k   Produce a one-line summary.

- Example:

  man cat

  displays the online manual explanation of `cat`.

Text Processing and Formatting

emacs   Display editor.

emacs *file*

See Chapter 6, "The emacs Editor," for more information.

join   Join lines from two files.

join *file1 file2*

- Options:

-t*c*	Use character *c* as a separator.
-j*n m*	Use field *m* of file *n* as the join field.

- Example:

    join names addresses

    joins lines common to both files. Note that files should be sorted first.

nroff   Advanced typesetting.

See Chapter 10, "More Text Processing: join, **sed**, and **nroff**," for details.

pr   Print partially formatted file.

pr [-*n*, -m, -t] *file...*

- Options:

-*n*	Arrange text into *n* columns.
-m	Print all files in multiple columns.
-t	Suppress heading on each page.

- Example:

    pr myths

    prints file **myths** onscreen.

vi   The screen-oriented text editor.

vi *file*

See Appendix E, "**vi** Command Reference," for more information.

Information Handling

awk   Pattern scanning and processing language.

See Chapter 11, "Information Processing: `grep`, `find`, and `awk`," and the `awk` manual.

find   Find designated files and act on them.

find *pathname searchcriteria action(s)*

- Search criteria:

-name *filename*	Files named *filename*
-size *n*	Files of size *n* blocks
-links *n*	Files with *n* links
-atime *n*	Files accessed *n* days ago
-mtime *n*	Files modified *n* days ago
-newer *filename*	Files modified more recently than the file *filename*

Note
n without a sign means exactly *n*; +*n* means greater than *n*; -*n* means less than *n*.

- Actions:

-print	Print the pathname of the found files.
-exec *command*\;	Execute the given command on finding a file; {} represents the found file.
-ok *command*\;	Similar to -**exec**, except your approval is requested before each execution; reply with a **y**.

- Example:

  find /usr/bob -mtime -10 -print

  finds all files in **usr/bob** directory that have been modified within 10 days and prints pathnames.

grep   Search a file for a pattern.

grep [-n, -i, -c, -w] *pattern file*...

- Options:

-n	Precede each matching line with its line number.
-i	Ignore the case of letters.
-c	Print only a count of matching lines.
-w	Match only complete words with the pattern.

- Example:

  grep -iw hop bugs

  searches the file bugs for the words hop, HOP, Hop, and so on.

head Look at the head of a file.

head [-n] *file*

- Option:

-*n*	Print *n* lines.

- Example:

  head -15 hunter

  prints the first 15 lines of the file hunter.

sort Sort and merge files.

sort [-b, -d, -f, -n, -o, -f] *file*...

- Options:

-b	Ignore initial blanks.
-d	"Dictionary" order.
-f	Ignore case of letters.
-n	Sort numbers by value.
-o *filename*	Output to file called *filename*.
-r	Sort in reverse order.

- Example:

  sort -fr -o sortbag grabbag

  sorts the file **grabbag** in reverse order, ignoring upper- and lowercase letters. The results are stored in **sortbag**.

spell Find spelling errors.

spell *file*...

tail   Give the last part of a file.

tail [-*n*] *file*

- Options:

-*n*	Start *n* lines from the end.

- Example:

tail -20 gate

prints the last 20 lines of the file gate.

uniq   Remove duplicated lines from file.

uniq [-u, -d, -c] *inputfile* [*outputfile*]

- Options:

-u	Print only lines with no duplicates.
-d	Print one copy of lines with duplicates.
-c	Print number of times the line is repeated.

- Example:

uniq -d ioulist urgent

scans the file **ioulist** for lines that appear more than once. One copy of each line is placed in the file **urgent**.

wc   Word count.

wc [-l, -w, -c, -p] *file*...

- Options:

-l	Counts lines
-w	Counts words
-c	Counts characters
-p	Counts pages (on older releases)

- Example:

wc -w Essay

counts the number of words in file **Essay**.

Running Jobs and Programs

cc   Compile C programs.

cc [-c, -o] *file*...

- Options

-c	Create object file that suppresses loading.
-o *filename*	Use *filename* for file a.out.

- Example:

  cc payroll.c

  compiles payroll.c file, with the executable program placed in a.out file.

jobs   List stopped and background jobs.

jobs [-1]

- Option:

-1	Give long listing that includes process identification number (PID).

kill   Terminate jobs.

kill [-9] *job_number_or_process_ID*

- Option:

-9	This is a sure kill.

- Example:

  kill 3

  or

  kill 3492

  kills job [3] or PID #3492.

ps   The Process Status Report.

ps [-a]

- Option:

-a	Displays ps information for all terminals.

tee   Split output.

tee [-i, -a] *file*

- Options:

-i	Ignore interrupts.
-a	Appends output to the named file if it exists or creates the file.

- Example:

ls -l /usr ¦ tee -a clutter

produces the long listing of the /usr directory onscreen and appends it to the end of the file clutter.

time   Time a command.

time *commandname*

- Example:

time cc woo.c

runs the command cc woo.c and prints the execution time when finished.

Adjusting Your Environment

alias   List aliases or make aliases.

alias
alias *abbreviation command*
unalias *abbreviation*

- Example:

alias list ls

makes list equivalent to ls.

History   Print a list of last commands given and provide abbreviations for running commands.

- Examples:

!!	Repeat the previous command.
!5	Run event 5 on the history list.

.login, .cshrc, .profile   Your personal startup file, depending on which UNIX shell your account was established with.

VI **COMMAND REFERENCE**

T he command for editing the file *filename* is

vi *filename*

If no such file exists yet, it will be created when this command is given.

Modes

Command mode lets you use the commands described in this appendix. You are placed in command mode when you invoke vi. To enter command mode from text mode, press Esc.

Text mode lets you use the keyboard to enter text. Any of the following commands will put you in text mode: a, i, o, 0, R, and c.

While in command mode, type a colon and follow it with the desired vi command—for example:

:g/dog/s/mango/g

or

:14,42w newfile

You are returned to regular command mode after the vi command is executed.

Cursor-Movement Commands

The vi cursor-movement commands take place at the cursor location in command mode. These commands help you place the cursor where you want it to be in the text. The cursor won't move beyond the bounds of the existing text.

j	Moves the cursor down one line
k	Moves the cursor up one line
h	Moves the cursor left one space character
l	Moves the cursor right one character space
Ctrl-d	Moves the screen down a half page

Ctrl-u	Moves the screen up a half page
Ctrl-w	Moves the screen up a full page
Ctrl-f	Moves the screen forward a full page
Ctrl-b	Moves the screen back a full page
*n*G	Moves the cursor to the *n*th line of file
Ctrl-g	Gives the line number where the cursor is located
Return	Moves the cursor down to the beginning of the next line

End this mode with Esc.

Text-Entering Commands

a	Appends text after cursor position
i	Inserts text before cursor position
o	Opens a new line below cursor position
O	Opens a new line above cursor position

Text-Deletion Commands

The following commands can be preceded by an integer to indicate the number of characters, words, and so on, to be affected.

x	Deletes character under cursor
dw	Deletes from cursor to beginning of next word
dd	Deletes line containing cursor
d)	Deletes rest of sentence
d}	Deletes rest of paragraph
Delete, #, Ctrl-h, or Rub	This backspace feature of the shell also works in the editor to move the cursor character by character leftward on a line, erasing each character from the buffer.

Text Alteration Commands

The R, cw, and c) commands need to be terminated with an Esc.

r	Replace character under cursor with next character typed.
R	Write over old text, beginning at cursor position.
cw	Change word (beginning at cursor) to new text.
c)	Change sentence (starting at cursor) to new text.
J	Join next line down to line with cursor.
u	Undo last command.
U	Undo all changes to line with cursor.

After these commands execute, you are returned to command mode.

Search Commands

/pattern	Search for next occurrence of *pattern*.
?pattern	Search for preceding occurrence of *pattern*.
n	Repeat the last search command given.

The Last Command

u	Undo the last command.
.	Repeat the last command.
U	Undo all changes on the current line.

Text-Moving Commands

Also see the text-deletion commands.

yy	Yank a copy of a line; place it in a buffer.
p	Put (paste) the last item yanked or deleted after the cursor.
P	Put the last item yanked or deleted before the cursor.
"cY	Yank a copy of a line, place it in buffer *c*, where *c* is any letter from *a* to *z*.
"cP	Put the contents of buffer *c* after the cursor.

Scopes to Use with Commands

e	From the cursor to the end of the current word
w	From the cursor to the beginning of the next word (including the space)
b	From the letter before the cursor backward to the beginning of the word
$	From the cursor to the end of the line
0	From just before the cursor to the beginning of the line
(	From just before the cursor backward to the beginning of the sentence containing the cursor
)	From the cursor to the beginning of the next sentence (a sentence is ended by ., !, or ? and followed by a Return)
{	From just before the cursor backward to the beginning of a paragraph (a paragraph begins after an empty line)
}	From the cursor to the end of a paragraph

Saving Text and Quitting the Editor

Editing takes place in a temporary work area and must be saved by writing it into a permanent file.

Esc :w	Write the current text into the permanent file.
Esc :q	Quit if no changes since last w.
Esc :q!	Emphatic form of quit: no changes written.
Esc :wq	Write and quit.
Esc ZZ	Write and quit.
Esc :n,kw file2	Write lines n through k into another file.
Esc :n,kw >> file2	Append lines n through k to another file.

Screen Enhancement Options

Esc :set nu	Show line numbers.
Esc :set wm=k	Wrap margin at k characters from right.
Esc :set redraw	Keep screen display current.
Plus others	

APPENDIX F

ENTERING AND EXITING THE UNIX SHELL

One major problem facing beginning UNIX users is how to go from the shell to various utilities and then return to the shell. The following are some commonly used commands for going back and forth:

In	Utility	Out
`learn`	`learn`	`bye`
`mail`	`mail`: Receive	EOF key
`mail username`	`mail`: Send	EOF key
`more filename`	`more`	Interrupt key or type `q`
`man command`	Online manual	Interrupt key
Ctrl-z	To suspend a job	`fg`
Ctrl-s	Terminal output	Ctrl-q
`loginname`	UNIX shell	EOF key or `logout`
`vi filename`	`vi` editor	`:wq` or `ZZ` or `:q!`

The following keys send commands to UNIX:

Interrupt key	The *interrupt* signal stops most processes. On most systems, the signal is sent by pressing Ctrl-c. Other common choices are the Delete or Rub keys.
EOF character	The *end-of-file* character is usually transmitted by typing Ctrl-d.

To see which characters are used to control your terminal input and output, type the UNIX command:

`stty all`

or

`stty -a`

You should be given a list of characters currently used to

- Erase character
- Erase line
- End of file
- Control terminal output
- Erase word
- Interrupt jobs
- Suspend jobs
- Other things

These control characters can be changed as described in Chapter 8, "The UNIX Shell: Command Lines, Redirection, and Shell Scripts."

ANSWERS TO CHAPTER REVIEW QUESTIONS

Chapter 2

Matching Commands and Descriptions

1. b
2. d
3. a
4. c
5. e

Questions

1. a. **1984**

   b. **09** and **2025**

   c. No argument

   d. **don**

2. **password** is a prompt from UNIX asking you to type your password; **passwd** is a UNIX command that initiates the process of changing your password.

3. b, of course.

4. Nothing happens; UNIX just sits patiently, waiting to be told that you are done and that it is now its turn to do something.

5. It means that you hold down Ctrl while pressing the s key once sharply.

6. It depends on the terminal you use. Generally, terminals use either Backspace, the Rub key, the Ctrl-h combination, or the # key.

7. Ctrl-c

8. The key repeats, sending the same character to the computer.

9. Use Ctrl-s to stop screen scroll and Ctrl-q to restart it.

10. A character that cancels a whole line instead of a single letter.

Chapter 3

1. Command mode and input mode. Command mode is used to read mail; input mode is used to send mail.

2. `mail` *`loginname`*

3. `s2 jobs`

4. Command mode to read your mail

5. `q`

6. Use `-v` to call the editor. Use `<Esc>:wq` to leave the editor. You are then back in the mail header.

7. `mail` can list or search Subject lines.

8. Just add login names after the command `mail`:

   `mail` *`loginname1 loginname2`*

9. Use `~?` in input mode and `?` in command mode.

10. `R` sends responses only to authors, not to carbon holders. It reduces the number of messages sent.

Chapter 4

1. d

2. a

3. c

4. b

5. e

6. g

7. f

Chapter 5

Matching Commands to Functions

1. j

2. g

3. f

4. k

5. d

6 i

7. b

8. c

9. a

10. e

Questions

1. The left column of the screen fills with tildes (~).

2. The commands `a`, `A`, `i`, `I`, `o`, and `0`

3. After the cursor

4. `:wq` or `:ZZ`

5. Before the cursor

6. `:1,3w` *filename*

7. Use Esc.

8. Position the cursor over `o` and type `ri`.

9. Position the cursor on the first line to be deleted and type `5dd`.

Chapter 6

1. Ctrl-x Ctrl-s

2. Ctrl-q

3. Ctrl-g

4. Use Ctrl-a to move to the beginning of the line; then press Ctrl-k.

5. Press Ctrl-k one or more times to kill lines; then press Ctrl-y.

6. `<Esc>x`

7. It's a help command used to look up a command. For example, to see which commands justify text, try `<Esc>x a justify`.

8. `<Esc>% county<Return>County<Return>`

9. A *region* is any text between *point* (the cursor) and *mark*. Mark is defined by typing Ctrl-@ or Ctrl-Spacebar.

10. `<Esc>x fill-region`

11. Set the right margin with `<Esc>`*n*`<Ctrl-x>f`, where *n* is the setting. Then to justify the current paragraph, enter `<Esc>q`.

Chapter 7

Matching Commands to Functions

1. i

2. g

3. c

4. d

5. h

6. b

7. a

8. e

9. j

10. f

Creating Commands

1. `ls`

2. `cat file2`

3. `cp file2 file5`

4. `mkdir D2`

5. `cd D2`

6. `mv ../file2.` or `cd home` and `mv file2/D2/file2`

7. `ls ../`

8. `cd` to go to your home directory; then `mkdir D3` or, in one step, `mkdir ../D3`

9. `date > D3/f8` or `cd D3` and `date > f8`

10. First, `cd D3`, second `pwd` to make sure you're there, then `rm *` (a powerful command!), then `cd` to get back home, and, finally, `rmdir D3`.

Chapter 8

1. a. `ls -l blackweb`; should be a space before the `-`.

   b. `ls -s rupart`; put the option in the right place.

   c. `ls -s -l` or `ls -sl`

d. This one is correct.

e. `cat duskhaven ¦ lp` or `lp duskhaven`. Either command sends the file `duskhaven` to the printer. The original command in this question would create a file called `lp` and place a copy of the contents of `duskhaven` there.

f. `cat jolly` or `cat < jolly`; the filename should be to the right of the redirection operator.

g. `set pal = "ginnie mae"`

h. `setenv NETWORTH 45`

2. The first command makes `fopman` into an executable file. The second makes `exc` into an executable file. Hereafter, the user can give commands like `exc nosecount`.

3. One way is to replace

```
echo You are
who am i
```

with

```
You are `myname`
```

The backquotes cause `` `myname` `` to be expanded by the shell and the result used.

4. One possibility is to use an alias:

```
alias cproj "cd /usr/lisa/prog/pasc/proj"
```

5. a. `cd English`

b. `cd /usr/nerkie/project.c`

c. `cd /usr/nerkie/project.c`

d. `head My.Summer Faulkner Tragedy ¦ more`

e. `vi Faulkner`

f. `wc My.Summer Faulkner Tragedy`

g. `more /usr/nerkie/project.c/guesses`

6. a. `rm -i junkfile` (UNIX asks you to confirm your `rm` order before acting.)

b. `cd; ls` (Change to home directory; list the files and directories there.)

c. `cd; ls junkdirectory` (Change to home directory but list the contents of `junkdirectory`—this will fail unless `junkdirectory` is a subdirectory of the home directory.) *Note*: `junkdirectory` is attached to `ls` rather than `cd` because `ls` is the command immediately preceding the directory name.

d. `cd junkdirectory; rm -i *` (Change to `junkdirectory`; then remove all files there, asking for confirmation.) *Note*: `junkdirectory` is attached to `cd` rather than `rm` because of the history substitution. The `rm -i` option is used because `rm` was redefined in another alias to mean that.

7. a. Resumes job [3], running it in foreground.

    b. Resumes job [1] because it is the current (+) job.

    c. Stops (suspends) job [2].

    d. Restarts job [3], running it in background.

    e. Terminates job [1].

Chapter 9

1. a. Changes modes or permission on files.

    b. Permits or denies messages from **write** and **talk**.

    c. Times a command.

    d. A reminder service.

    e. Sorts a file.

    f. Identifies your terminal.

    g. Sends material to a line printer.

2. a. **wc -w blackweb**; counts words in the file **blackweb**.

    b. Correct; shows the last 10 lines of the file **blackweb**.

    c. **sort -f -n iou.list** or **sort -fn iou.list**; sorts the contents of **iou.list** in machine-collating order, but ignores the difference between capital and small letters and sorts numbers numerically.

    d. **tail -15 blackweb**; shows the last 15 lines of **blackweb**. The incorrect version that we gave would have shown the last 10 lines of **blackweb** and would then have looked for a file called **-15**. Of course, if you had had a file by that name, the original instruction would have been correct.

    e. **cat Rupart ¦ lpr** or **lpr Rupart**; sends the file **Rupart** to be printed on the line printer. The original command given would create a file called **lpr** and would place a copy of the contents on **Rupart** there.

    f. **wc < blackweb** or **wc blackweb**; counts the lines, words, and characters in the file **blackweb**. The < and > operators require a command or executable file on the left and a filename on the right.

Chapter 10

1. a. `spell piffle`

   b. `join -t# flip flop`

   c. `nroff -ms staid`

2. a. `sed 's/Edgar/Elgar/g' essay`

   b. `sed -n '10,15p' essay`

   c. `sed 's/San Francisco Treat/"&"/g' essay`

   d. `sed '/ude/d\`
      `/aked/d' essay`

Chapter 11

Using `grep` to Match Patterns

1. b, c, d

2. a, b, d

3. a, c, e

Using `find`

1. Searches your home directory recursively for files whose names end in `.c` and moves them to the directory `$HOME/cdirect`.

2. Searches your current working directory recursively for files whose names end in `.c` and have a size in excess of three blocks. Then, for each found file, asks user whether it should be removed.

3. Searches the `/usr` directory recursively for all files that either are bigger than 10 blocks and haven't been used in more than 20 days or are bigger than 30 blocks. Prints the pathnames of these files.

Questions

1. a.

```
Antibody:Aristotle:Asis:26 Furtz Way:RedviLLe:OH:40822
Morgan:Joe::315 Second Street:Redville:OH:40817
Morgan:Joe::315 Second Street:Hot'n'wet:TX:72727
Morgan:Joe::315 Second Street:Riesenstadt:CA:94707
Vegetable:Joe:Fritz:1002 Market Pl.:Riesenstadt:CA:94707
Zircon:Bilbo:Nagy:1313 Ratgut Blvd.:Hot'n'wet:TX:72702
```

b.

```
Antibody:Aristotle:Asis:26 Furtz Way:Redville:OH:40822
Morgan:Joe::315 Second Street:Riesenstadt:CA:94707
Morgan:Joe::315 Second Street:Hot'n'wet:TX:72727
Morgan:Joe::315 Second Street:Redville:OH:40817
Vegetable:Joe:Fritz:1002 Market Pl.:Riesenstadt:CA:94707
Zircon:Bilbo:Nagy:1313 Ratgut Blvd.:Hot'n'wet:TX:72702
```

c.

```
Zircon:Bilbo:Nagy:1313 Ratgut Blvd.:Hot'n'wet:TX:72702
Morgan:Joe::315 Second Street:Riesenstadt:CA:94707
Vegetable:Joe:Fritz:1002 Market Pl.:Riesenstadt:CA:94707
Morgan:Joe::315 Second Street:Redville:OH:40817
Antibody:Aristotle:Asis:26 Furtz Way:Redville:OH:40822
Morgan:Joe::315 Second Street:Hot'n'wet:TX:72727
```

2. `sort -t: +5 -6 +4 -5 +0 maillist`

Chapter 12

1. No.

2. Only the last command.

3. Because you might want to run an **ex** command that uses the same single letter—for example, :r, :a, or :w. The abbreviation would expand these single letters.

4. An abbreviation works in text input mode; a **map** macro works in command mode.

5. Yes, by placing a **cw** operation in the macro.

6. Pressing Return or Esc while in the **map** macro leaves the **map** command. To insert these keystrokes in the **map** macro, they must be escaped with Ctrl-v.

7. Use Ctrl-v in **map** macros and the \ character in regular expressions.

8. The .* stands for any number of any characters. It's very broad. The example would replace not only **receive** but also the words **recalled the damage done by the river**.

9. An unmarked dot is a metacharacter standing for any single character. An escaped dot (\.) stands for a period or dot.

10. It lets you respond with a yes or no before carrying out each substitution.

11. The .exrc file is sourced on starting the **vi** editor.

12. Use Ctrl-d.

INDEX

D

E

F

T